Conducting Authentic Historical Inquiry

Conducting Authentic Historical Inquiry

Engaging Learners with SOURCES and Emerging Technologies

Scott M. Waring
Richard Hartshorne

TEACHERS COLLEGE PRESS
TEACHERS COLLEGE | COLUMBIA UNIVERSITY
NEW YORK AND LONDON

Published by Teachers College Press,® 1234 Amsterdam Avenue, New York, NY 10027

All front cover images from the United States Library of Congress's Prints and Photographs division unless noted otherwise. Clockwise from top left: Woman drilling "Vengeance" dive bomber, 1943; Postcard, The Circus Procession, 1888, via Wikimedia Commons; Baseball card, Cap Anson, Chicago White Stockings, 1888; "Destitute peapickers in California," by Dorothea Lange, 1936; U.S. Army recruitment poster designed by Frances Adams Halsted and painted by V. Aderente, 1916; Men of Fort Story operate an azimuth instrument; Congresswoman Shirley Chisholm announcing her candidacy for presidential nomination, 1972.

Library of Congress Cataloging-in-Publication Data

Names: Waring, Scott Monroe, author. | Hartshorne, Richard, 1971– author.
Title: Conducting authentic historical inquiry : engaging learners with SOURCES and emerging technologies / Scott M. Waring, Richard Hartshorne.
Description: New York, NY : Teachers College Press, [2020] | Includes bibliographical references and index.
Identifiers: LCCN 2020013696 (print) | LCCN 2020013697 (ebook) | ISBN 9780807764053 (hardcover) | ISBN 9780807764046 (paperback) | ISBN 9780807778647 (ebook)
Subjects: LCSH: History—Study and teaching (Elementary)—United States. | History—Study and teaching (Secondary)—United States. | History—Sources—Study and teaching—United States. | History—Computer-assisted instruction.
Classification: LCC LB1582.U6 W37 2020 (print) | LCC LB1582.U6 (ebook) | DDC 372.89—dc23
LC record available at https://lccn.loc.gov/2020013696
LC ebook record available at https://lccn.loc.gov/2020013697

ISBN 978-0-8077-6404-6 (paper)
ISBN 978-0-8077-6405-3 (hardcover)
ISBN 978-0-8077-7864-7 (ebook)

Printed on acid-free paper
Manufactured in the United States of America

Contents

Preface

In *Conducting Authentic Historical Inquiry: Engaging Learners with SOURCES and Emerging Technologies*, we will address the power of integrating emerging technologies alongside the SOURCES Framework for Teaching with Primary and Secondary Sources as a comprehensive pedagogical approach for supporting active, collaborative, inquiry-based learning (Cowgill & Waring, 2015; Herlihy & Waring, 2015; LaVallee, Purdin, & Waring, 2019; LaVallee & Waring, 2015; Terry & Waring, 2017; Waring, 2017; Waring & Herlihy, 2015; Waring, LaVallee, & Purdin, 2018; Waring & Scheiner-Fisher, 2014; Waring & Tapia-Moreno, 2015). We argue that educators can simultaneously meet the pedagogical and technological needs and expectations of today's learners and that those individuals empowered with these skills and modes of thinking help to form a more active and informed citizenry.

As context for your understanding of what is presented in this book, as well as for use in your instruction, we define *primary sources* as the direct evidence related to a topic of study. These are the sources that were created by individuals present at the event, place, and/or time under study. Primary sources can be any item that can help someone create a narrative, a story, or a better understanding about a subject, issue, or theme being investigated or learned. These can include documents, letters, cookbooks, clothing, scientific or mathematical equipment, ephemera, maps, musical instruments, textbooks, or literally any item directly related to the content being studied. *Secondary sources* differ from primary sources in that they are not the items or sources that were created by someone directly present or linked to the topic of study. They are items that were created after an event, by someone not present at an event, place, and/or time under study, or by an individual not directly connected to the specific topic of study. Examples of secondary sources could include textbooks, biographies, documentaries, newspapers, paintings, or any other item not directly related to the content being studied.

In Part I of this book, we will provide a deeper and more complex look at what primary and secondary sources are and ways in which teachers can help students to understand the differences between primary and secondary sources, how to utilize sources in instruction, and how to build a more complex way of thinking and approaching historical content. We will outline the SOURCES Framework for Teaching with Primary and Secondary Sources, present explanations for each of the seven stages of the framework, and provide multiple examples of ways to incorporate the framework into the teaching of history content.

In Part II, we will provide a detailed collection and rationale for the implementation of a wide array of emerging technological applications into the teaching and learning process, particularly in support of the SOURCES framework, such as:

- Backchannel platforms (e.g., Backchannel Chat) and real-time collaborative questioning tools (e.g., Crowdsignal) that facilitate initial student engagement and support multiple approaches to scrutinizing fundamental sources;
- Cloud-based collaborative concept mapping tools (e.g., Coggle) that allow students to map and organize their thoughts and visualize connections and disconnections between content and events;
- Personalized multimedia-based collaborative participatory tools (e.g., VoiceThread) that give the user opportunities for complex contexts to be explored in depth from multiple perspectives;
- Authoring and curating tools (e.g., Tes Teach with Blendspace) that permit students to "read between the lines" and find information that is not explicitly stated, but can be inferred through observations;
- Categorization, annotation, and sharing tools that facilitate the collection and organization of varied resources (e.g., Zotero), allowing students to corroborate and refute their analysis and provide supporting documentation to back up positions; and,
- Collaborative development tools (e.g., Weebly) that assist students in authoring, developing, and publishing through the establishment of a plausible narrative and to summarize final thoughts.

Along the way, we will explore the role of the individual technology tools in supporting each phase of the SOURCES pedagogical framework, and provide varied examples of the merging of technological and pedagogical applications in the social studies classroom.

Our hope is that educators find *Conducting Authentic Historical Inquiry: Engaging Learners with SOURCES and Emerging Technologies* to be a thought-provoking and engaging book that inspires the reader to find varieties of ways to engage learners in diverse learning opportunities that focus on the use of primary and secondary sources. We anticipate that readers will then find ways in their own classrooms to move students toward more independent, critical, and engaged ways of thinking, and, along the way, will seamlessly integrate a variety of emerging technologies into the learning opportunities provided to their own student populations. Ultimately, we hope that you really enjoy reading this book!

Part I

UNDERSTANDING THE SOURCES FRAMEWORK

CHAPTER 1

The SOURCES Framework

An Introduction

Far too often in classrooms across the United States, there is an overutilization of textbooks, lecturing, and instructional methods that focus on the superficial memorization of "facts" and the use of methods devoid of authentic and disciplined-based inquiry. Approaches such as these lead to disengagement and a general distaste for the subject being covered (Allen, 1994; Black & Blake, 2001; Zhao & Hoge, 2005). These methods of presenting content can also oversimplify the importance of various events, items, and topics, as well as the individuals involved, and remove them from the complex contexts in which they were involved. One method of strengthening instruction, building higher-level and critical-thinking skills, and improving understanding and retention for students is to embed opportunities to engage with primary and secondary sources—which are directly related to the complex environments from which they occurred—throughout the learning process (National Council for the Social Studies, 2010, 2013; National Governors Association Center for Best Practices and Council of Chief State School Officers, 2010). Primary and secondary sources are particularly effective in supplementing the student learning experience in social studies by providing multiple perspectives and allowing for the construction of more authentic and in-depth evidence-based narratives and understandings (Britt & Howe, 2014; Callison, 2013; Lamb, 2014; White, O'Brien, Smith, Moretensen, & Hileman, 2006; Woyshner, 2010).

Primary sources can be defined as the direct evidence related to a topic of study. These are the sources that were created by individuals present at the event, place, and/or time under study. Engaging students with primary sources, especially in social studies, can help them foster critical-thinking and deductive reasoning skills while also allowing teachers an opportunity to personalize learning environments, making learning more engaging and appealing for students. Making learning *active* is a critical component of student learning, as that is how students construct meaning and refine their understanding of historical events. Therefore, teachers can utilize both primary and secondary sources to expand student understandings and provide students with opportunities to authentically construct their own evidence-based narratives, replicating methods utilized by experts in various fields of study (Barton, 2005; Barton & Levstik, 2003; Wineburg, 2010).

> **The SOURCES Framework for Teaching with Primary and Secondary Sources**
>
> 1. Scrutinizing the Fundamental Source(s)
> 2. Organizing Thoughts
> 3. Understanding the Context
> 4. Reading Between the Lines
> 5. Corroborating and Refuting
> 6. Establishing a Plausible Narrative
> 7. Summarizing Final Thoughts

However, simply inserting primary and secondary sources into the classroom is not sufficient to improve student learning and does not adequately serve the fundamental purpose of education, which is to "help young people develop the ability to make informed and reasoned decisions for the public good as citizens of a culturally diverse, democratic society in an interdependent world" (National Council for the Social Studies, 1994, p. 157). For more in-depth and authentic engagement, teachers should employ a comprehensive and structured pedagogical framework that facilitates students actively engaging in inquiry, perspective-taking, and meaning-making in order to develop the habits of mind that are important for the rights and responsibilities of 21st-century citizenship. The SOURCES Framework for Teaching with Primary and Secondary Sources was developed as a structure to support teachers to harness the power of primary sources in pedagogically appropriate ways to construct effective and powerful learning opportunities for their student populations. Through the seven stages of the SOURCES framework, the learning process is scaffolded to allow individual students opportunities to examine primary and secondary sources, question their understandings about a historical event, develop background knowledge, find supporting and corroborating evidence, construct source-based narratives, and critically analyze the learning process and findings, as well as consider questions that were not answered. The seven SOURCES stages will be discussed further later in the chapter, but before considering this framework, it is vital to properly prepare students to think historically, allow them to understand what primary and secondary sources are, and demonstrate how best to utilize sources throughout the entire historical inquiry process.

STEPS TO PREPARING STUDENTS TO THINK HISTORICALLY AND UTILIZE PRIMARY SOURCES

Students' first exposure to utilizing primary sources in the history classroom is typically through the use of document-based question assignments or similar approaches. Using this as an introduction to primary sources easily stifles excitement for history and causes great frustration for many, as they are not prepared to think historically and often cannot even define the term *primary source*. Prior to expecting students to analyze primary sources in isolation or as a set, especially in a case when students are given the task of trying to create

Publications About SOURCES

LaVallee, C., Purdin, T., & Waring, S. M. (2019). Civil liberties, the Bill of Rights, and SOURCES: Engaging students in the past in order to prepare citizens of the future. In J. Hubbard (Ed.), *Extending the ground of public confidence: Teaching civil liberties in K–16 social studies education* (pp. 3–32). Charlotte, NC: Information Age Publishing.

Waring, S. M., LaVallee, C., & Purdin, T. (2018). The power of agentic women and SOURCES. *Social Studies Research and Practice, 13*(2), 270–278.

Terry, K., & Waring, S. M. (2017). Expanding historical narratives: Using SOURCES to assess the successes and failures of Operation Anthropoid. *Social Studies Journal, 37*(2), 59–71.

Waring, S. M. (2017). Engaging history students through the use of the SOURCES framework. *In Context, 1*(1), 2–4.

Cowgill, D., & Waring, S. M. (2015). Using SOURCES to examine the American Constitution and events leading to its construction. *The Councilor: A Journal of the Social Studies, 76*(2), 1–14.

Waring, S. M., & Herlihy, C. (2015). Are we alone in the universe? Using primary sources to address a fundamental question. *The Science Teacher, 82*(7), 63–66.

Herlihy, C., & Waring, S. M. (2015). Using the SOURCES framework to examine the Little Rock Nine. *Oregon Journal of the Social Studies, 3*(2), 44–51.

LaVallee, C., & Waring, S. M. (2015). Using SOURCES to examine the Nadir of Race Relations (1890–1920). *The Clearing House, 88*, 133–139.

Waring, S. M., & Tapia-Moreno, D. (2015). Examining the conditions of Andersonville Prison through the use of SOURCES. *The Social Studies, 106*(4), 170–177.

Waring, S. M., & Scheiner-Fisher, C. (2014). Using SOURCES to allow digital natives to explore the Lewis and Clark expedition. *Middle School Journal, 45*(4), 3–12.

a narrative or thesis statement based on the evidence provided to them, students need to be able to define the terms *primary* and *secondary sources*.

One way to get students to understand the term *primary source* is to conduct an approach entitled *Leaving Evidence of Our Lives* (www.loc.gov/teachers/professionaldevelopment/tpsdirect/pdf/Leaving-Evidence-of-Our-Lives.pdf). In this activity, students are asked to think about a 24-hour period of their lives. While they are doing so, the students should determine what sorts of activities took place, what individuals they interacted with, what technologies were utilized, and anything else that would help somebody to create a narrative about their day. Once they have had a sufficient amount of time to think about their day, students should write down all of the evidence that they left behind during their day. This might include things such as garbage, dirty dishes in the sink, a bicycle forgotten at school, homework they completed, or clothes that were placed in a laundry hamper. Students should be given an opportunity to discuss their list in small groups of peers before class discussion ensues, and talk about specific items that they listed and what type of items might remain and be most easily accessible by others wanting to learn about their day.

Once a class discussion begins, the teacher should show how each of the items on the composite lists is important to be able to construct a narrative about the day in the life of each individual in the classroom in order to better understand the activities in which they were involved. Students can also be asked to consider how they might be able to relate the "daily" items that they are listing to any of the content being covered in the class. In one instance, a student shouted out in the middle of the activity that these items are very similar to sources they discussed and examined during their recent unit on Pompeii. The nearly 2,000-year-old items they had discussed, and those that social scientists were using to develop narratives about what life was like and what happened on the fateful day when Mt. Vesuvius erupted, were not unlike the items they listed. A discussion of how social scientists might develop narratives about various content can be considered when examining the past. Furthermore, the importance of sources in creating compelling and well-developed narratives should be examined.

By the end of this activity, students should understand that each of the items they listed from the day in their life is a primary source. Together, as a class, a working definition of the term *primary source* should be constructed, as well as specific items that could be considered as primary sources. Students should be asked if they might have a sense of what a secondary source might be, given their understanding of the term *primary source*. A working definition of *secondary source* should be constructed as well. These definitions can be compared to that provided by the Library of Congress (2019): "Primary sources are the raw materials of history—original documents and objects which were created at the time under study. They are different from secondary sources, accounts or interpretations of events created by someone without firsthand experience" (para. 1). Even as the students work on the definitions and on creating lists of sources, there can be some confusion as to whether a specific piece of evidence is a primary source or a secondary source. It should be made clear to them that anything can be a primary source, as it depends upon what your question is or what it is that you are trying to determine. For example, a textbook can be considered as a secondary source, as the creators were not present for all of the events presented in the text, and a level of analysis and synthesis occurred during its creation. If one is using a textbook to try and determine what happened at the Battle of Lexington Green, then the textbook is a secondary source. However, if a professor of history education is using the textbook to answer the question, "How do textbooks represent what happened at the Battle of Lexington Green?," then the textbook, as well as others including narratives about the battle, would be considered primary sources. Students should continually be reminded that it all depends upon the question being asked. Another example of this is when one student inquired as to whether paintings depicting various events throughout history completed by her grandfather would be primary or secondary sources. She added that he was present for some of the events that he painted but not the majority of them. Once asked what she was really trying to determine, this student noted that she was interested in depictions of impactful and historical events by her grandfather and others like him. Because her question was focused on the representations rather than the events themselves, these paintings are primary sources. Thus, when trying to determine whether a source is primary or secondary, it all depends upon what question you are trying to answer.

In preparing students to think historically and utilize primary sources in the creation of authentic and evidence-based historical narratives, the next step is to ask them to analyze one source, preferably a photograph, to learn basic skills necessary to understand and learn from sources. As a typical classroom includes students with a variety of cognitive, linguistic, and intellectual abilities, a simple image for which most would have predeveloped schema may allow for the greatest number of students to find success, in comparison to using text-heavy sources or complex visuals. It is suggested that the use of an image of a classroom environment be utilized, as students will have sufficient schema developed in order to permit them to critically examine, question, and make hypotheses about what they are viewing. An ideal image for this entry-level activity is the *Daily Inspection of Teeth and Finger Nails* (www.loc.gov/pictures/item/2018678589; Figure 1.1), which can be found on the Library of Congress's website.

Proper scaffolding for the analysis of primary sources is essential to novice-level learners, so the utilization of the *Observe, Reflect, and Question* Analysis Sheet from Library of Congress (www.loc.gov/teachers/usingprimarysources/resources/Primary_Source_Analysis_Tool.pdf; Figure 1.2) is a perfect way to get students to begin to understand the process of analyzing primary sources.

The Library of Congress also provides teacher guides (www.loc.gov/teachers/usingprimarysources/guides.html) for analyzing different types of sources, such as manuscripts, motion pictures, political cartoons, sound recordings, and maps. In the first column of the analysis sheet (*Observe*), students are asked to write down any items or thoughts that they can concretely say exist within the source. For example, when looking at the photograph of the daily inspection of fingernails and teeth, the students could note that there are boys and girls represented in the image, only Caucasian individuals, or that wooden furniture is lined up in rows. It would not be appropriate to note that there is a teacher in the classroom, as it cannot be concretely determined that it is a school classroom or that any individual seen in the image is definitively a teacher and not an administrator or even a guest visiting the classroom from the local community. It often can be a difficult process for students to list only items that can be definitively observed and to make concrete and undebatable statements about them.

Figure 1.1. Daily Inspection of Teeth and Finger Nails

Figure 1.2. Primary Source Analysis Sheet

PRIMARY SOURCE ANALYSIS TOOL

OBSERVE · REFLECT · QUESTION

OBSERVE	REFLECT	QUESTION

FURTHER INVESTIGATION

LIBRARY LIBRARY OF CONGRESS | LOC.gov/teachers

As students move to the second column of the analysis sheet (*Reflect*), they are expected to make inferences and hypotheses about what they think is occurring in the image. It would be completely appropriate for students to list items, such as the image is of a classroom, the students are of mixed ages, the individual in the foreground of the image is pregnant, or that there are multiple adults present within this classroom. As long as the student has rationale and evidence for a comment in the reflecting column, the teacher should allow them to list their thoughts; in this stage, teachers should encourage critical and deep thinking, and considering any and all possibilities.

In the third column (*Question*), students are asked to list any questions they may have about the image that they are analyzing, especially those for which they do not feel there is a sufficient amount of information in the image to concretely determine an answer. It should be noted that these three columns can be completed in any order and it is not a linear process that must be completed left to right. A student may start with having three or four questions before even attending to an observation; however, students should be encouraged to have multiple items listed under each column header. The *Observe, Reflect, and Question* Analysis Sheet is a perfect way to introduce the use of primary sources to students at a novice level of thinking and can be equally effective with more advanced students. As they become more proficient at analysis using multiple primary sources or sets of sources, more complex analysis sheets may be necessary, but this analysis sheet can and should be used with learners at all levels.

Once students have had an opportunity to carefully analyze one image, begin introducing other types of primary sources to the students, such as letters, diary entries, short video and audio clips, maps, and political cartoons, to give them the opportunity to analyze various types of sources. When using different types of sources, teachers may use the *Observe, Reflect, and Question* Analysis Sheet from the Library of Congress or utilize other analysis sheets available from the National Archives (www.archives.gov/education/lessons/worksheets), the Maryland Historical Society (www.mdhs.org/education/teachers/primary-source-worksheets), The History Project (www.calisphere.universityofcalifornia.edu/themed_collections/pdf/6cs_primary_source.pdf), or some of the other analysis sheets available online from other creators and organizations.

Works that have been edited can be powerful sources to utilize in the classroom, as students can see how thoughts of the creator changed and how even powerful and notable people had to edit their work. A good source to introduce to students is an item written by Rosa Parks (www.loc.gov/resource/mss85943.001810/?sp=27; Figure 1.3) in regard to the decision she made when forced with the prospect of sitting at the back of the bus. One can directly see Rosa's edits and read her associated thoughts as she explains what she was thinking at that time:

> I had been pushed around all my life and felt at this moment that I could not take it anymore. When I asked the policeman why we had to be pushed around? He said he didn't know. "The law is the law. You are under arrest." I did not resist.

Another powerful source to share with students as an example of edited work is an original typed draft of President Franklin Delano Roosevelt's *Day of Infamy Speech* (www.archives.gov/files/publications/prologue/images/day-of-infamy-draft1-page1.jpg; Figure 1.4). Students can read that he initially intended to say that this was a "date which will live in world history."

Lines were drawn through the words "world history" and above this edit is written the stronger word "infamy." Besides this monumental modification, there are many other edits found in this one-page draft. This is also a nice reminder to students about the need to edit their own writing.

Figure 1.3. Image 27 of Rosa Parks Papers: Writings, Notes, and Statements, 1956–1998

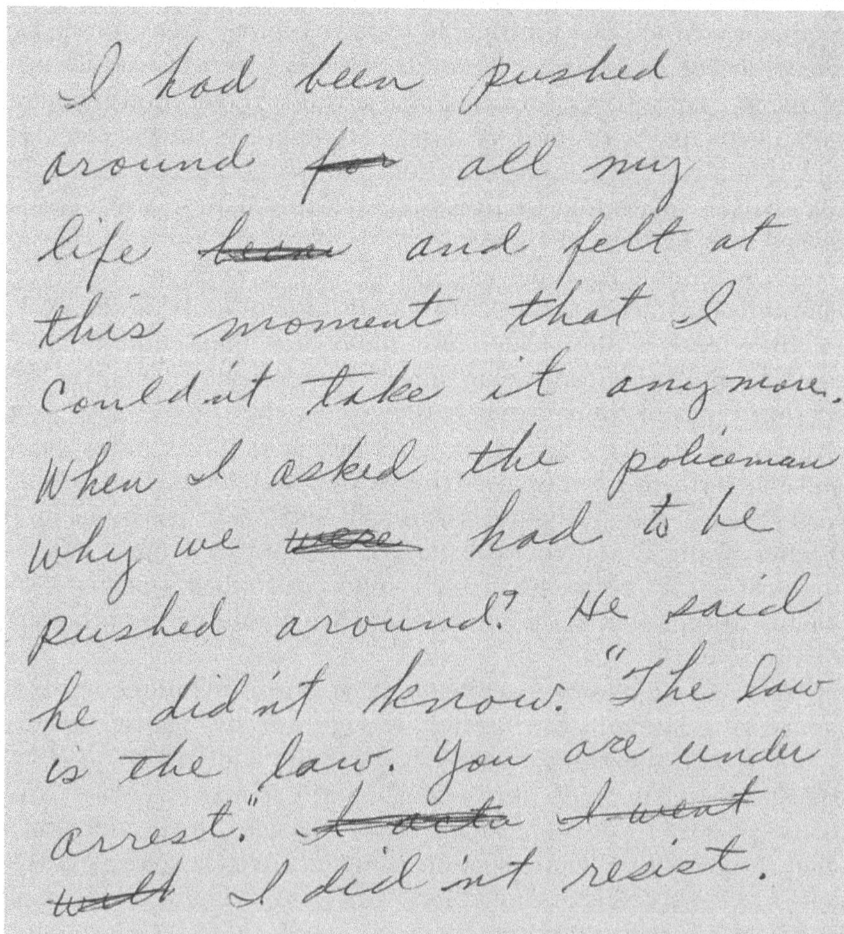

I had been pushed
around ~~for~~ all my
life and felt at
this moment that I
Could'nt take it anymore.
When I asked the policeman
why we ~~were~~ had to be
pushed around? He said
he did'nt know. "The law
is the law. You are under
arrest." ~~I went~~
I did'nt resist.

Figure 1.4. FDR's "Day of Infamy" Speech

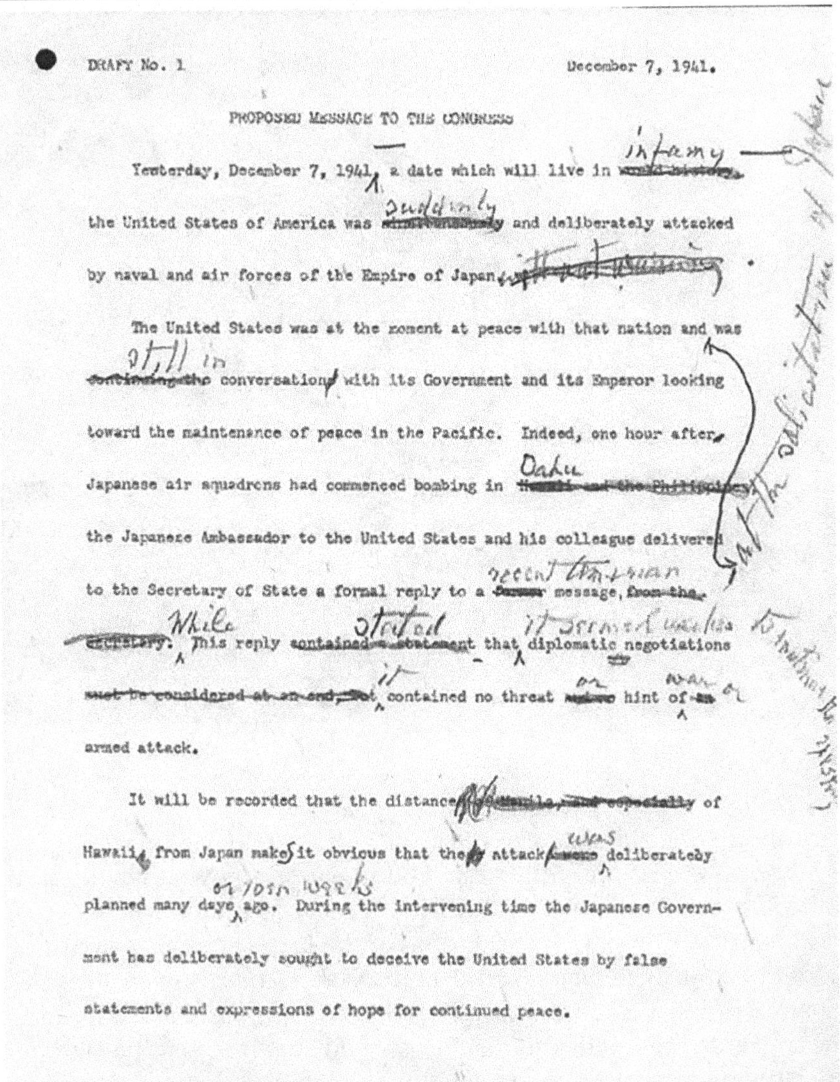

DRAFT No. 1 December 7, 1941.

PROPOSED MESSAGE TO THE CONGRESS

Yesterday, December 7, 1941, a date which will live in infamy, the United States of America was suddenly and deliberately attacked by naval and air forces of the Empire of Japan.

The United States was at the moment at peace with that nation and was still in conversation with its Government and its Emperor looking toward the maintenance of peace in the Pacific. Indeed, one hour after Japanese air squadrons had commenced bombing in Oahu the Japanese Ambassador to the United States and his colleague delivered to the Secretary of State a formal reply to a recent American message. While this reply stated that diplomatic negotiations it contained no threat or hint of war or armed attack.

It will be recorded that the distance of Hawaii from Japan makes it obvious that the attack was deliberately planned many days or even weeks ago. During the intervening time the Japanese Government has deliberately sought to deceive the United States by false statements and expressions of hope for continued peace.

CRITICAL EXAMINATION OF SOURCES

Home of the Rebel Sharpshooter

To help students become critical consumers of sources and question each source with which they come in contact, they should be introduced to powerful images such as the *Home of the Rebel Sharpshooter* (www.loc.gov/resource/cwpb.04337; Figure 1.5).

Figure 1.5. Gettysburg, Pennsylvania: *Home of the Rebel Sharpshooter*

Students should be asked to carefully examine the image and go through the stages of observing, reflecting, and questioning what is seen in the image. As the students respond to what they see, what they think they see, and the questions that they have, a class list can be generated on a board or by using the online tool provided on the Library of Congress website (www.loc.gov/teachers/primary-source-analysis-tool). Once a sufficient amount of analysis has been completed, the teacher should read the first paragraph from the entry that accompanies the image in Alexander Gardner's *Photographic Sketch Book of the War* (rmc.library.cornell.edu/7milVol/plate41.html), published in 1865–66, so that the students can hear what the creator of the image thought, in his own words, when the image was captured. The students learn that "The artist, in passing over the scene of the previous days' engagements, found in a lonely place the covert of a rebel sharpshooter, and photographed the scene presented here." They also discover that Gardner noted:

> The Confederate soldier had built up between two huge rocks, a stone wall, from the crevices of which he had directed his shots, and, in comparative security, picked off our officers. The side of the rock on the left shows, by the little white

> spots, how our sharpshooters and infantry had endeavored to dislodge him. The trees in the vicinity were splintered, and their branches cut off, while the front of the wall looked as if just recovering from and (sic) attack of geological small-pox. The sharpshooter had evidently been wounded in the head by a fragment of shell which had exploded over him, and had laid down upon his blanket to await death. There was no means of judging how long he had lived after receiving his wound, but the disordered clothing shows that his sufferings must have been intense. (rmc.library.cornell.edu/7milVol/plate41.html)

Reading this passage significantly adds to the understanding of the image and clarifies or corroborates many of the thoughts already reflected upon by the students. The last portion of the first paragraph of Gardner's entry urges the reader to think about the family and loved ones left behind by this Confederate sharpshooter:

> Was he delirious with agony, or did death come slowly to his relief, while memories of home grew dearer as the field of carnage faded before him? What visions, of loved ones far away, may have hovered above his stony pillow! What familiar voices may he not have heard, like whispers beneath the roar of battle, as his eyes grew heavy in their long, last sleep!

With this new information, a deeper discussion can ensue, and the idea of corroborating evidence can be introduced. Students can discuss how the second source added to understandings, modified their thoughts, made the past more personable, or in what ways more than one source can be beneficial to the process of thinking critically about the past. Especially with the emotional nature of this source coupled with Gardner's narrative, students typically talk about how this humanized the process for them and allowed them to think of the American Civil War combatants as humans and individuals, not just a large mass of soldiers. After students have thoroughly discussed their thoughts, the teacher can ask if they would be troubled or upset to learn that Alexander Gardner, possibly along with his colleagues Timothy O'Sullivan and James Gibson, dragged the body across a field and set up the body, along with a prop gun, to stage the image that he entitled *The Home of the Rebel Sharpshooter.* These arguments were made by an artist and illustrator (Frederick Ray) for *Civil War Times Illustrated,* in 1961, by looking at the similarities between two different photographs captured by Alexander Gardner at Gettysburg. In 1975, historian William Frassanito decided to go a step further with Ray's observations, and outline the probable process that Gardner undertook in transporting the body more than 70 yards and setting the scene to his liking. Once they have been able to digest this new information, students should take a look at the second paragraph of Alexander Gardner's entry for the *Home of the Rebel Sharpshooter* from the *Photographic Sketch Book*:

> On the nineteenth of November, the artist attended the consecration of the Gettysburg Cemetery, and again visited the "Sharpshooter's Home." The musket, rusted by many storms, still leaned against the rock, and the skeleton of the soldier lay undisturbed within the mouldering uniform, as did the cold form of the dead four months before. None of those who went up and down the fields to bury the fallen, had found him. "Missing," was all that could have been known of him at home, and some mother may yet be patiently watching for the return of her boy, whose bones lie bleaching, unrecognized and alone, between the rocks at Gettysburg.

This narrative and the fact that the body was moved typically disturbs students and opens up a conversation about what the teacher should do and think when encountering primary and secondary sources. The idea of whether an image must depict what happened and the thought of whether utilizing corroborating information is always necessarily sufficient becomes a topic of discussion and one that is a vitally important one to broach.

July 2, 1776, as the Date of Independence

To encourage students to think more critically about what they believe they know and about what they are told, the date of the declaration of our nation's independence can be examined. This process will help allow students to be more critical in their thinking, prepare them for Stage 1 (Scrutinizing the Fundamental Source[s]) of the SOURCES framework, and will set them up nicely to begin any historical investigation. This activity should begin with a listing of thoughts that come to students' minds when July 4th is mentioned. Students may reference fireworks, celebrations, family gatherings, and other visions associated with the date in 1776 when, they are traditionally told, the declaration occurred. Images for fireworks displays in Washington, DC, can be displayed while the discussion is held. Next, a discussion of the Committee of Five (John Adams, Benjamin Franklin, Thomas Jefferson, Robert Livingston, and Roger Sherman) and the painting of *The Declaration of Independence, July 4, 1776* by John Trumbull (b02.deliver.odai.yale.edu/4b/83/4b836cfe-f3de-47b7-9899-31df7970b30b/ag-obj-69-0001-pub-large.jpg; Figure 1.6) should be displayed and examined.

Students should be asked to share what they know about this image, what they interpret to be happening, and how the title helps them to better understand what the painting is depicting. For more information about this painting, one can visit the Yale University Art Gallery webpage (artgallery.yale.edu/collections/objects/69), where the history of this painting and a number of issues and inaccuracies are discussed.

Once a sufficient conversation has been held, a letter from John Adams to his wife, Abigail Adams (www.masshist.org/digitaladams/archive/popup?id=

Figure 1.6. The Declaration of Independence, July 4, 1776

L17760703jasecond&page=L17760703jasecond_1; Figure 1.7) should be shared with the students.

The teacher should begin by asking students to determine the date of the letter and to put this into the context of what has been discussed. They should note that, by looking at the top right portion of the letter, the reader could surmise that the letter was written in Philadelphia on July 3, 1776. If none state it clearly, they should be reminded that this letter was written by one of the Committee of Five on the day before the signing of the Declaration of Independence, now known as Independence Day. The following section, found on pages 2–3, should be read to the students, where John Adams boldly and decisively proclaims:

> The Second Day of July 1776, will be the most memorable Epocha, in the History of America. I am apt to believe that it will be celebrated, by succeeding Generations, as the great anniversary Festival. It ought to be commemorated, as the Day of Deliverance by solemn Acts of Devotion to God Almighty. It ought to be solemnized with Pomp and Parade, with Shews, Games, Sports, Guns, Bells, Bonfires and Illuminations from one End of this Continent to the other from this Time forward forever more.

Figure 1.7. Letter from John Adams to Abigail Adams, July 3, 1776

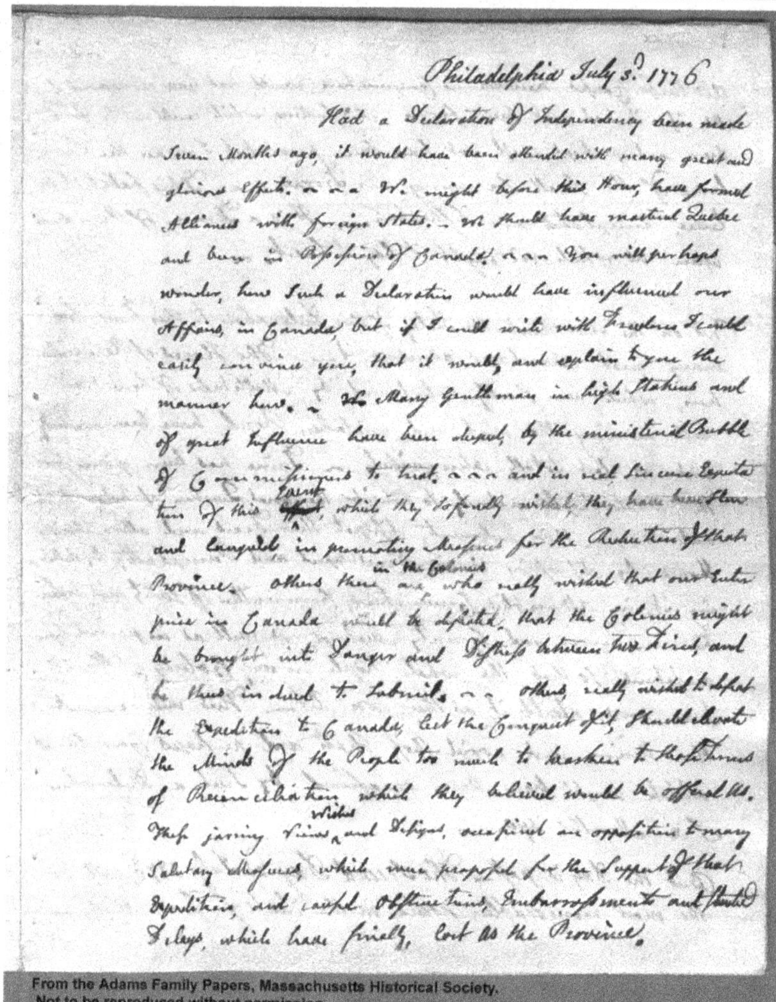

Philadelphia July 3. 1776

Had a Declaration of Independency been made seven Months ago, it would have been attended with many great and glorious Effects. . . We might before this Hour, have formed Alliances with foreign States.—We should have mastered Quebec and been in Possession of Canada. . . You will perhaps wonder, how such a Declaration would have influenced our Affairs, in Canada, but if I could write with Freedom I could easily convince you, that it would, and explain to you the manner how.—Many Gentlemen in high Stations and of great Influence have been duped, by the ministerial Bubble of Commissioners to treat. . . And in real, sincere Expectation of this Event, which they so fondly wished, they have been slow and languid, in promoting Measures for the Reduction of that Province. Others there are in the Colonies who really wished that our Enterprize in Canada would be defeated, that the Colonies might be brought into Danger and Distress between two Fires, and be thus induced to submit. . . Others really wished to defeat the Expedition to Canada, lest the Conquest of it, should elevate the Minds of the People too much to hearken to those Terms of Reconciliation which they believed would be offered Us. These jarring Views, Wishes and Designs, occasioned an opposition to many salutary Measures, which were proposed for the Support of that Expedition, and caused Obstructions, Embarrassments and studied Delays, which have finally, lost Us the Province.

Students should be asked to summarize what John Adams was suggesting as he wrote this letter on July 3, 1776, and in what ways this causes them to question the validity of celebrating the date of our nation's independence as July 4 each year. They should be asked what other sources they would need to corroborate this belief, because this is a letter from just one person on the committee and may not necessarily be reliable. As the teacher wraps up this activity, further discussion of the Trumbull painting should occur. Certain troubling elements should be addressed, among them the fact that the painting took more than 3 decades to complete; that many depicted in the painting were not present for the signing, opposed the declaration, and never signed; and even that some of the figures were not the actual individuals themselves but likenesses of their sons or other stand-ins. Other sources that can be shared at this point include the broadside of the Declaration of Independence produced by John Dunlap on July 4, 1776 (www.wdl.org/en/item/2716) and an engrossed copy of the Declaration, dated July 4, 1776 (www.archives.gov/founding-docs/declaration). Once again, students should think critically about the validity and accuracy of utilizing a single source, such as a painting, to determine what happened in the past or to construct a narrative about any topic of study.

EVALUATION OF SOURCES

As students learn to be more critical of the sources they encounter, they should be given the opportunity to evaluate and weigh the importance of particular sources against others. They should be provided with various historical questions and associated sources for them to determine which source, of those available, best allows them to answer the historical question. For example, students could be asked the question "Why were Lewis and Clark traveling west?" They could be provided with two sources: a letter from Thomas Jefferson to Meriwether Lewis on June 20, 1803, outlining the mission proposed by Jefferson (image: www.visitthecapitol.gov/exhibitions/artifact/president-thomas-jeffersons-instructions-meriwether-lewis-june-20-1803; transcription: www.loc.gov/exhibits/lewisandclark/transcript57.html) and a portion of a documentary film, such as the one created by Ken Burns (www.pbs.org/show/lewis-clark), which focuses on the lives of Meriwether Lewis and William Clark. The students would need to discuss the two sources provided to them and decide:

- Which source is better for assisting you with answering the historical question?
- Could you use both sources?
- If you were to have the opportunity to examine other sources, what would they be?

One could also present two narratives from a similar type of source, such as two articles from different newspapers about a single event. For example, one may examine two news stories about an event such as Patrick Gilmore's peace jubilee, which was held in Boston, Massachusetts, in June 1869. On June 26, 1869, the *Albany* (Oregon) *Register* published a piece (chroniclingamerica.loc.gov/lccn/sn84022643/1869-06-26/ed-1/seq-1) about this gathering that characterized the event as having "from ten to twelve thousand persons. The audience was probably 25,000, notwithstanding a heavy shower." The author of this piece wraps it up by stating that at the end of the performance:

> The audience stood on the seats, shouted and made an extraordinary demonstration. The last piece was repeated by the whole mass again. At the conclusion there were repeated cheers from the audience and the performers. The building was soon vacated and every person was loud in praise of the success of the inaugural day of Jubilee.

On July 7, 1869, the *Democratic Enquirer* (Ohio) ran a piece in which the author states that:

> The Mongrel party has had what they call a "peace jubilee" . . . hundreds of thousands of dollars were squandered. . . . They shouted, sang, and made huge noises with anvils, cannon, and musical instruments—all in mockery of the woes of the nation at this time.

As one can see from short sections of the two different depictions, these narratives almost do not seem to be depicting the same event. This is a good example to remind students that all sources are biased, and so often this bias is demonstrated in the sources themselves. It is typical for students to believe that if it is a primary source it must be true and free of distortion. A discussion about the inherent bias in all sources is necessary. This contributes to the argument for a need for multiple sources from multiple perspectives, and the use of a mix of sources that both corroborate and refute.

As a follow-up to this, students can be provided engaging questions of interest, along with two associated sources to determine which they prefer and find to be more reliable. The Stanford History Education Group has constructed a lesson in which they provide a handout with historical questions for students to consider, such as "Who was present at the signing of the Declaration of Independence?," "What was the layout of the Nazi concentration camp Auschwitz?," and "Did American soldiers commit atrocities during the Vietnam War in 1969?" (sheg.stanford.edu/history-lessons/evaluating-sources). This is an excellent resource for helping to create discerning students.

Teachers should discuss with students what their thoughts are regarding sources that have information missing, such as an isolated sentence, a paragraph, or an abridged version of a speech or document. For example, in the process of researching George Washington, a student may come across his *Farewell Address*. Students typically do not have an understanding of what an ellipsis—the three dots indicating that information has been left out—means and how this might impact the message being conveyed in a document. Other possible issues with acquiring the intended message of the creator should be addressed. This includes transcriptions and modern-day readings of historical documents and speeches. For example, the reading of Frederick Douglass's speech *The Meaning of July Fourth for the Negro* can be quite powerful, especially when it is read by James Earl Jones (www.youtube.com

/watch?v=8tTkHJWxfP0); however, because much of the speech is left out and even portions of it moved around, the reader should question this as a legitimate source to be used when learning about the past. Additionally, because James Earl Jones has a familiar voice associated with Darth Vader from *Star Wars*, Mufasa from *The Lion King*, and CNN, this may be confusing for students and may lead to misunderstandings about Frederick Douglass.

It is vital for students to develop skills to evaluate evidence, weigh the importance of a variety of sources to a particular narrative or argument, and understand what they see in sources as well as transcripts and translations of text. This is also important because in the next stage, students will engage with sets of primary sources and weigh conflicting, as well as confirming, evidence against other sources focused around a theme or topic.

PRIMARY SOURCE SETS

When students become comfortable working with a single source or pair of sources, teachers should provide primary source sets (Figure 1.8) of multiple items for them to analyze. These sets may focus on topics for which primary sources can be elucidative, such as

- The Seven Years' War (www.mountvernon.org/education/lesson-plans/lesson/seven-years-war-primary-source-set)
- The Civil War: The Nation Moves Towards War, 1850–61 (www.loc.gov/teachers/classroommaterials/primarysourcesets/civil-war-approach)
- Civil War Images: Depictions of African Americans in the War Effort (loc.gov/teachers/classroommaterials/primarysourcesets/african-american-civil-war-depictions)
- The Treaty of Versailles and the End of World War I (dp.la/primary-source-sets/treaty-of-versailles-and-the-end-of-world-war-i)

As students are analyzing the sets, they still are expected to carefully *observe, reflect,* and *question* each of the sources; however, an additional goal will be for them to determine the purpose of each of the sources included, why this source set has been created, and the overall significance of the set.

Lincoln's Pockets

A model example that could be introduced to the students is one created by the Library of Congress entitled *Lincoln's Pockets* (www.loc.gov/teachers/professionaldevelopment/tpsdirect/pdf/Lincolns-Pockets.pdf; Figure 1.9). Within this set, students will be able to see items worn by President Abraham

Figure 1.8. Sample Primary Source Set

Lincoln or found in his pockets on the night he was assassinated. The powerful thing about this particular set is that these sources were found on a person considered a great and powerful man, but, when considered carefully, they are fairly ordinary in nature and used by a variety of people at that period in time or even today. This helps students recognize that all sources are useful, even the items found on an individual at any point in time.

Teachers may introduce this in a variety of ways; however, it would be best to introduce one source at a time to groups of 3–4 students. This way, the students can analyze each source one at a time and continually reexamine what they think the significance of the set might be. After a sufficient amount

Figure 1.9. Contents of President Lincoln's Pockets on the Night of His Assassination

of time has elapsed, a second source should be added, and then a third, and so on until all the sources have been given to the students. Depending on the students' comfort level with analyzing primary sources and on the purpose for the teacher, an analysis sheet may not be necessary when examining a set such as this one. The ultimate goal for this exercise is to allow the students to see how one source in isolation does not create a proper understanding or narrative about the past. Students will see that their understandings evolve as each new source is acquired. Once students have examined all of the sources from this set and have thought about a title for the collection or a statement of the significance of the collection of sources, a classroom discussion should be held to evaluate various options for what the set represents. Additionally, the teacher should ensure that all students understand what each source is and how each is significant to the whole collection of sources.

Lincoln's Whiskers

Now that students understand the terms *primary* and *secondary sources,* and have had an opportunity to analyze various sources and see the importance of sets of sources to the creation of historical narratives, children's literature can be introduced as a way to serve as a basis for historical inquiry and the creation of unique primary source sets. An approach known as a *book backdrop* can be introduced. With this approach, the teacher shares a piece of children's literature with the students. While they are enjoying the narrative, they are asked to create a list of primary sources associated with the content presented in the story, such as sources that would allow them to further illustrate their understanding of the narrative, help to provide a counternarrative to the piece of literature, or assist in filling in missing information not fully established in the story.

A story that works well with this approach is *Mr. Lincoln's Whiskers*, by Karen Winnick. As the story is read, students learn about an 11-year-old girl named Grace Bedell and her effort to get presidential candidate Abraham Lincoln to grow facial hair. Grace notes in a letter that she writes Lincoln (www.loc.gov/loc/lcib/0903/detail/letter02.html; Figure 1.10) that he "would look a great deal better for [his] face is so thin. All the ladies like whiskers and they would tease their husband's to vote for you and then you would be President." As the story is read to the students, their list should grow with a variety of primary sources to serve as a backdrop to the literature being shared. Among these sources could be images of Lincoln with and without whiskers, the letter

Figure 1.10. Correspondence Between Candidate Lincoln and 11-year-old Grace Bedell in 1860

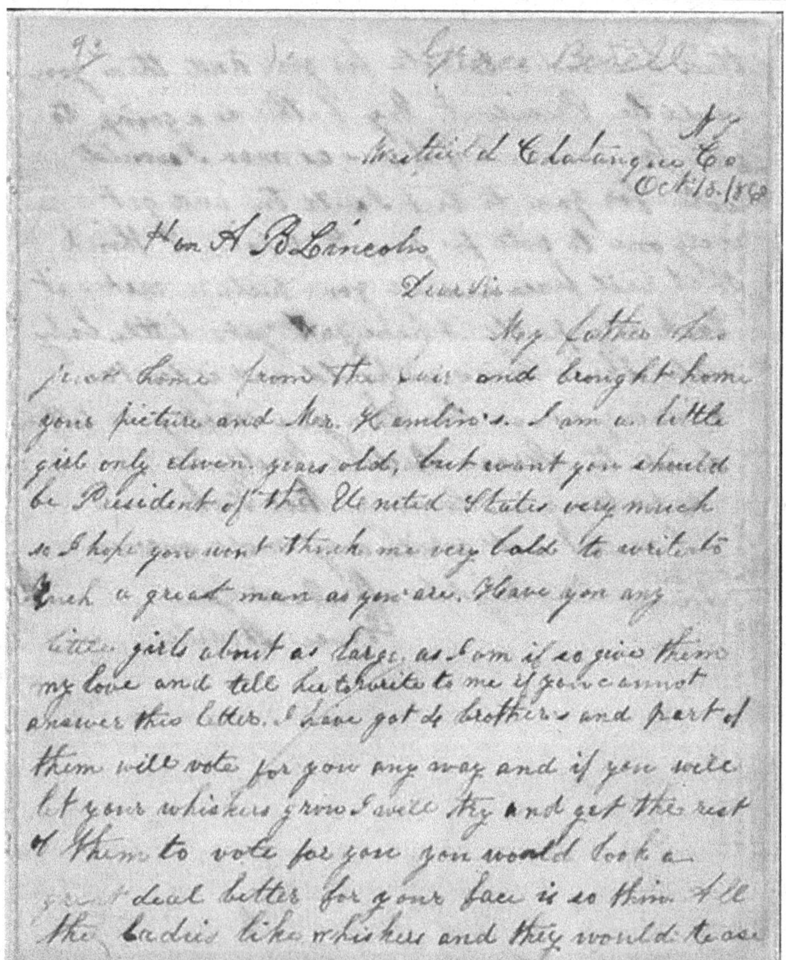

NY
Westfield Chatauque Co
Oct 15. 1860

Hon A B Lincoln

Dear Sir

My father has just home from the fair and brought home your picture and Mr. Hamlin's. I am a little girl only eleven years old, but want you should be President of the United States very much so I hope you wont think me very bold to write to such a great man as you are. Have you any little girls about as large as I am if so give them my love and tell her to write to me if you cannot answer this letter. I have got 4 brothers and part of them will vote for you any way and if you will let your whiskers grow I will try and get the rest of them to vote for you you would look a great deal better for your face is so thin. All the ladies like whiskers and they would tease that Grace writes to candidate Lincoln and his response, election ballots, and postage stamps from that time. Students see how primary sources can help to corroborate a narrative or even provide another perspective that one may not have considered. On the Library of Congress website, there is a primary source set for *Mr. Lincoln's Whiskers* (www.loc.gov/teachers/professionaldevelopment/tpsdirect/pdf/Book-Backdrops.pdf) that can be shared.

THE SOURCES FRAMEWORK FOR TEACHING WITH PRIMARY SOURCES

Once students have been empowered with a variety of skills related to working with primary and secondary sources, it would be appropriate to engage in more complex and authentic historical inquiry-based activities and investigations. Because history students are afforded various ways to learn about and engage with the past, it is essential that educators think critically about how they frame, scaffold, and facilitate their students' educational opportunities. Thus, it is important to properly guide students and structure the historical inquiry process to carefully determine how primary sources will be introduced, especially because many may not have learned how to effectively or correctly engage with and analyze primary sources. Through the use of the SOURCES framework for teaching with primary sources, students are provided a structure and scaffolding to direct their investigations. In the following section, the SOURCES framework is outlined for use in the history classroom. However, this framework easily may be utilized in all content areas.

In the first stage of the SOURCES framework, *Scrutinizing the Fundamental Source(s)*, students are asked to analyze a primary source related to the selected topic of study. Two sources may be used if they are both deemed crucial, but for this initial stage, the use of one source is optimal. The fundamental source is the one that would be considered vital to any proper study of the topic being considered. To help scaffold the process of examining this fundamental source, the teacher should supply a fundamental question that will guide the entire historical inquiry process associated with the topic of study. These questions should not be dichotomous in nature and should not allow for an easy, common answer; rather, they should encourage students to think critically and should necessitate careful examination of the sources provided throughout the entire process. Examples of fundamental questions for this sort of inquiry could be "What

The SOURCES Framework for Teaching with Primary and Secondary Sources

1. Scrutinizing the Fundamental Source(s)
2. Organizing Thoughts
3. Understanding the Context
4. Reading Between the Lines
5. Corroborating and Refuting
6. Establishing a Plausible Narrative
7. Summarizing Final Thoughts

historical and social impacts can be associated with the assassination of John F. Kennedy?," "To what extent did the end of slavery improve the lives of African Americans in the South?," or "What are some of the events that led to the writing of the United States Constitution, and how did those events impact the content of this document?" In addition to providing a fundamental question to facilitate the historical inquiry process, it is essential to provide students with other proper scaffolds, analysis sheets, and guiding questions or prompts, such as those in the analysis sheet shown in Figure 1.11 (www.sourcesconference.com/uploads/1/0/4/0/10400589/sources_framework_1_.pdf).

For the second stage of this inquiry process, students are asked to *Organize Thoughts* associated with the fundamental source, the fundamental question, and any other information gleaned at this point in time. Students should ask themselves what they know about the topic or theme that is emerging and what more they need to know to properly analyze the fundamental source, as well as others to come. Additionally, students will need to critically think about the fundamental question and ensure that they understand what is being asked and how they might go about answering it.

During the third stage, *Understanding the Context,* students are given an opportunity to think about what they know about the historical context related to the fundamental question and fill in gaps in their understanding. Depending on the ability level and content knowledge of the students, this can be provided by the teacher through children's literature, brief videos, primary and secondary sources, guest speakers, or whatever method is most appropriate. Alternatively, students can independently find necessary information to form a more complete understanding of the associated context.

Now that the students have formed a better understanding about the topic of study and can formulate thoughts regarding the fundamental question, they are asked to revisit the fundamental source and carefully *Read Between the Lines* to interpret the rationale and purpose for the creation of the fundamental source. Students must think critically about what they know about this source presently and what knowledge has emerged since they first encountered the source. Teachers can provide specific prompts, questions, and scaffolds to assist students in this analysis. This is an essential step in the historical

Figure 1.11. SOURCES Analysis Sheet

What do you know?	What do you think you know?	What do you wonder?

thinking process; students will then understand that a source's creator(s) often had deliberate reasons for its creation that typically are not apparent from the initial analysis of the source.

Depending upon the expertise of the students conducting the SOURCES inquiry, the *Corroborating and Refuting* stage can vary in structure. If students are more adept at analyzing sources and working independently, the teacher can assign students the task of finding sources that will corroborate or refute their understandings, in regard to the fundamental question. If the students are at a less advanced level, the teacher can instead provide a set of primary and secondary sources, scaffolding questions, analysis sheets, and any other necessary information that will help them to develop a more complex and diverse understanding of the topic of study.

Now, students should be prepared to *Establish a Plausible Narrative.* This can be created in the form of a traditional paper, documentary movie, historical marker, play or skit, diary, or whatever artifact the teacher decides is the best product for allowing for assessment of each student's acquisition of the desired content. Lastly, in the *Summarizing Final Thoughts* stage, students are asked to think about the process that was undertaken, the procedures and patterns of thought they engaged in that mimic what a historian does, what they have learned about the topic of study and the fundamental question, how they came to know what they know, and what questions still exist.

Engaging with the past, especially when utilizing primary sources, is a valuable and educational experience for students of various abilities and ages. It is essential that the process be properly scaffolded in order to help ensure success and, hopefully, engender interest and passion for learning history. The SOURCES framework is one tool that can help history teachers in this endeavor.

In the following chapters, the authors will present several examples of different topics that have been used in history classrooms. The readers should consider how each of the investigations might work in their classroom, how modifications might be made, and how existing curriculum might be enhanced through the use of the SOURCES framework. If teachers are flexible in thought and approach, have the proper primary and secondary sources, and desire an authentic historical engagement for their students, the SOURCES framework is the perfect structure for bringing historical content and thinking to life in any classroom.

CHAPTER 2

What Would Historians Write About Thomas Garber?

An Application of a SOURCES Lesson

In the following lesson example, students are asked to find out: "What would historians write about Thomas Garber?" The SOURCES framework for teaching with primary sources provides the structure and scaffolding to guide the students throughout the investigation. This lesson is presented for many reasons, but mainly because this is the first example constructed and tested using the SOURCES framework, over a span of more than 20 years, and has proven to be an engaging and successful example of what authentic historical engagement and inquiry in the history classroom can and should be.

SCRUTINIZING THE FUNDAMENTAL SOURCE(S)

In this first stage of the framework, students should scrutinize a fundamental source. To begin a historical investigation utilizing the SOURCES framework, the teacher should provide students with one or, if necessary, two sources that are deemed vital to the topic of study and the inquiry to follow. In this case, the source chosen to frame and encourage engagement is a letter from Thomas Garber to Addie Garber dated August 15, 1862 (valley.lib.virginia.edu/papers/A0806; Figure 2.1) from Camp Gordonsville, Virginia. In this letter, Thomas writes home to his family to inform them about the military company that he has joined and some of his activities, and to inquire about family members and their health. Students can read the letter individually, but it would be best if the teacher read the letter aloud to the class. As the letter is read aloud, students should listen for information that may be interesting, specific dates and names, or anything else that catches their attention. The teacher should complete a What do you know?, What do you think you know?, and What do you wonder? analysis sheet (refer to Figure 1.11), or similar graphic organizer, with the class. For the first column of the chart, students will need to tell what they know about the time frame, content, or Thomas Garber from the letter that was read aloud to them. Students often mention comments about him joining Captain C. J. O'Ferral's company from Warren County, Virginia,

Figure 2.1. Augusta County: Thomas Garber to Addie Garber, August 15, 1862

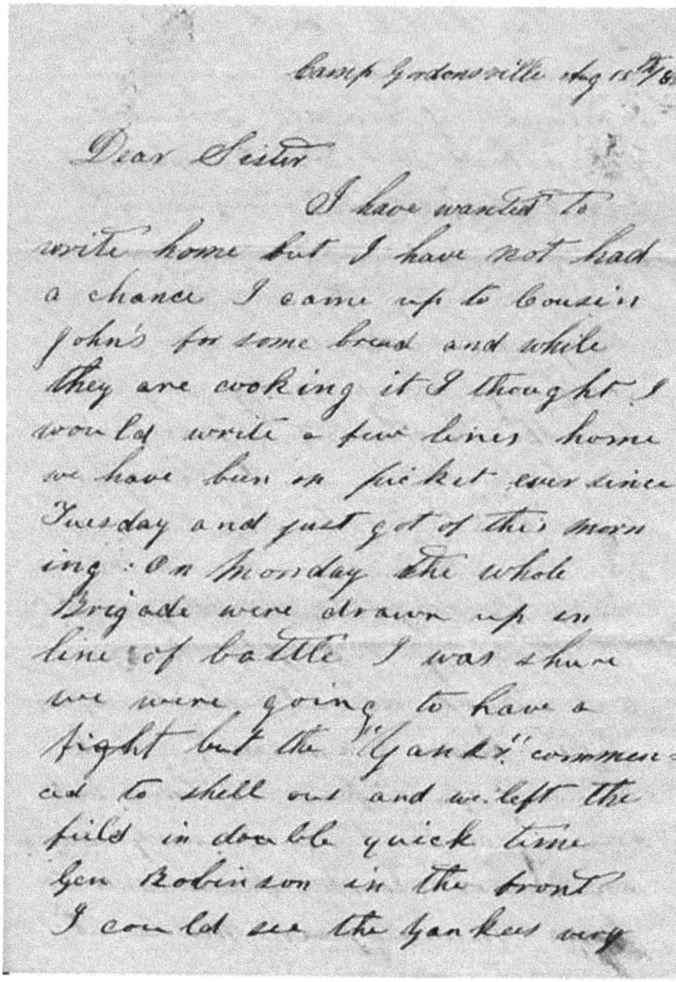
Camp Gordonsville Aug 15th/62

Dear Sister

I have wanted to write home but I have not had a chance I come up to Cousin John's for some bread and while they are cooking it I thought I would write a few lines home we have bin on picket ever since Tuesday and just got of this morning. On Monday the whole Brigade were drawn up in line of battle I was sure we were going to have a fight but the "Yanks" commenced to shell out and we left the field in double quick time Gen Robinson in the front I could see the Yankees way

that he is carrying the colors for the regiment, he is having difficulty managing his horse, that he was carrying a dispatch to General Jackson, and that he has seen Ash and Mike several times but has not seen Ned but once. He also asked specifically about sister Seal and mentions that he hopes she is not very sick. He ends the letter by asking Addie to give his love to Sister Seal, Pa, Ma, Kate, Nelly, and all others who ask about him. He also makes a comment about writing a good many times and putting an unfinished letter in his pocket and that once he was able to get back to writing the letter, he would learn that the letter was "spoiled."

For the middle column of the chart, students should use their own understandings and information gained from the letter to make educated guesses or hypotheses about what is happening to Thomas at this point in time, or what the information shared means. Students have made statements that "Sister Seal" is not really a biological sister but is, in fact, a nun who is close with the Garber family. Some also think that Thomas is brave, that the Garber family might have been slave owners, and that Thomas will not survive through the end of the war.

In the third column of the analysis sheet (Figure 1.11), the students are asked to think about what they might want to know and what they wonder about at this point in time in regard to Thomas Garber, the time period, or any other information that we shared in the letter. Students often ask questions specifically about Thomas Garber, his family, what life was like for typical soldiers of the time period, and why a letter would spoil. Questions about Thomas focus on his age, what his responsibilities in the army might be, why he is fighting, where he travels during the war, and whether Thomas even survived the war. All of these questions should be captured and written on the board or projected onto a screen from a computer so that the diversity of thoughts and questions can be discussed and analyzed. This is an important step in wrapping up the first stage of the framework and can help to enhance understandings related to the fundamental source and engender interest in the topic and investigation to come.

ORGANIZING THOUGHTS

In this step students create a graphic organizer or a foldable to collect their thoughts and questions. A six-door organizer works perfectly for this lesson. Students are asked to choose six questions of interest and to write them in their organizer. They are allowed to use any of the questions that came up in class, and/or they may add ones of their own. These questions may include things such as the following:

- What did you learn about Thomas Garber from reading this letter?
- What does this tell you about the life of a Civil War soldier?
- What else would you like to know about Thomas Garber?
- How could you find the answers to these questions?
- Do you think Thomas was afraid?
- Do you think Thomas missed his family?
- What do you think was Thomas's job in the army?
- How old do you think Thomas was when he wrote this letter?
- Was Thomas killed in the war?
- Did Thomas have other brothers and sisters?
- Who were Thomas's parents?
- What was life like during the Civil War for the average family?
- What was it like to be a teenager during the Civil War?

Once students have written down their questions on their graphic organizers, the teacher can begin a discussion about how a historian may go about answering these questions. An excellent resource for determining Thomas's age or for learning more about his family is the 1860 census data for Augusta County, Virginia (valley.lib.virginia.edu/population_census), provided by the Virginia Center for Digital History. When initiating the search, students can learn that Thomas Garber was 14 years old when the census was conducted in 1860 (Figure 2.2). Therefore, they will be able to determine that Thomas was around 16 years old when the letter was written in 1862. According to the census data, Thomas had attended school in the past year, but the data indicate that he could not read or write. Once students learn this, they often ask how is it possible that Thomas wrote home. This is a great opportunity to get students to start thinking about various options regarding how this letter from Thomas was actually written. Typically, as a class, it can be determined that possibilities include things such as:

- Thomas wrote the letter;
- He may not have had the ability in 1860 to be considered literate but that he learned enough in school to write the letter in 1862;
- The information collected in the census data was not accurate;
- The census data was entered into the online database incorrectly; or,
- Somebody who was literate wrote the letter for Thomas.

Figure 2.2. Census Data, 1860, for Thomas Garber

Personal Information

Name:	Thomas Garber
Age:	14
Order in Family:	6
Sex:	Male
Race:	White
Birth Place:	Va.
Attended School in Past Year:	yes
Can Read:	no
Can Write:	no

Location

County:	Augusta
District:	North Subdiv.

Census Record Information

Page Number:	965
Dwelling Number:	1020
Family Number:	1025

Figure 2.3. Search Tool—Finding the Garber Family

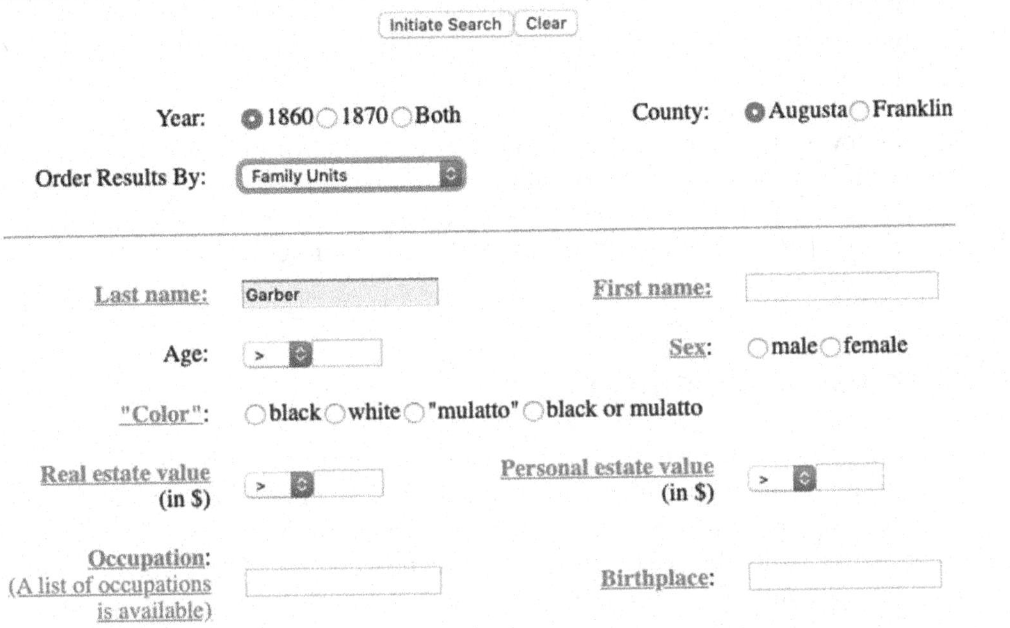

Using the information that is found here, one can then learn more about Thomas's family and determine that he is the sixth of eight family members in the "family number" 1025. If you return to the original page where you were able to search the U.S. Census for 1860, you may search Augusta County for those individuals with the last name of Garber to learn more about the family. It is crucial to use the drop-down menu for "order results by" to include the results by "family units" (Figure 2.3). When doing this, you can see that there are eight family members in the Garber household (Figure 2.4). The father of the household is Albert, age 56, and he is a farmer who was born in Virginia.

The mother is Mary, age 48. She was born in Pennsylvania and does not have an occupation. There are six children in the Garber household, three

Figure 2.4. Results for the Garber Family in the 1860 Census (Family Number 1025)

1025	7	Garber	Katherine	12	Female	White		North Subdiv.
1025	8	Garber	Ellen	6	Female	White		North Subdiv.
1025	2	Garber	Mary	48	Female	White		North Subdiv.
1025	3	Garber	Asher	25	Male	White	Machinist	North Subdiv.
1025	4	Garber	Michael	18	Male	White	Moulder	North Subdiv.
1025	5	Garber	Martha	16	Female	White		North Subdiv.
1025	6	Garber	Thomas	14	Male	White		North Subdiv.
1025	1	Garber	Albert	56	Male	White	Farmer	North Subdiv.

girls and three boys. Thomas is the fourth oldest of six children. When looking more closely at all of the family members, the census data records indicate that none of the family members are able to read or write. The census data records answer several of the questions that students have, including the ages of family members and other information about their schooling and literacy; however, the examination of the records often brings about new questions of interest. When it is the most appropriate moment to share information about schooling and literacy, inform the class that literacy was not recorded for any minors at this time, so, in the census records, no child would be described as able to read or write.

UNDERSTANDING THE CONTEXT

In this next stage, students have the opportunity to share their questions and tentative understandings with classmates and think about what information they know about this time period, about the American Civil War, about life as a soldier, and about any other content related to the investigation. Situating the material within the overall context is critical to a comprehensive understanding of events, and this can be done in one of a number of ways, providing a more holistic examination and development of a deeper understanding. For example, reading an effective piece of children's literature can often activate knowledge, thoughts, and questions, and provide the information needed to further investigate the questions of interest to the students. Good options for children's literature would be books and stories that focus on the lives of soldiers during the Civil War, especially any that include main characters who are younger than the students might imagine. Documentaries, websites, additional primary and secondary sources, and a class discussion about the content can be provided as well, if necessary. Such resources, whether teacher-introduced or student-selected, can be used as tools to provide additional context and information related to the topic or event under examination, and used in future phases of the SOURCES framework, such as *Reading Between the Lines* or *Corroborating and Refuting*.

READING BETWEEN THE LINES

In the *Reading Between the Lines* stage of the SOURCES framework, the teacher should guide students in a process of going back to the fundamental source with their newfound knowledge regarding the source and the topic of study. Students are asked to once again engage with the fundamental source and think about their initial impressions and how their understandings acquired since the first time that they viewed the source have changed. This thought

Suggestions for Civil War–Related Children's Literature

Pink and Say—by Patricia Polacco
Now or Never: 54th Massachusetts Infantry's War to End Slavery—by Ray Anthony Shepard
Soldier Song: A True Story of the Civil War—by Debbie Levy
John Lincoln Clem: Civil War Drummer Boy (Based on a True Story)—by E. F. Abbott
Louisa May's Battle: How the Civil War Led to Little Women—by Kathleen Krull
Nurse, Soldier, Spy: The Story of Sarah Edmonds, A Civil War Hero—by Marissa Moss
The Mostly True Adventures of Homer P. Figg—by Rodman Philbrick
I'll Pass for Your Comrade: Women Soldiers in the Civil War—by Anita Silvey
Two Girls of Gettysburg—by Lisa Klein

process should help deepen understanding but should also encourage them to think about other questions of interest and how the investigation could proceed.

Now that the students have a deeper understanding of the lives of soldiers during the American Civil War, each student should be given a copy of the initial letter written by Thomas Garber to his sister Addie. With better contextual understanding of the time period and the fact that children were often fighting, the students should be able to more deeply understand the content provided in this letter and think about what Thomas might have experienced. Students should revisit the questions that were written into the graphic organizer and think about the questions posed by classmates. Guidance can be provided, and questions of particular interest can be asked of the students, such as:

- What more did you learn about Thomas Garber from rereading this letter?
- What else would you like to know about Thomas Garber now?
- Do you wonder where Thomas traveled during the American Civil War?
- Did you consider whether he survived the war?
- Do you think that Thomas was afraid or had fears related to serving in the Confederate army?
- What are you thinking about the Garber family or individuals in the family?
- How could you find the answers to these questions?

Questions such as these focus students and prepare them to analyze their thought processes and understanding at this point in time, especially with regard to the fundamental question posed for the investigation. At this point, they are ready to and should consider evidence that may corroborate or refute their hypotheses and understanding.

CORROBORATING AND REFUTING

During this stage of the framework, teachers will be leading students through a process in which they are to think about and utilize primary and secondary sources that will corroborate and refute their tentative understandings or answers to the fundamental question provided earlier in the investigation. For this example, teachers should arrange students into mixed-ability groups of four to five students. The students should discuss the questions that they wrote down on their six-door organizers as well as methods for how they might go about answering them. After a sufficient interval, the teacher should provide a set of letters to each group. These letters include correspondence sent from Thomas to his father and other family members, as well as letters from Thomas's cousins to the family. In small groups, students analyze:

- Asher Harman to Albert Garber, September 24, 1862 (valley.lib.virginia.edu/papers/A0808)
- Thomas Garber to Albert Garber, September 25, 1862 (valley.lib.virginia.edu/papers/A0809)
- Thomas Garber to Addie Garber, December 6, 1862 (valley.lib.virginia.edu/papers/A0811)
- Thomas Garber to Albert Garber, April 15, 1863 (valley.lib.virginia.edu/papers/A0813)
- Thomas Garber to Addie Garber, May 29, 1863 (valley.lib.virginia.edu/papers/A0812)

If a teacher feels it necessary and has the time, it often works best to have five groups of students, where each group is assigned only one letter for which they are to become an expert. Students would analyze the letter to see how it might attend to the questions posed by all members within the group and found within the six-door organizers. They are then to provide an overall synopsis of the letter and discuss any findings related to the questions of interest with the group. Then, students can be jigsawed into new groups, where each newly formed group has one expert on each of the letters. During this period of time, all of the questions, as well as any new ones that surface, should be discussed, and students should record any answers to their questions and any evidence in their organizers.

After the students have had a sufficient amount of time to analyze and discuss the set of letters, the teacher may read them a letter from Thomas's

Figure 2.5. Letter from M. G. Harman to Albert Garber, June 20, 1863

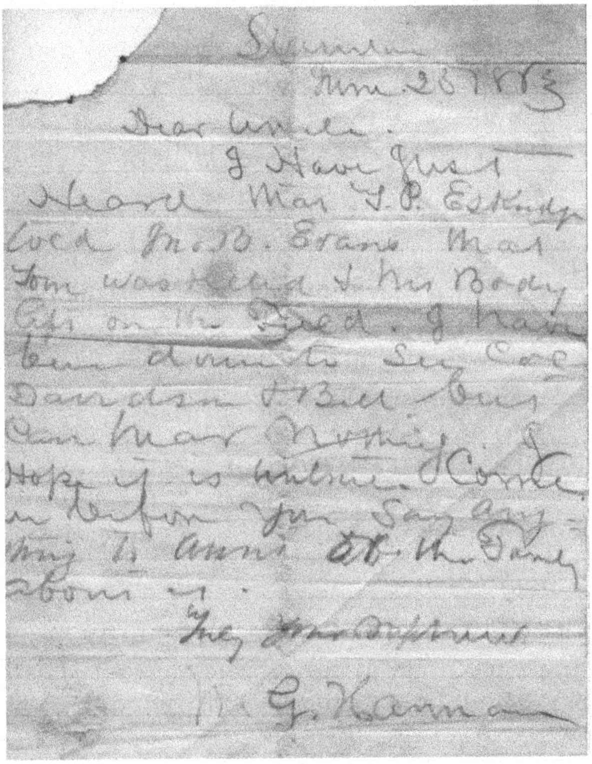

Staunton
June 20 1863
Dear Uncle.
I Have Just Heard that Maj T. P. Eskridge told Mr. B. Evans that Tom was killed & his Body Left on the Field. I have been down to see Col Davidson & Bill but can hear nothing. I Hope it is untrue. Come in before you say anything to Aunt or the Family about it.
Very Affectionately
M. G. Harman

cousin, M. G. Harman, to Thomas's father, Albert Garber, dated June 20, 1863 (Figure 2.5). In this letter, M. G. informs the Garber family that:

> I have just Heard Maj T. P. Eskridge told Mr. B. Evans that Tom was killed & his body left on the Field. I have been down to see Col Davidson & Bill but can hear *nothing*. I Hope it is untrue. Come in before you say anything to Aunt or the Family about it.

At this point, students are asked what new information they have obtained and their current understandings and beliefs, especially in regard to the questions posed in the six-door organizer. Typically, someone responds that they know that Thomas is dead. It is important to pause and wait for any response from other students. Hopefully, a student will note that they are not sure if Thomas is dead. Not only is there a need for corroboration of evidence, but also there is specific language found within this letter, such as "I Hope it is untrue," and speculation rather than facts presented. Students should be asked what some of the possibilities, at this point in time, would be. Students may provide thoughts, such as the fact that he may possibly still be living, that he might have in fact died, that it might have been a case of misidentification, or other ideas.

Students should be asked where one might find more information to corroborate the idea that Thomas has died. They might offer up several suggestions, including utilizing census data records. If not, the teacher can bring up the idea of revisiting the census data for 1870 to conduct a search for Thomas Garber in the Augusta County records. When this is completed, a result of "there were no matches for the search you requested" is provided. Students should be asked what this means, and typically, at least one student informs the class that this means that Thomas is dead. Other students may suggest that this does not mean that he is dead, as Thomas may have moved to another county or the census data might be wrong. Students may suggest that he may have moved to Lexington to attend school, referencing evidence found within an earlier letter (May 29, 1863). As mentioned earlier in the chapter, some explain that census data records may have errors in them and, additionally, the individual who transcribed the information to the website may have made an error. These sorts of questions and further analysis help to inform the students' thinking and are important to the *Corroborating and Refuting* stage in the SOURCES framework. These sorts of skills and ways of thinking are vital to authentic historical engagement but are also necessary in the navigation of opinions, stories, and theories encountered in everyday life.

The teacher should next conduct a search looking for the Garber family (Family Number 1025) in the 1870 Census records and be sure to specify Augusta County and choose the drop-down menu so that the results are ordered by family unit. The results will show that there are no results for any Garber family members in Family Number 1025. Students should be questioned as to why this might be. Responses may include the thought that the whole family died, the whole family moved, and issues with census data reporting or transcription. The suggestion should be made that a search be conducted looking for Thomas's father, Albert Garber, as he might have been too old to fight but young enough to be alive in 1870. When the search is conducted, students will see that Albert is found but that he no longer has an occupation and that he has lost a considerable amount of land. Discussions about why a Confederate farm owner may have less land after the American Civil War should be conducted. Students should notice that the family number has changed at this point in time to 686, so they should be questioned as to why the family number changed. Responses typically focus on the fact that the population decreased as a result of the American Civil War or that the census data collection procedures may have changed. Another search can be conducted at this point for the Garber family in 1870 (Figure 2.6). When looking for the new family unit number of 686, students will see that all the male family members, except for Albert, are no longer listed within this family unit. This brings up thoughts of whether all the male children died during the

Figure 2.6. Results for the Garber Family in the 1870 Census (Family Number 686)

686	1	Garber	Albert J.	66	Male	White	No Occupation		
686	2	Garber	Mary J.	58	Female	White	Housekeeping	1st District	Staunton
686	3	Garber	Kate M.	20	Female	White	No Occupation	1st District	Staunton
686	4	Garber	Jane E.	18	Female	White	School	1st District	Staunton
686	5	Garber	Helen	25	Female	Black	Domestic	1st District	Staunton

Civil War, if they started families of their own, if they moved out of the county, or other feasible options. One entry of note is the listing of a Black domestic family member named Helen. As she was not listed in the 1860 Census but is present in the 1870 Census within this family unit, it brings up thoughts of whether this family owned slaves. The discussion of how African Americans were counted in the census data prior to the American Civil War occurs. It is also interesting for students to see that Helen is able to read and write.

After a sufficient amount of discussion has occurred, the teacher should read a letter from Thomas's cousin Lewis Harman to Thomas's sister Addie Garber dated July 20, 1863, informing his cousin that he is sending Thomas's belongings back home following his death. In this letter, Lewis notes that he "started Dear Tom's knapsack home," that he has "Tom's knife & Testament," and goes on to inform the family that he

> did not see dear Tom on the morning after he died, as we moved forward at dawn in pursuit of the enemy, when I had gotten back in the evening he had been buried by a party of his Company who had been sent to bury the dear fellow. The poor fellow suffered very little Dear Cousin, & I am sure he died as I wish to die & all other brave soldiers fighting in our most just cause.

Students are typically satisfied with the level of corroboration among the sources that have been examined. Although the idea of corroboration has been the primary focus during this stage of the Garber example, all of the sources provided may in fact have been used by students to refute inaccurate or misguided understandings and can allow students to modify hypotheses and thoughts throughout the entire stage.

At this point, some students would like to have further evidence to be fully satisfied with the notion that Thomas has died. To help with this, the teacher may reference a newspaper article from the *Staunton Vindicator*, dated July 3, 1863. In the article, one may read that "Thomas Garber of Augusta County was wounded in fighting in Upperville and has since died." Additional research can be conducted on the Battle of Upperville to learn more about this battle and the progress of Thomas's unit.

To help students think critically, the teacher may ask students why one would find a newspaper clipping about Thomas Garber in the *Staunton Vindicator* from May 11, 1866. Students typically inform the teacher that this could be a newspaper article about another Thomas Garber who perhaps did not die, or that there might be a memorial that has been dedicated to Thomas. After discussion has occurred about this new piece of evidence, students should be given the opportunity to view the text of the article:

> The remains of our gallant young townsman, Thos. M. Garber, youngest son of Albert J. Garber, Esq., color bearer of the 12th Virginia Cavalry, who fell mortally wounded in a cavalry engagement near Upperville, Va., were brought to Staunton on Tuesday week and re-interred in Thornrose Cemetery.

If there were concerns about the validity of the narrative that has been constructed to this point, this last piece of evidence typically eliminates any doubt.

Two final primary sources should be shared with the students to help with answering any additional questions and to build a deeper narrative about the life of Thomas Garber. The first is an illustration by Arthur R. Waud in the *Harper's Weekly* periodical (Figure 2.7). On July 11, 1863, there is the inclusion of an image from the "Battle Near Upperville." The caption reads:

> On page 445 we reproduce a sketch by Mr. A. R. Waud, illustrating THE BATTLE NEAR UPPERVILLE, Ashby's Gap in the distance. The square inclosure is called the vineyard; on the right on the rise is a stone-wall; against this a charge was made, the men returning to form again a little to the left. On the extreme left five rebel regiments came out with their large flags to charge our men before they could form, but the First and Sixth regulars, sweeping round the hill, charged upon them while the band played Hail Columbia.

Figure 2.7. The Army of the Potomac—Skirmish Near Upperville—Ashby's Gap in the Distance

The teacher should walk students through the thought process around what Thomas's role was in his regiment (color bearer) and lead them to understand that the last moments of Thomas's life were recorded in the image drawn by Arthur Waud and that he even makes mention that the "regiments came out with their large flags to charge our men."

The final source to be shared is an autobiography by Charles O'Ferrall (Figure 2.8) entitled *Forty Years of Active Service*. As the investigation can take on a life of its own and an end may be difficult to find if one were to consider all of the possible questions and avenues in which the investigation could travel, this source was chosen to be the last. It brings the inquiry back full circle to the initial fundamental source, as Charles O'Ferrall is mentioned by Thomas in his letter to his sister. If needed, the students should be reminded that in the initial letter that was read, Thomas mentions that he has "joined Capt. C. J. O'Ferral's from Warren County Va." Thus, this book is written by Thomas's commanding officer. On pages 79–80 of the autobiography, Charles writes:

> For some time prior to the Battle of Upperville the color-bearer of the Twelfth Cavalry was Tom Garber, a member of my company. Colonel Harman was Tom's cousin, and when Tom came to the regiment he asked his advice as to what company he should join, and the Colonel told him he thought Company I would suit him, so he enlisted in my company.

Figure 2.8. "Forty Years of Active Service"

> It did not take me long to determine of what metal he was made. In a fight he was in his element, and the hotter it was the better he liked it. He was only seventeen years of age, yet he was over six feet in height, splendidly built, and much more mature every way than most boys of his age. He had been raised in the saddle and was a superb rider. A vacancy occurred in the color sergeancy of the regiment—how it occurred I do not now remember, and Tom applied for the position and it was given to him, and never in any war, on any field, were the colors of an army more grandly and heroically borne.
>
> He entered the charge at Upperville in the van, with his colors streaming in the breezes above his head as he charged down the field to the stone fence. There under the rain of lead he stood waving the stars and bars until just as I was shot, when he reeled in his saddle, and still clinging to his flag staff he fell to the ground dead. He was the brother of Major A. H. Garber, of Richmond, whose record as the commander of Garber's battery is too well known to require any encomiums from me. Of all the brave and intrepid boys whom it was my pleasure and privilege to observe during four years of strife I never saw one who was superior of Tom Garber; and as brave and dashing as our calvalrymen were generally, I do not detract from them when I declare that I recall comparatively few who were his equals, taking him all and all. He rests in Thornrose Cemetery at Staunton, beneath the sod of old Augusta, and while she can boast of many gallant sons, she had none more gallant that the young color-bearer of the Twelfth Calvary who yielded up his life at Upperville.

This statement from Thomas's superior officer is a powerful and concrete way to conclude the inquiry and serves as a testament to the kind of person Thomas was. This is a powerful narrative and one that can nicely wrap up the corroborating and refuting stage of the investigation.

ESTABLISHING A PLAUSIBLE NARRATIVE

During the *Establishing a Plausible Narrative* stage of the SOURCES framework, students should think about the fundamental question, the investigation that ensued, and how they might be able to best answer the question that was to frame the inquiry process. This narrative can come in a variety of formats and should serve as an excellent opportunity for the teacher to assess the students' understanding and ability to think historically and to formulate and propose an evidence-based response to a critical question of interest. In order to assess the students' understanding of who Thomas was and the life that he lived during the American Civil War, they should create whatever assessment piece is deemed appropriate by the teacher or, if appropriate, by the students themselves. A good option is for the students to create a historical marker for Thomas Garber at the location of the Battle of Upperville or in his hometown. They could also write a letter to a local historical society outlining why Thomas Garber should be remembered, create a documentary film, write a piece of children's literature or a graphic novella, or whatever option is best to ascertain that the students acquired the desired information from the lesson. Students should also use any and all resources available, such as the Garber Family Letters found on the *Valley of the Shadow* website (valley .lib.virginia.edu/VoS/personalpapers/collections/augusta/garber.html). This opportunity to establish an original and evidence-based narrative is extremely important, not only for the historical inquiry process but also as a process necessary for civic engagement, as students need these skills to be able to critically examine sources and develop a response to a question posed to them. This leads them into the final stage, in which metacognitive awareness and thinking are employed.

SUMMARIZING FINAL THOUGHTS

In this final stage, students are asked to revisit the inquiry process and think about what they have learned from the Garber lesson, explicitly focusing on the questions that they posed in the *Organizing Thoughts* stage of the framework at the beginning of the investigation. Students should be asked to consider:

- How do I know what I know?
- What do historians do?
- Did I replicate what historians might do?
- What questions still exist?
- Is it okay that questions still exist?
- How might I answer questions that still exist?

This is building up on the analysis sheet (Figure 1.11) utilized at the beginning of the inquiry. The students should be encouraged to think about what they still wonder, want to know, or can answer. These thoughts should be recorded and discussed.

CONCLUSION

Through the utilization of the SOURCES Framework for Teaching with Primary and Secondary Sources, students are taken through an authentic historical inquiry process, focusing on an American Civil War soldier possibly not far off in age from them. Students are able to engage with the past and answer their unique questions with real sources from the time period. They are able to go through thought processes similar to those used by experts in social sciences and history and, at the same time, learn and practice skills vital to being critically-thinking and engaged citizens in society. In fact, these students should be considered as junior historians, and given additional opportunities to engage in further authentic history inquiry; their skills, knowledge, and critical-thinking abilities will only be enhanced. In the example found in the next chapter, students move from someone obscure like Thomas Garber to one of the founding brothers and our first president, George Washington, and examine and assess his plan, as Commander of the Continental Army, to attack Princeton at the beginning of 1777.

CHAPTER 3

Assessing General Washington's Plan to Attack Princeton at the Beginning of 1777

An Application of the SOURCES Framework

> For my part my Lucy I look up to Heaven & most devoutly thank the great Governor of the Universe for producing this turn in our affairs of America—& this sentiment I hope will so prevail on the Hearts of the people . . .
>
> —Henry Knox to Lucy Knox

In the opening statement from one of General George Washington's most trusted advisors and officers—and his eventual choice as the first Secretary of War—Henry Knox states the vital importance of the Battle of Princeton to the morale of those on the home front and to the success of the efforts for an independent American nation. In the following investigation scaffolded by the SOURCES framework, students are asked to assess the decisions made by General Washington and his choice to attack Princeton at the beginning of 1777, not only through the sources provided but in light of the statement made by Henry Knox about the importance of this battle.

As the end of 1776 drew near, control of the colonies in North America hung in the balance. General William Howe, the British commanding officer, decided to suspend military operations until the spring. In the Continental Army, morale was low, and, to make matters worse, the enlistment term for most of the Continentals was due to expire at midnight on December 31. General George Washington decided that "desperate diseases require desperate Remedies" (Washington, December 20, 1776, p. 382) and determined that the time for an attack was now, and that Trenton, New Jersey, was the perfect location for it. After a decisive victory at Trenton over the Hessians, many began to consider General Washington a truly brilliant leader (Wertenbaker, 1922). Initially, Washington determined that further operations at that time would not be wise and retreated across the Delaware River (Washington, December 27, 1776). With this critical victory and after heavy solicitation from Washington and others, many of Washington's veteran soldiers reenlisted.

After hearing of the rebel victory at Trenton, General Howe readied his 8,000 troops to combat the assorted group of 5,000 men assembled by Washington, who had once again crossed the Delaware River and occupied Trenton. Howe dispatched General James Grant with all of the available troops to Princeton. On January 2, 1777, General Cornwallis left Princeton with more than 5,000 men to push back the rebels to the Delaware River and to destroy them there. In Princeton, Colonel Mawhood was left with three regiments of infantry and light horse and was given orders to follow on the next day. At this time, Washington sent forward Colonel Joseph Reed, with 12 men, on a reconnaissance expedition to determine the intentions of General Howe, as well as to assess current troop strength. Reed determined that the British forces were numerous and that the outposts were heavily defended; however, on his return trip to Trenton, he was able to surprise a detachment of 12 British soldiers on a scouting mission. From the interrogation of these prisoners, Washington was able to determine that Cornwallis was rapidly approaching with a large force and that he must prepare for the worst.

In the late hours of January 2, 1777, Washington brought together a war council to determine the proper course of action. There were three possible options that Washington posed: stand and fight; retreat down the Delaware River and attempt to cross into Pennsylvania; or travel south around the British flank and move up toward Princeton (Ketchum, 1973). Washington, and others, believed that if the army were to remain in its present position, it most certainly meant a disastrous defeat and would possibly risk the entire Revolutionary cause. To retreat to the Delaware River would lead to inevitable surrender (Wertenbaker, 1922). It was thought that the only option was to escape around the British left flank and move up the New Jersey highlands. Although this could be a risky maneuver, Washington knew that staying put would be costly, if not completely detrimental, and also wanted to avoid the appearance of retreat. Following days of warmer weather, which made the ground marsh-like and travel difficult, the Continental Army got lucky. Temperatures steadily fell through the night, and the ground began to freeze. This "providential change of weather" (Stryker, 1898, p. 273), as Washington would later describe it, allowed the option of traveling around the British flank, through Princeton, and on toward New Brunswick more feasible and, additionally, would bring the prospect of procuring much-needed supplies. Ultimately, Washington determined that the most prudent decision was to take his 6,000 troops and proceed toward Princeton in the early hours of January 3, 1777, before continuing north toward New Brunswick.

Before this was to be done, Washington decided that he would try to lead Cornwallis into thinking that he and his troops had remained in camp at Assunpink (Trenton) by ordering his men to construct earthwork defenses there and by doubling the numbers of guards posted. When it was time to leave, fires were left burning, and about 500 men and two cannons stayed behind in order to help deceive Cornwallis into thinking that the entire army remained. Any details that would add to the charade of a defensive stance were considered and, if possible, employed. The troops left behind in Assunpink were ordered to leave just before dawn and follow, as expeditiously as possible. The ultimate plan was for Washington and his men to take Princeton and eventually move on to New Brunswick, capturing any enemy combatants and supplies along the way. There is debate as to whether the decision to leave the fires burning and using the flanking maneuver to move past the oncoming British troops was Washington's alone; however, as commander in chief, he deserves full credit for what may have been the most brilliant strategy conceived during the Revolutionary War (Wertenbaker, 1922).

One of the primary sources that assisted Washington in deciding to prepare this deception and to move toward Princeton, around the British left flank, was a reconnaissance map that was provided to Washington by Colonel John Cadwalader (www.loc.gov/item/gm71000925; Figure 3.1). This spy map provided an overview of the area surrounding Princeton, as well as the strength, numbers, and positions of the British and their batteries. Specifically, it showed the weakest point at which to attack the enemy, as well as how to reach it and the best methods for taking advantage of its limitations. Today the Cadwalader map is considered a somewhat inaccurate, but highly valuable, map that significantly helped General Washington plan for the success of that

Figure 3.1. Plan of Princeton, December 31, 1776

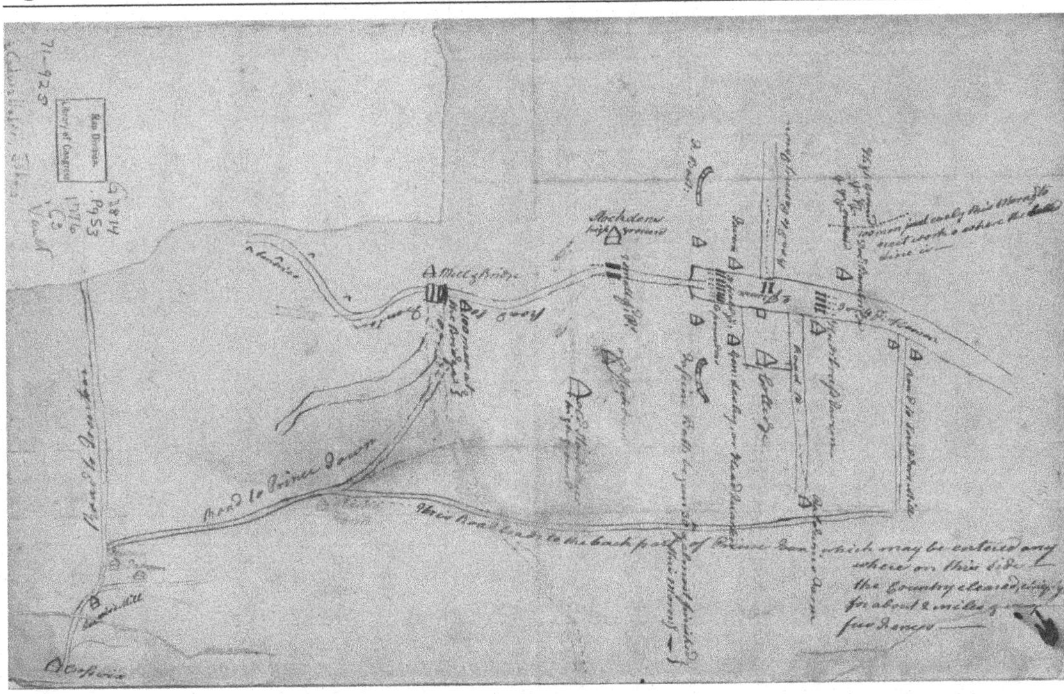

campaign (Library of Congress, n.d.). This map, *Plan of Princeton, Dec. 31, 1776,* allows students to better conceptually understand and engage with the content associated with the Battle of Princeton.

SCRUTINIZING THE FUNDAMENTAL SOURCE(S) AND ORGANIZING THOUGHTS

In the first stage of the SOURCES framework, *Scrutinizing the Fundamental Source(s),* students are asked to analyze the Cadwalader spy map and associated letter (hdl.loc.gov/loc.gmd/g3814p.ct000076; Figure 3.2; transcription available at founders.archives.gov/documents/Washington/03-07-02-0386) that was sent to General Washington from Colonel Cadwalader on December 31, 1776, using the What do you know?, What do you think you know?, and What do you wonder? analysis sheet. If deemed necessary, specific questions can be used to help guide in the analysis of maps for key elements that include:

1. What do you know? Have students identify and note details.
   a. Describe what you see.
   b. What do you notice first?

Figure 3.2. John Cadwalader to George Washington, December 31, 1776

   c. What graphical elements do you see?
   d. What place or places does the map show?
   e. What, if any, words do you see?
   f. What on the map looks strange or unfamiliar?
2. What do you think you know? Encourage students to generate and test hypotheses about the source.
   a. Why do you think this map was made?
   b. Who do you think the audience was for this map?
   c. What does this map tell you about what the people who made it knew and what they didn't?
   d. If this map were made today, what would be different?
3. What do you wonder? Have students ask questions to lead to more observations and reflections.
   a. What do you wonder about?
   b. Who? What? When? Where? Why? How?
   c. What more do you want to know, and how can you find out?

In the accompanying letter from Cadwalader to Washington, students can gain additional information about the British troop numbers and actions. They can be provided guiding questions and analysis sheets to better analyze and understand the letter. Teachers' guides and primary source analysis tools from the Library of Congress are of further use (www.loc.gov/teachers/usingprimarysources/guides.html). To better understand the map, a video provided by the Library of Congress, *How to Get into Princeton* (www.loc.gov/item/myloc19), could be viewed. This video includes a narration by Library of Congress historian John Hebert, in which he clearly describes details of the letter and the importance of this particular map. The video complements the Cadwalader map and letter.

ORGANIZING THOUGHTS AND UNDERSTANDING THE CONTEXT

During the second (*Organizing Thoughts*) and third stages (*Understanding the Context*) of the SOURCES framework, students consider what they know about the fundamental source(s) and related content. These stages will typically be utilized independently; however, for this lesson, they will be presented together.

To begin, students need to organize their thoughts and understanding as they relate to the American Revolution, General George Washington, and the process undertaken in the creation of the United States of America as a nation independent of the British Empire. Next, teachers should instruct students to complete background work associated with the fundamental source and question to better understand the historical context related to the time period and historic event under study. In order to assist students in better understanding this particular source and the events leading up to the Battle of Princeton, they can be provided with a variety of primary and secondary sources to develop a deeper understanding of the geography, time frame, and historical context, as well as Washington's decision to move his troops toward Princeton.

Imagery can be powerful and extremely helpful in assisting students to better understand the context of an historic event. Two images in particular, *Washington Crossing the Delaware: On the Evening of Dec 25th, 1776, Previous to the Battle of Trenton* (www.loc.gov/pictures/item/2002698169) and *Washington Passing the Delaware, Evening Previous to the Battle of Trenton, Dec. 25th, 1776* (www.loc.gov/pictures/item/98501385), can bolster their understanding and paint a picture illustrating the conditions, weather, and logistics of moving more than 5,000 men and associated supplies; however, any inaccuracies in these sources should also be discussed. Additionally, many letters can be utilized to help students, especially these letters from the Library of Congress: Washington to Alexander McDougall (December 28, 1776); William Maxwell (December 28, 1776); the Morristown, New Jersey, Detachment Commanding Officer (December 30, 1776); and the Continental Congress Governing Committee (January 1, 1777).

- *George Washington to Alexander McDougall, December 28, 1776;* The George Washington Papers at the Library of Congress, 1741–1799. Available at www.loc.gov/item/mgw446294/
- *George Washington to William Maxwell, December 28, 1776;* The George Washington Papers at the Library of Congress, 1741–1799. Transcript available at founders.archives.gov/documents/Washington/03-07-02-0367
- *George Washington to Morristown, New Jersey, Detachment Commanding Officer, December 30, 1776;* The George Washington Papers at the Library of Congress, 1741–1799. Available at www.loc.gov/item/mgw446307/
- *George Washington to Continental Congress Governing Committee, January 1, 1777;* The George Washington Papers at the Library of Congress, 1741–1799. Available at www.loc.gov/item/mgw446332/

Several websites that can help students fill in gaps in understanding historical context include: *History*'s site for *Battles of Trenton and Princeton* (www.history.com/topics/american-revolution/battles-of-trenton-and-princeton), PBS's site *George Washington: Founding Father* (www.pbs.org/foundingfather/), and the State of New Jersey's *Hangout NJ* site for the Battle of Princeton (www.state.nj.us/hangout_nj/200401_princeton_p2.html). Books that may be of interest to teachers include David Hackett Fischer's *Washington's Crossing* (2004), Richard Ketchum's *The Winter Soldiers: The Battles for Trenton and Princeton* (1973), and William Stryker's *The Battles of Trenton and Princeton* (1898).

READING BETWEEN THE LINES

Now that the students have a better understanding of the context, in the fourth stage, *Reading Between the Lines*, they are asked to revisit the fundamental source(s). At this stage of the SOURCES framework, students should have a better understanding of the importance of the Cadwalader map and be able to more clearly consider its significance and the impact that this source had on the decisions that needed to be made by General Washington. They should be able to gain a better understanding of the area surrounding Princeton, and since many may not have previously considered the position of the British and their batteries as well as the strength and numbers of the enemy, this map, along with the new contextual understanding, allows students to better comprehend why General Washington determined the location for where to attack the enemy, where the British forces might be the weakest, and the best way to turn the British limitations into advantages for the American army. If necessary, additional guiding questions and analysis sheets can be provided for the novice-level learners.

CORROBORATING AND REFUTING

For the fifth stage (*Corroborating and Refuting*), students are asked to conduct research to find sources that provide corroborating evidence and/or those that may refute an argument that they are constructing in response to the fundamental question guiding the inquiry. Teachers can scaffold this process as much or as little as needed. For this lesson, students are asked to consider the following question: In your estimation, to what extent was the campaign on Princeton a prudent and successful one? As students grapple with how to answer this, they can be provided a list of possible sources for reference, or they can be set to conducting research on their own if they have already been properly instructed on how to successfully do this. Additionally, students who have been properly trained to think critically and to utilize sources in this manner will not see this as a leading question and will feel compelled to respond along an entire spectrum of thoughts and responses.

Numerous sources can be provided to students as they construct a response to the fundamental question. One of the sources that may help students to combat historical presentism is the painting entitled *Washington at Princeton* (www.loc.gov/pictures/item/2003671527; Figure 3.3).

Often, novice historians place the historical events they are studying in a present-day context. Although there can be some historical inaccuracies inherent within images, paintings and other images can combat this urge to see the past through a present-day lens. Paintings, photographs, and other

Figure 3.3. Washington at Princeton, January 3, 1777

visuals provide students with sources that can be quite powerful when used for comparison, corroboration, and consideration, especially when conducting an investigation exclusively utilizing written and other nonvisual sources. Additional images that can be helpful with the development of contextual understanding of what military maneuvers and forces looked like in the late 1700s, specifically Washington's army at Princeton, are *Washington at Princeton January 3d. 1777* (Figure 3.4), published by Currier and Ives, and *The Battle at Princeton* (Figure 3.5), by John Trumbull.

Although the Cadwalader map is vital to grappling with Washington's understanding of the British forces present in Princeton, it does not provide an overview of the area between and surrounding Trenton and Princeton. The *Plan of the Operations of General Washington Against the King's Troops in New Jersey* (Figure 3.6) is a map showing the area from Newtown, Pennsylvania, to Kingston, New Jersey, with routes of British and American forces.

If a different perspective of the "Affair of Princeton" is desired, one can examine the map constructed by Henry Schenck Tanner in 1816 (graphicarts.princeton.edu/2014/05/17/affair-of-princeton-january-3-1777).

Furthermore, specific letters that can provide details in answering the fundamental question are ones written on January 5, 1777, from George Washington to the Continental Congress (Figure 3.7), Israel Putnam (Figure 3.8), William Heath (Figure 3.9), and the New York Committee of Safety (founders.archives.gov/documents/Washington/03-07-02-0414).

Figure 3.4. Washington at Princeton, January 3rd, 1777

Library of Congress Prints and Photographs Division. Available at loc.gov/pictures/item/2002698168/

Figure 3.5. The Battle at Princeton

Library of Congress Prints and Photographs Division. Available at www.loc.gov/pictures/item/98501341

Figure 3.6. Plan of the Operations of General Washington Against the King's Troops in New Jersey, from the 26th of December 1776 to the 3rd of January 1777

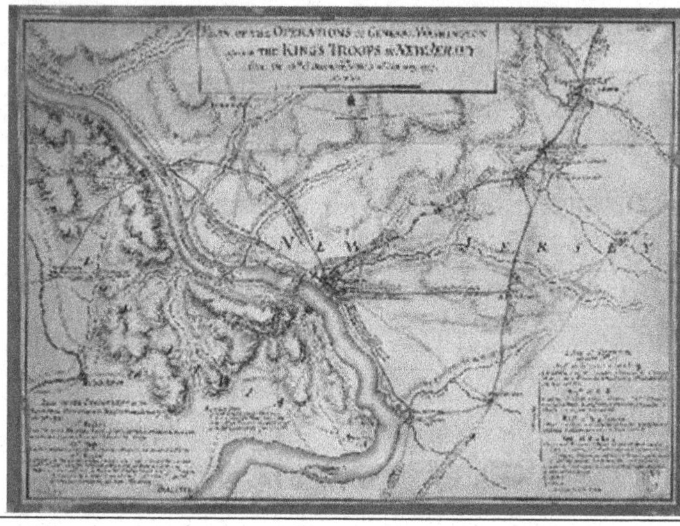

Library of Congress Geography and Map Division. Available at www.loc.gov/item/gm71000654

Figure 3.7. George Washington to Continental Congress, January 5, 1777

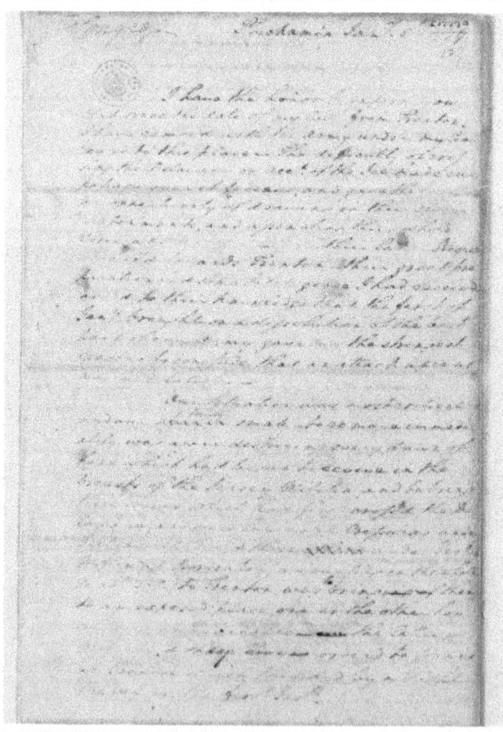

The George Washington Papers at the Library of Congress, 1741–1799. Available at www.loc.gov/item/mgw446345/

Figure 3.8. George Washington to Israel Putnam, January 5, 1777

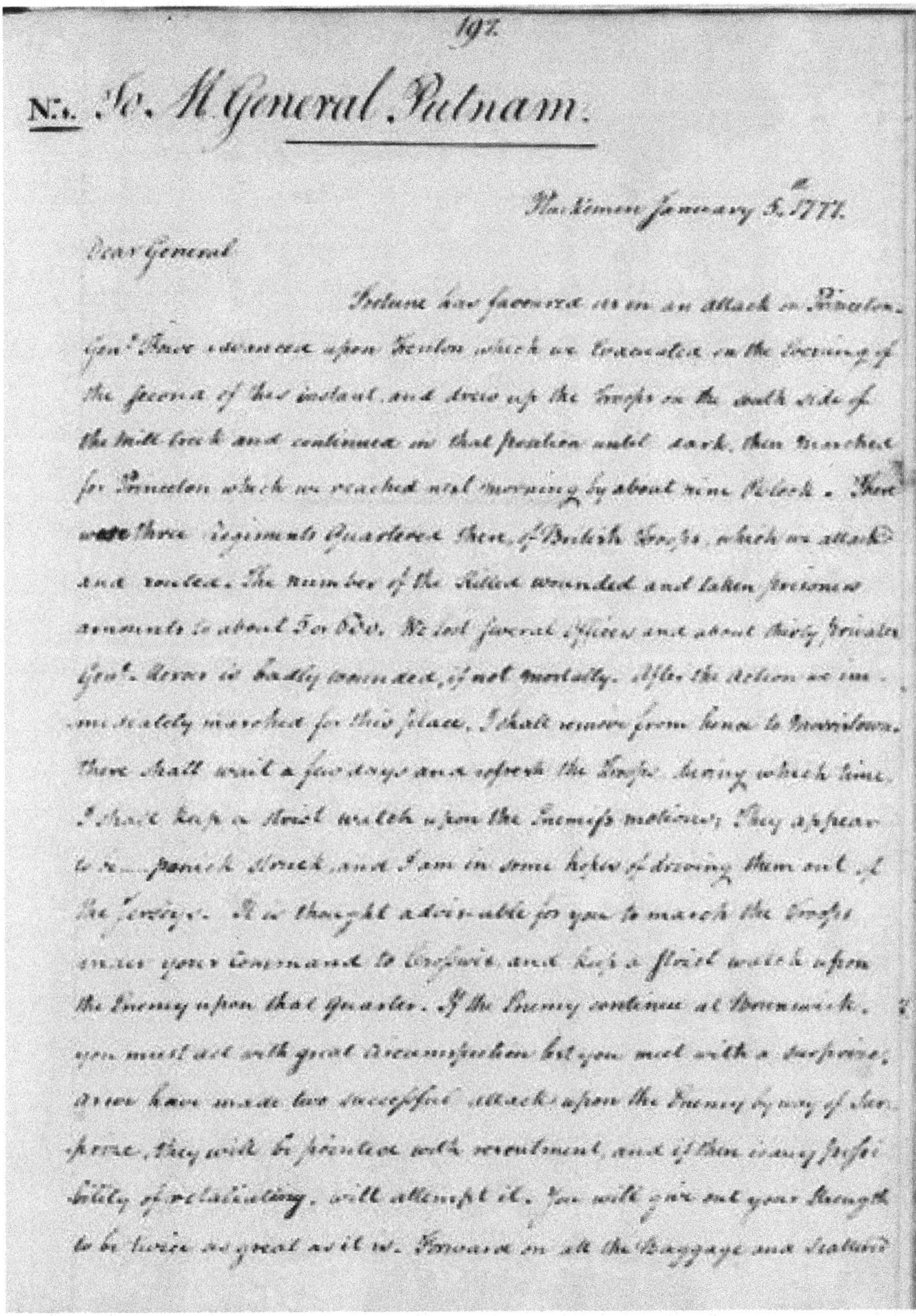

197

No. 1. To Mr General Putnam.

Pluckemin January 5th 1777.

Dear General

Fortune has favored us in an Attack on Princeton. Genl. Howe advanced upon Trenton which we evacuated in the Evening of the second of this instant, and drew up the Troops on the south side of the Mill Creek and continued in that position until dark, then marched for Princeton which we reached next morning by about nine o'Clock. There were three Regiments Quartered there of British Troops, which we attacked and routed. The number of the killed wounded and taken prisoners amounts to about 5 or 600. We lost several officers and about thirty privates. Genl. Mercer is badly wounded, if not mortally. After the Action we immediately marched for this place. I shall remove from hence to Morristown, there shall wait a few days and refresh the Troops during which time I shall keep a strict watch upon the Enemy's motions; They appear to be panick struck, and I am in some hopes of driving them out of the Jerseys. It is thought advisable for you to march the Troops under your Command to Crosswix and keep a strict watch upon the Enemy upon that Quarter. If the Enemy continue at Brunswick, you must act with great circumspection lest you meet with a surprize; As we have made two successful attacks upon the Enemy by way of Surprize, they will be pointed with resentment, and if there is any possibility of retaliating, will attempt it. You will give out your Strength to be twice as great as it is. Forward on all the Baggage and scattered

The George Washington Papers at the Library of Congress, 1741–1799. Available at www.loc.gov/item/mgw3b.002/

Figure 3.9. George Washington to William Heath, January 5, 1777

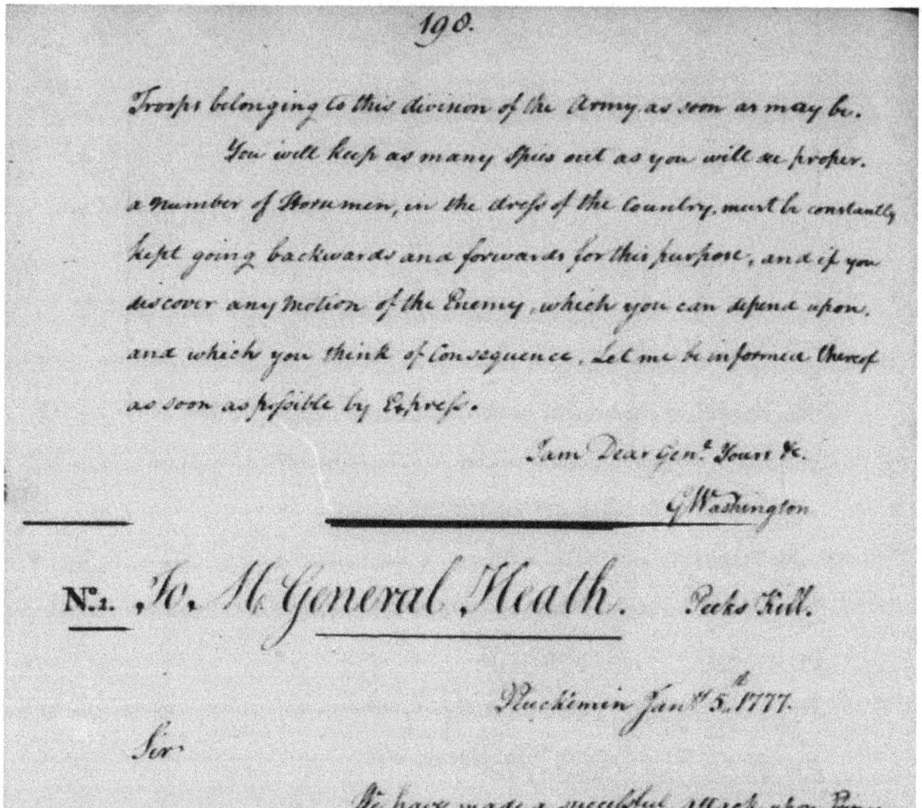

190.

Troops belonging to this division of the Army as soon as may be.

You will keep as many Spies out as you will see proper. a Number of Horsemen, in the dress of the Country, must be constantly kept going backwards and forwards for this purpose, and if you discover any Motion of the Enemy, which you can depend upon, and which you think of Consequence, Let me be informed thereof as soon as possible by Express.

I am Dear Genl. Yours &c.

G Washington

No. 1. To M. General Heath. Pecks Kill.

Pluckemin Jany 5th 1777.

Sir

We have made a successful attack upon Princeton. Genl. Howe advanced upon Trenton, we evacuated the Town and lay on the otherside of the Mill Creek, until dark, then stole a march and attacked Princeton about nine o'clock in the morning; There was three Regiments quartered there, the killed, wounded, and taken Prisoners amounts to about 500. The Enemy are in great consternation, and as the Panick affords us a favourable opportunity to drive them out of the Jerseys, It has been determined in Council, that you should move down towards New York with a considerable force, as if you had a design upon the City. That being an Object of great importance, the

The George Washington Papers at the Library of Congress, 1741–1799. Available at www.loc.gov/item/mgw3b.002/. Transcription available at founders.archives.gov/documents/Washington/03-07-02-0412

From these sources one can find excerpts that may be useful in attending to the creation of an overall narrative and in providing evidence in answering the fundamental question. These include passages such as Washington's overall thoughts summarized in his statement to Israel Putnam:

> Fortune has favord us in an attack on Princeton. . . . march't for Princeton which we reacht next morning by about Nine oClock—There was three Regiments Quarterd there of British Troops—which we Attackt and Routed. . . . As we have made two successful Attacks upon the Enemy—by way of surprise—they will be pointed with resentment and if there is any possibillity of retalliateing will Attempt it. (Washington, 1777)

In this source, Washington was notified by John Hancock that:

> Congress are infinitely anxious to hear the Event; and humbly hope, that Victory has declared in Favour of those, whose sacred Cause should inspire them with Ardour, on every solemn Appeal to that Being, who hateth all Injustice, Tyranny, and Oppression. (Hancock, 1777)

Washington also received a letter from the Continental Congress Executive Committee that informed him that "We waited with Impatience to learn the consequence of your late movements and have been highly gratified" (Continental Congress Executive Committee, 1777, para. 1). To gather additional sources of information, students can perform a search of *The George Washington Papers* at the Library of Congress, 1741–1799 (www.loc.gov/collections/george-washington-papers/) and the National Archives and Records Administration's *Founders Online* website (founders.archives.gov), using keywords of Washington and/or Cadwalader and dates of December 1776 and January 1777.

Several accounts constructed by participants at the Battle of Princeton were published years later and can provide additional insight. Two such examples include:

- Sergeant R_______, "The Battle of Princeton," *The Pennsylvania Magazine of History and Biography* 20, no. 4 (1896): 515–519; and
- Thomas Sullivan, "The Battle of Princeton," *The Pennsylvania Magazine of History and Biography* 32, no. 1 (1908): 54–57.

Much can be learned from these primary sources that can help corroborate and/or refute the student's constructed argument, but additional information can be gleaned from websites mentioned earlier, as well as other sites, such as the Clarke House Volunteers' *Visit Princeton Battlefield* (www.visitprincetonbattlefield.org/visit-princeton-battlefield/ten-crucial-days/battle-of-princeton). Additionally, children's books such as Elaine Landau's

George Washington Crosses the Delaware: Would You Risk the Revolution? (2009) and Margery Cuyler's *The Battlefield Ghost* (2011) are valuable resources for students when constructing better conceptual understandings and narratives about the past. Lastly, teachers can provide historian accounts, so that students can read powerful commentary from experts, such as the thought that "Howe and Cornwallis had been completely outgeneraled, outwitted, outfought" and that the major impact from this battle was to show the world that "British regulars could be routed, shattered, and captured in large numbers" (Wertenbaker, 1922).

ESTABLISHING A PLAUSIBLE NARRATIVE

During the sixth stage (*Establishing a Plausible Narrative*), students take the information gathered during the first five stages to construct a plausible narrative, based on the available evidence, to answer the fundamental question: In your estimation, to what extent was the campaign on Princeton a prudent and successful one? This can be done in numerous ways. In addition to traditional text-based narratives, students can construct websites, documentary videos, computer-based presentations, dioramas, or other creations to demonstrate the understandings that they have developed throughout the previous stages and to adequately address the fundamental guiding question.

SUMMARIZING FINAL THOUGHTS

In the final stage (*Summarizing Final Thoughts*), students are asked to revisit the investigation they conducted throughout the SOURCES process and metacognitively analyze what was learned, how the knowledge was acquired, how differences in opinion present in the sources were handled, and what questions were left unanswered. They should discuss this with classmates and, if time permits, determine a plan for approaching historical investigation with primary sources in the future, and specifically how to attend to lingering questions particular to this exploration. Although additional questions and thoughts may persist, students should have been able to go through the stages of thinking historically and been able to provide an evidence-based narrative to answer the fundamental question posed at the beginning of the investigation.

CONCLUSION

Through the investigation of a variety of sources and by using the SOURCES framework to scaffold the inquiry process, students can construct their own evidence-based argumentative narrative to respond to the fundamental question: In your estimation, to what extent was the campaign on Princeton a prudent and successful one? Students can debate the prudence and success of this campaign. Most will come to an understanding that there were many different factors and elements facing General Washington in early January 1777, and crucial decisions that impacted the outcome of the revolution had to be made in a limited period of time. Regardless, the evidence will show that the Princeton campaign was a resounding success and was probably the most prudent decision that could have been made at that time, considering the confounding factors that were present.

After this investigation, some students may wonder what happened next and want to learn about whether Washington continued on to New Brunswick. Additional sources can show that Washington gave up the plan of continuing on to New Brunswick, as he felt that with the "harassed state of our troops (many of them having no rest for two nights and a day), and the danger of losing the advantage we had gained by aiming at too much, induced me, by the advice of my officers, to relinquish the attempt" (Washington, 1777). Students can learn that Washington and the Continental Army ended the day in Millstone, continued on to Pluckemin, and on the fifth day arrived at Morristown, where they spent the winter. Unfortunately, the British stores and munitions taken at Princeton were minimal, including the acquisition of blankets, shoes, and a few other items. Although the Continental Army did not cause significant damage to the British, the victories at Trenton and Princeton did force Howe to rethink his tactics and, more importantly, increased morale and public opinion (Ellis, 2004). Henry Knox noted that if they had had 1,000 additional fresh men, they could have moved on to New Brunswick and "struck one of the most brilliant strokes in all history" (Knox, 1777).

CHAPTER 4

Building Capacity for Student Agency

Using Baseball-Related Primary Sources and the SOURCES Framework

Because many students have interest in and knowledge about sports, one way to demonstrate the capacity for individuals and groups to impact their community and serve as change agents is through the historical investigation of America's pastime of baseball. Through a variety of sources from different periods of time in American history and with the use of the SOURCES framework, students are able to authentically think about the question "How have Americans used sports as a tool for agency or civic engagement?" To pique interest, students can begin by looking at the poem entitled "Base-Ball" (www.loc.gov/resource/rbc0001.2003juv05880/?sp=51; Figure 4.1), found in *A Little*

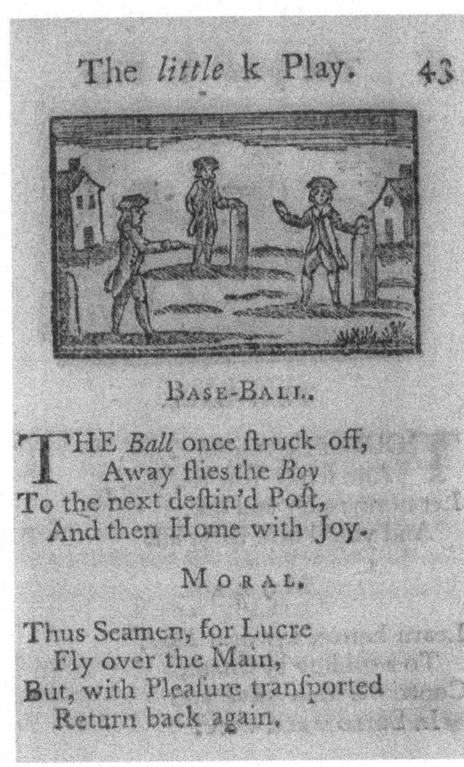
The *little* k Play. 43

BASE-BALL.

THE *Ball* once ſtruck off,
Away flies the *Boy*
To the next deſtin'd Poſt,
And then Home with Joy.

MORAL.

Thus Seamen, for Lucre
Fly over the Main,
But, with Pleaſure tranſported
Return back again.

Figure 4.1. "Base-Ball"—From *A Little Pretty Pocket-Book*

Pretty Pocket-Book, first published in England in 1744 about outdoor activities suitable to "instruct and amuse" children. The first American edition was published in Worcester, Massachusetts, in 1787. Although legend has it that Abner Doubleday invented the sport in 1839, this source, as well as many others, helps to debunk that myth. By investigating various sources, the teacher can also discuss with students the evolution of the name of the game itself from Base-Ball (1787), to base-ball (1799), to base ball (1818), to Base Ball (1845), and eventually to baseball (1899).

SCRUTINIZING THE FUNDAMENTAL SOURCE(S)

Once students have thought about the game of baseball, the teacher can inquire as to how a sport such as baseball can be used as a tool for civic engagement. The fundamental question to be posed for this investigation then can be something like "How have Americans used sports as a tool for agency or civic engagement?" In a source from 1916, "Girls Organize Sure 'Nough Ball Club—Know How to Play" (chroniclingamerica.loc.gov/lccn/sn83045487/1916-01-06/ed-1/seq-5; Figure 4.2), students can learn how Ida Schnall felt the need for the creation of a female baseball team in Los Angeles, especially after seeing the success of the New York Female Giants and given the absence of any teams on the West Coast of the United States. She decided to replicate in her home of Los Angeles what she had seen in New York. Students should be reminded that this is during a time when women were denied the right to vote, so many may have been discouraged when thinking about the prospect of creating an all-women's baseball team. When examining this newspaper article, students can learn that more than 20 players showed up for the first tryout and the numbers increased daily. This was considered a testament to the interest in an all-women's team, and it was ultimately a good problem to have, as Schnall's "greatest difficulty now seems to be the final choice of first team players." Students can conclude that there was an apparent interest in having a female team in the Los Angeles area, and, thanks to Ida, this became a reality.

ORGANIZING THOUGHTS

After examining the fundamental source and having a better understanding of what the source is, students need to consider what they know about the historical context in which the source is located, what they know about the source, what they think they know, what they wonder about the source, and what they do not know. To help them in engaging with this source and putting it into context, students should be asked to think about any extracurricular

Figure 4.2. Girls Organize Sure 'Nough Ball Club—Know How to Play—From *The Day Book*

GIRLS ORGANIZE SURE 'NOUGH BALL CLUB—KNOW HOW TO PLAY

Ida Schnall, Captain of the Feminine Baseball Club at Los Angeles.

A feminine baseball club composed of girls who really understand the game has been organized by motion picture actresses at Los Angeles.

Daily tryouts for places on the team are being held, suits and equipment have been ordered and a schedule of games with similar organizations throughout the state is being made.

Miss Ida Schnall, as captain and manager, has her hands full attending to the various details of the new club and looking over the fair recruits, who are besieging the diamond in an attempt to land on the team. She was formerly captain of the New York Female Giants.

Miss Schnall, who is an expert swimmer and diver, came west from

activities in which they are involved. Those who play sports and musical instruments, are scouts, have been members of academic clubs, and/or have participated in other organizations should be asked to think critically about how they became members, how they think those groups came to be, and what if the groups had not existed. All students should be asked to think about what clubs or groups they might wish existed. Then they should think about the steps necessary for the creation of these sorts of groups or organizations and how the level of difficulty in creating them today would differ from the level at various points in time in American history, especially during the second decade of the 20th century.

UNDERSTANDING THE CONTEXT

Depending on the age of the students, it may be difficult for them to truly grasp the complexity of advocating for and creating a women's baseball team in 1916. To help students gain a better understanding, further historical contextual information can be discussed. Students should be instructed that this team came together when women were denied the right to vote and that the 19th Amendment to the Constitution of the United States was not passed by Congress until June 4, 1919.

They can also be informed that in 1916, a dozen eggs cost 38¢, a gallon of milk delivered to one's home cost 36¢, and a pound of coffee cost 30¢ (United States Bureau of the Census, 1975). Thus, it was a very different time, and societal norms and standards were quite different from today's.

To further bolster their knowledge, various selections from children's literature can be shared with the students. In *Bloomer Girls: Women Baseball Pioneers (Sport and Society)*, Debra A. Shattuck uses various primary sources to document the history of women's organized baseball clubs and tells how the women involved were treated with condescension, faced countless obstacles, became agents of the women's rights movement, and transformed society's perceptions of women's physical and mental capacity. Other books, like *No Girls in the Clubhouse: The Exclusion of Women from Baseball* by Marilyn Cohen and the *Encyclopedia of Women and Baseball* by Leslie A. Heaphy, can help create a better understanding of the struggles in the creation of female baseball teams and leagues. Students may also be interested in the All-American Girls Professional Baseball League, which was founded and first hosted games in 1943. Films like *A League of Their Own*, and books such as *Players in Pigtails* by Shana Corey and *Mama Played Baseball* by David A. Adler, provide students with more information and context related to this league. Students could also learn about the creation of the Girl Scouts in 1912 by reading *Here Come the Girl Scouts! The Amazing All-True Story of Juliette "Daisy" Gordon Low and Her Great Adventure* by Shana Corey. Books about the women's suffrage movement, such as *Bold & Brave: Ten Heroes Who Won Women the Right to Vote* by Kirsten Gillibrand and *Miss Paul and the President: The Creative Campaign for Women's Right to Vote* by Dean Robbins, can allow students to gain a better understanding of the struggles facing women in the early 20th century.

READING BETWEEN THE LINES

With a better understanding of the time period, of obstacles facing women in the early 20th century, and of how one might go about constructing women's teams and organizations at that time, students should revisit the fundamental source ("Girls Organize Sure 'Nough Ball Club—Know How to Play") and think about how their understanding of this source has changed. They can be asked to focus on the line "Miss Ida Schnall, as captain and manager, has her hands full attending to the various details of the new club" and what this might mean, especially considering the obstacles and resistance that the creation of a female baseball club might encounter. Once they have considered this, placed the sources within the proper context, and have a better understanding of the content, the students are ready to construct a tentative mental narrative and to move to the *Corroborating and Refuting* stage.

CORROBORATING AND REFUTING

Around the same time as the creation of the female baseball team in Los Angeles, there were increased efforts to make the lives of America's youth better, such as greater focus on various health-related issues and conditions, increased educational opportunities, and limitations on child labor. With this in mind, students can examine and discuss a source published in 1914 entitled "Playground baseball league takes boys off streets and puts them into health" (chroniclingamerica.loc.gov/lccn/sn83045487/1914-02-26/ed-1/seq-27; Figure 4.3). From this source, one can learn that Radowe Abeken, "the young and enthusiastic head of the playgrounds in St. Louis, has started a vigorous campaign to organize every playground system of the large cites of the Unites States into one great league of municipal amateur baseball teams" so that collectively they may be able to "keep many boys away from the street corner gangs."

This can provide an opportunity to discuss ways in which individuals have utilized sports to improve conditions and lives throughout history and then transition into how this is being done today and how one might use sports to help others. This way, students can think about how Americans, as well as people across the globe, continue to use sports as a tool for agency and civic engagement.

Conversations also can be had about how baseball was used during wartime. In the image *Union Prisoners at Salisbury, N.C.* (Figure 4.4), students can view how the American Civil War added to the popularity of baseball. Union officers encouraged off-duty soldiers to play the game in order to increase morale and foster camaraderie; additionally, Union prisoners held in Confederate camps taught Southerners about the game and played baseball games within the camps.

Figure 4.3. Playground Baseball League Takes Boys Off Streets and Puts Them Into Health

PLAYGROUND BASEBALL LEAGUE TAKES BOYS OFF STREETS AND PUTS THEM INTO HEALTH

Hy Hugh S. Fullerton.

St. Louis may the joke of major league baseball, but that city has advanced and developed an idea which, if extended to every city and town in America, would be the greatest possible development of our national game, and one of the greatest things for the youth of American cities ever planned.

The Playground Baseball League of St. Louis has proved such a success that several other cities are taking up the plan. Cincinnati, Cleveland and Pittsburgh authorities have studied it.

Radowe Abeken, the young and enthusiastic head of the playgrounds in St. Louis, has started a vigorous campaign to organize every playground system of the large cities of the United States into one great league of municipal amateur baseball teams, directly controlled by the playground officials of the cities. At the recent meeting of the National Association of Amateur Baseball Clubs, held in Chicago, Abeken appealed to the promoters to indorse his municipal league and have the amateur teams from the playgrounds of different cities meet each fall for a national championship.

The St. Louis plan is the first comprehensive one put into effect, although many of the other cities have their playground teams. Abeken, when he left college, went into the playground work with the idea that the greatest success could be attained through devoting the most attention to the game most popular among he boys. He threw open the playgrounds of St. Louis to all the boy teams of the city.

At the start little effort was made to control the teams save to allot to them the playing hours. In this way the boys came to look upon the playground authorities as the proper ones to decide disputes, and they became the real government of amateur baseball in St. Louis.

Within a short time even outside teams appealed to the playground authorities for decisions. The move,

Figure 4.4. Union Prisoners at Salisbury, N.C.

Available at www.loc.gov/item/94508290/)

As baseball gained popularity through the second half of the 19th century, Japanese Americans began to see baseball as "a critical force in shaping identity, binding ethnic enclaves, forging ties with Japanese culture and promoting civil rights" (Maloney, 2018). Because baseball leagues in the United States were not integrated, they were prohibited from playing in organized leagues, so many Japanese Americans created their own leagues. The first team fielding Japanese Americans arose in San Francisco in 1903, with the creation of the Fuji Athletic Club. As leagues and teams consisting of Japanese Americans continued to develop and evolve, first-generation immigrants began to see baseball as a modern equivalent of kendo or judo, with many seeing it as a sport that illustrated their dedication to American ideals and presented an opportunity to keep children away from "boozing, drugging or gambling their lives away in American environs" (blogs.loc.gov/loc/2018/05/japanese-americas-pastime-baseball/). After the bombing of Pearl Harbor and the introduction of internment camps for those of Japanese ancestry, many of the internees turned to baseball to preserve some semblance of a normal life and provide a distraction from the life within the camps. In a photograph included in the *Manzanar Free Press* newspaper (Manzanar, California), from July 27, 1942, students can see an image of baseball being played in Manzanar with a caption that reads, "Baseball . . . Manzanar's favorite sport. One of 180 teams in action" (www.loc.gov/item/sn84025948/1942-07-27/ed-1; Figure 4.5). This is just one example out of many of Japanese American internees using baseball to raise dipping morale in Japanese internment camps. To take this investigation a step further, the teacher can read *Baseball Saved Us*, by Ken Mochizuki, and utilize various sources found on the Library of Congress website, as well as those in the Japanese Internment Camp primary source set (www.loc.gov/teachers/classroommaterials/primarysourcesets/internment/).

Another source that builds understanding and allows for corroboration and refuting outlines the creation of the All-American Girls Professional Baseball League in 1943. Due to the fact that many young men were being drafted into the service, professional baseball teams were having difficulty fielding teams, and baseball stadium owners were fearful of what might happen with an absence of baseball (All-American Girls Professional Baseball League, n.d.). Phillip J. Wrigley, the owner of the Chicago Cubs, introduced the idea of the creation of a women's softball league that could utilize the now empty stadiums. During the existence of the league from 1943 to 1954, more than 600 women had the opportunity to play professional baseball. To allow students to understand the importance of this league to the women who played it, the theme song co-written by players Pepper Paire and Nalda Bird can be examined:

Figure 4.5. Photograph by Ansel Adams from 1943 entitled "Baseball game, Manzanar Relocation Center, Calif."

Victory Song

Batter up! Hear that call!
The time has come for one and all
To play ball.

We are the members of the All-American League
We come from cities near and far
We've got Canadians, Irishmen, and Swedes,
We're all for one, we're one for all
We're all Americans!!

Each girl stands, her head so proudly high,
Her motto "Do or Die"
She's not the one to use or need an alibi.

Our chaperones are not too soft,
They're not too tough,
Our managers are on the ball.
We've got a president who really knows his stuff,
We're all for one, we're one for all,
We're All-Americans!

Portions of the fictionalized feature film about this baseball league, *A League of Their Own*, such as the scene when the players sing the league theme song, can be shared to increase understanding and empathy. Additionally, students may enjoy reading *The Rules of Conduct* (chicagology.com/baseball/allamericangirlsbaseballleague/) and learning that uniforms, hairstyles, and even how members conducted themselves when not playing was regulated. The players faced a fine of $5 for a first offense, $10 for a second, and would be suspended for a third infraction of the league rules. Additional sources may be utilized, but those presented here should allow each of the students an opportunity to establish an evidence-based narrative in response to the fundamental question posed at the beginning of the investigation.

ESTABLISHING A PLAUSIBLE NARRATIVE

There are many ways in which students could go about demonstrating knowledge and understanding of "How have Americans used sports as a tool for agency or civic engagement?" The creation of a website documenting their thoughts in response to the fundamental question is one good option. A website can be quite a powerful way for them to demonstrate their understanding and show how they formulated an evidence-based response to wrap up the investigation. This can be enjoyable for the students, can easily be shared with family and friends, and can allow an easy way for the students to link to sources beyond those used in class. Further examples and ideas will be presented in Part II of this book, and the authors will demonstrate how students can harness the power of the Internet by using images, audio, video, and more in the creation of plausible narratives.

SUMMARIZING FINAL THOUGHTS

In the final stage, students need to examine their thoughts regarding the investigation, but teachers should also engage with them and prompt further considerations. By tying this all to the present and to more contemporary issues, teachers may help to empower students to become change agents. Teachers can provide more contemporary examples of children becoming civically engaged through various types of sports. Instances of current youth involvement and activism, such as efforts for heads-up tackling in football, erasing racism in soccer and other sports, and the creation of community teams and leagues can all be discussed in the classroom. This may lead to opportunities for the students to become more actively involved in sports or other youth programs in their communities and to gain a better appreciation of the ability of athletes to enable change.

CONCLUSION

By using primary sources in the classroom, students are able to examine multiple perspectives to enrich their critical-thinking and problem-solving skills. Rather than telling students what they can do, teachers can allow them the freedom to examine and discuss what others have done to bring about change; this empowers them and encourages civic engagement, whether individually or through community collaborations. Using primary sources when teaching civic ideals and instilling civic-mindedness can go way beyond founding documents, as teachers can find a variety of primary sources related to the interests of their students, such as sports, to effectively accomplish this. Utilizing the SOURCES framework gives students the skills and ability to interact with and analyze sources from the past, and even those of today—skills that will help them more effectively examine and question sources they encounter on a daily basis. The ultimate goal of examining sources in this manner is to help students realize and believe that citizenship is not a spectator sport, and that without action there is no positive change.

CHAPTER 5

What Motivated the Wright Brothers?

An Application of the SOURCES Framework

Although the Wright Brothers are often credited with being the first in flight, as Orville Wright is considered the first person to successfully accomplish a sustained flight in a heavier-than-air mechanically powered plane, some wish to debate as to whether Glenn H. Curtiss, Clément Ader, Gustave Whitehead, Alberto Santos-Dumont, or other candidates for this honor should receive the credit. Despite this, it is a fact that on December 17, 1903, at Kitty Hawk, North Carolina, the plane, known as the Wright Flyer, that Orville piloted flew over a distance of 120 feet and remained aloft for more than 12 seconds. Through the analysis of primary sources, one can learn a tremendous amount about the Wright Brothers; their plans; the design, construction, fabric, propulsion system, and flight controls of the Flyer; and details about the trials and successes of Orville and Wilbur Wright (see airandspace.si.edu/exhibitions/wright-brothers/online/). Despite the debate that exists, one thing that is certain is that the Wright brothers were interested in mechanical flight, and one inquiry that can capture students' interest is to try to determine where this desire to fly originated, how serious it was, and through what means it was facilitated. As the topic of first flight, how people impacted history, and the rapid acceleration of innovations from the time of the Wright Brothers' first flight are typical topics covered in the history classroom, the SOURCES framework is an excellent scaffold to facilitate the exploration of the Wright Brothers' motivation.

SCRUTINIZING THE FUNDAMENTAL SOURCE(S)

Even though one could easily begin a historical inquiry about the Wright Brothers with questions focusing on their early life or their collaboration as printers (*West Side News*), bicycle-shop founders (Wright Cycle Company), or inventors, this SOURCES investigation begins on May 30, 1899, with a letter written by Wilbur to the Smithsonian Institution (siarchives.si.edu/history/featured-topics/stories/letter-dated-may-30-1899; Figure 5.1, transcript available on website). It is thought to be the first documented evidence pointing

Figure 5.1. Letter from Wilbur Wright Dated May 30, 1899

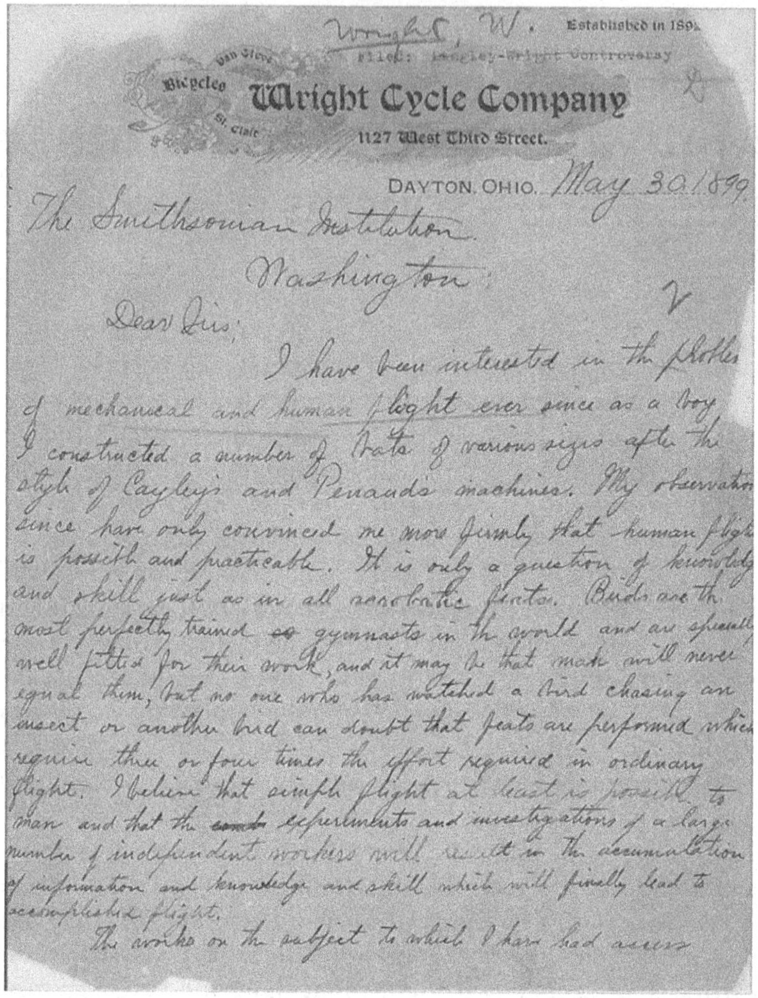

Wright, W. Established in 1892
File: Langley-Wright Controversy

Van Cleve Bicycles St. Clair

Wright Cycle Company
1127 West Third Street.

DAYTON, OHIO. May 30, 1899

The Smithsonian Institution
Washington.

Dear Sirs;

I have been interested in the problem of mechanical and human flight ever since as a boy I constructed a number of bats of various sizes after the style of Cayley's and Penaud's machines. My observations since have only convinced me more firmly that human flight is possible and practicable. It is only a question of knowledge and skill just as in all acrobatic feats. Birds are the most perfectly trained gymnasts in the world and are specially well fitted for their work, and it may be that man will never equal them, but no one who has watched a bird chasing an insect or another bird can doubt that feats are performed which require three or four times the effort required in ordinary flight. I believe that simple flight at least is possible to man and that the experiments and investigations of a large number of independent workers will result in the accumulation of information and knowledge and skill which will finally lead to accomplished flight.

The works on the subject to which I have had access

Transcript available at siarchives.si.edu/history/featured-topics/stories/letter-dated-may-30-1899

toward the Wright Brothers' serious interest in the possibility of mechanical and human flight.

As students analyze the letter, they should think about the fundamental questions for this SOURCES-based exploration: What motivated the Wright Brothers? Was it passion, just a way to pass the time, and/or simply a paycheck? In the letter Wilbur writes that he has been "interested in the problem of mechanical and human flight ever since as a boy I constructed a number of bats of various sizes" and he has determined that his "observations since have only convinced me more firmly that human flight is possible and practicable." Analysis of the letter allows the readers to gain insight into his thinking and what has led him to pursue human flight. He states that flight is "only a question of knowledge and skill just as in all acrobatic feats." He discusses observations he has made of birds and that he is going to begin a "systematic study of the subject in preparation for practical work to which I expect to devote what time I can spare from my regular business." He contacts the Smithsonian because he wishes to obtain papers and any writings that they have focusing on studies, theories, and thoughts regarding flights. He concludes the letter by offering his services to fellow researchers and providing assurance to the recipient that he is "an enthusiast, but not a crank in the sense that I have some pet theories as to the proper construction of a flying machine."

The letter written by Wilbur on May 30, 1899, can be followed with another letter from Wilbur, dated May 13, 1900 (www.loc.gov/item/wright002804/; Figure 5.2). This letter is written to aviation pioneer Octave Chanute, who is living in Chicago, Illinois, at the time. The choice of words that Wilbur uses even in the introduction is powerful, as one can get a sense of his passion for flight. He writes:

> For some years I have been afflicted with the belief that flight is possible to man. My disease has increased in severity and I feel that it will soon cost me an increased amount of money if not my life.

He argues to Mr. Chanute that it is "possible to fly without motors, but not without knowledge & skill," which is "fortunate, for man, by reason of his greater intellect, can more reasonably hope to equal birds in knowledge, than to equal nature in the perfection of her machinery." The main purpose of the letter is for Wilbur to detail

> the plan and apparatus it is my intention to test. In explaining these, my object is to learn to what extent similar plans have been tested and found to be failures and also to obtain such suggestions as your great knowledge and experience might enable you to give me.

As one considers his true intentions, it can be read that Wilbur believes that

> no financial profit will accrue to the inventor of the first flying machine, and that only those who are willing to give as well as to receive suggestions can hope to link their names with the honor of its discovery. The problem is too great for one man alone and unaided to solve in secret.

Wilbur goes on to explain in clear detail his plans for achieving flight. He notes his observations of buzzards, his knowledge of previous attempts, including Mr. Chanute's efforts in 1896–1897, and how his plan differs from others:

Figure 5.2. Octave Chanute Papers: Special Correspondence—Wright Brothers, 1900

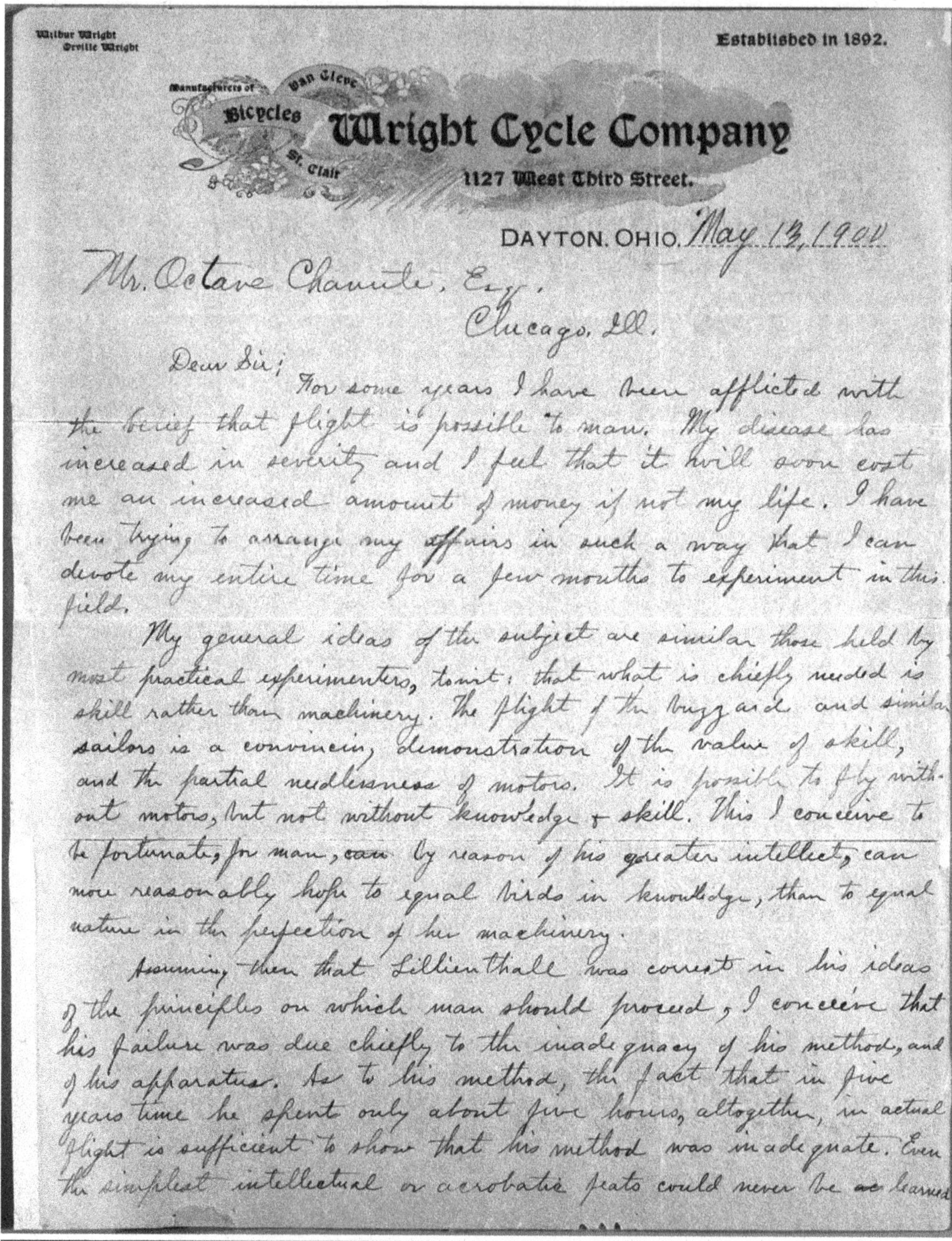

Wilbur Wright
Orville Wright

Established in 1892.

Manufacturers of Van Cleve Bicycles St. Clair

Wright Cycle Company
1127 West Third Street.

DAYTON, OHIO, May 13, 1900

Mr. Octave Chanute, Esq.
Chicago, Ill.

Dear Sir;

For some years I have been afflicted with the belief that flight is possible to man. My disease has increased in severity and I feel that it will soon cost me an increased amount of money if not my life. I have been trying to arrange my affairs in such a way that I can devote my entire time for a few months to experiment in this field.

My general ideas of the subject are similar those held by most practical experimenters, to wit: that what is chiefly needed is skill rather than machinery. The flight of the buzzard and similar sailors is a convincing demonstration of the value of skill, and the partial needlessness of motors. It is possible to fly without motors, but not without knowledge & skill. This I conceive to be fortunate, for man, ~~can~~ by reason of his greater intellect, can more reasonably hope to equal birds in knowledge, than to equal nature in the perfection of her machinery.

Assuming then that Lillienthall was correct in his ideas of the principles on which man should proceed, I conceive that his failure was due chiefly to the inadequacy of his method, and of his apparatus. As to his method, the fact that in five years time he spent only about five hours, altogether, in actual flight is sufficient to show that his method was inadequate. Even the simplest intellectual or acrobatic feats could never be ~~as~~ learned

Transcript available at invention.psychology.msstate.edu/i/Wrights/library/Chanute_Wright_correspond/May13-1900.html

> cross-stays which prevent the upper plane from moving forward and backward are removed, and each end of the upper plane is independently moved forward or backward with respect to the lower plane by a suitable lever or other arrangement. By this plan the whole upper plane may be moved forward or backward, to attain longitudinal equilibrium, by moving both hands forward or backward together. Lateral equilibrium is gained by moving one end more than the other or by moving them in opposite directions. . . . My plan is to attach the tail rigidly to the rear upright stays which connect the planes, the effect of which will be that when the upper plane is thrown forward the end of the tail is elevated, so that the tail assists gravity in restoring longitudinal balance.

Wilber also notes that he "would be particularly thankful for advice as to a suitable locality where I could depend on winds of about fifteen miles per hour without rain or too inclement weather. I am certain that such localities are rare." It is interesting to read in Octave Chanute's response on May 17, 1900, that several locations may be suitable but that he believes that "better locations can be found on the Atlantic coasts of South Carolina or Georgia." After careful examination of the fundamental source and consideration of current understanding, it is time for students to organize their thoughts.

ORGANIZING THOUGHTS

During the *Organizing Thoughts* stage, students should think about what they knew prior to reading the letters authored by Wilbur Wright. They can work individually or in small groups, but it may be most beneficial at this point if the teacher leads them in a class discussion about what they knew, how the letter added to or modified their understanding, and what else they would like to know. Students can be given several minutes to Think, Pair, and Share their thinking in small groups of two or three and to develop questions to guide the remainder of the lesson, while focusing on the fundamental question posed for the investigation. A perfect scaffold to utilize here and have the students complete in small groups is the SOURCES Analysis Sheet (Figure 1.11).

UNDERSTANDING THE CONTEXT

There are many resources available to assist students in building their content knowledge and to help them to better *Understand the Context.* The historical context is vital to understanding the time period in which the source is situated and the sources to be examined. Such knowledge empowers the students to properly attend to the fundamental question. The following are excellent books for helping students to put this investigation into proper context and to learn more about the thoughts, intentions, and lives of Orville and Wilbur Wright:

Borden, L., & Marx, T. (2003). *Touching the sky: The flying adventures of Wilbur and Orville Wright*. New York, NY: Margaret K. McElderry Books.

Buckley, J. (2014). *Who were the Wright Brothers?* New York, NY: Grosset and Dunlap.

Busby, P. (2002). *First to fly: How Wilbur and Orville Wright invented the airplane*. New York, NY: Crown Publishers.

Collins, M. (2003). *Airborne: A photobiography of Wilbur and Orville Wright*. Washington, DC: National Geographic.

Freedman, R. (1991). *The Wright Brothers: How they invented the airplane*. New York, NY: Holiday House.

Glass, A. (2003). *The wondrous whirligig: The Wright Brothers' first flying machine*. New York, NY: Holiday House.

Gutman, D. (2003). *Race for the sky: The Kitty Hawk diaries of Johnny Moore*. New York, NY: Simon and Schuster.

READING BETWEEN THE LINES

At this stage of the inquiry process, provide students with copies of the two fundamental sources that started the investigation, the two letters written by Wilbur Wright (May 30, 1899, and May 13, 1900). Encourage students to think about how they interpreted what they read in these letters initially and how their understanding has changed. They should think about what has changed and what it was that made them modify their understanding of the possible motivations of Orville and Wilbur Wright to pursue flight at Kitty Hawk and beyond.

CORROBORATING AND REFUTING

As students develop their understanding of what truly motivated the Wright brothers and what their intentions were as they pursued mechanical flight, they should be given an opportunity to begin developing a narrative in response to the fundamental questions guiding the investigation, as well as any of their own. Each of the following sources refer to the motivations of the Wright brothers. Thus, each source helps students build an appropriate, evidence-based response:

- Orville Wright letter to his father on September 3, 1900
  - cdn.loc.gov/master/mss/mwright/02/02055/0001d.jpg
  - Letter where he notes that flight is possible and that he is doing his experiments for pleasure, not profit.

- Orville Wright's diary entry of December 17, 1903
  - » www.libraries.wright.edu/special/wrightbrothers/educational/orville
  - » What did Orville feel like after he made the first flight? Read his diary entry of December 17, 1903, to find out.
- Wright Brothers' patent for the 1903 Flyer
  - » www.libraries.wright.edu/special/wrightbrothers/patents
  - » This patent was granted to the Wrights in 1906 and protected them from other inventors who might have tried to steal their ideas.
- "The Wright Brother's Aëroplane" by Orville and Wilbur Wright
  - » invention.psychology.msstate.edu/inventors/i/Wrights/library/Century.html
  - » Orville and Wilbur wrote this article, which appeared in the September 1908 issue of *Century Magazine*, to give people a first-person account of how they invented flight.
- "Girls Flew Too"
  - » www.libraries.wright.edu/special/wrightbrothers/educational/girls
  - » A reminiscence by Ivonette Wright Miller, niece of the Wright brothers. Ivonette Wright Miller was one of the first girls to fly in the United States. In this source she remembers what it was like to fly with her Uncle Orville in 1911.

If the teacher wants to include more open inquiry for the students, some of these sites are useful:

- siarchives.si.edu/history/featured-topics/stories/wright-brothers-pioneers-aviation
- www.libraries.wright.edu/special/wrightbrothers/
- primarysourcenexus.org/2012/12/today-in-history-wright-brothers-first-flight/
- www.nps.gov/wrbr/learn/historyculture/theroadtothefirstflight.htm
- airandspace.si.edu/exhibitions/wright-brothers/online/classroomActivities/8-12_step1.cfm
- www.airspacemag.com/as-interview/david-mccullough-wright-brothers-180955344/

ESTABLISHING A PLAUSIBLE NARRATIVE

In this second-to-last stage of the SOURCES framework, students are expected to create their own original, evidence-based narrative responding to the fundamental questions posed at the beginning of the investigation: What motivated the Wright Brothers? Throughout the stages of the framework, some students may consider whether their major motivator was primarily a passion for flight, maybe just a way to pass the time or earn a paycheck, or any number of reasons. There are many ways to assess student knowledge about the Wright Brothers and their motivations, but we suggest assigning the students a construction project: a historical marker for the Wright brothers' hometown of Dayton, Ohio, or for the site of their flight in Kitty Hawk, North Carolina. They will be expected to provide essential information regarding the brothers' motivations and intentions on the marker, as well as imagery to help convey their understandings.

SUMMARIZING FINAL THOUGHTS

In this last stage, students should *Summarize Final Thoughts.* One way to accomplish this is through small-group discussions, which can help each student to contemplate his or her thoughts about the Wright brothers and their motivations, explore their own feelings about the inquiry process and about how knowledge was acquired, and address any remaining questions. To assist students, the following questions can be posted for their consideration as they reflect upon the entire inquiry process:

- How effective was the inquiry process for you?
- What would you change for next time?
- What content was acquired?
- How was it acquired?
- What questions are left lingering?

CONCLUSION

Through this examination of the motivation of the Wright brothers, students have an opportunity to engage in authentic historical inquiry. They are able to examine original sources, contemplate essential questions, and develop evidence-based narratives. Thus, students are given the opportunity to replicate processes and thinking engaged in by experts focusing on the social sciences and history.

Part II

ENGAGING LEARNERS WITH WEB 2.0 TOOLS AND EMERGING TECHNOLOGIES

A Step-by-Step Guide with the SOURCES Framework

CHAPTER 6

Defining Web 2.0 and Other Emerging Technologies

Since the early 2000s, a wave of Internet applications, Web 2.0, has emerged with potential to further support instructional settings that facilitate inquiry-based pedagogical aims, while also serving to fulfill some of the technological expectations of students (Hartshorne & Ajjan, 2009). The current generation of students has grown up on the technologies powering computers, tablets, smartphones, and the Internet. They also use Web 2.0 applications such as social networks, social bookmarking, media sharing, and mash-ups on a regular basis. These and related applications have the potential to enable active participation of students, promote opportunities and environments for student publication and reflection, and foster a collaborative and active community of learners, as well as offer multiple pedagogical benefits (Alexander, 2006; Franklin & van Harmelen, 2007). For example, many Web 2.0 tools support active and social learning, provide venues for student publication, and allow for the organization and curation of resources—characteristics that many constructivist theorists believe are as critical to effective learning environments and supportive of the intellectual processes necessary for students to be active and engaged citizens (Ferdig, 2007).

Web 2.0 applications depend on user contributions and interactions as driving forces, providing settings and opportunities for social connectivity and collaborative environments, important elements of effective teaching and learning environments. Furthermore, the integration of Web 2.0 tools into the teaching and learning environment has shown the potential to result in more positive attitudes toward content areas, elevated motivation levels, and increased student achievement, and can result in more reflective learning environments (Maloney, 2007). This integration supports individual growth and development and provides opportunities to explore content and problems in new and different ways, providing a clear and purposeful visualization of one's work while also providing venues for sharing work and solutions globally. Finally, Web 2.0 tools provide numerous opportunities for interactions in the learning environment between teachers and students, as well as with more knowledgeable others, such as parents, peers, and subject-matter experts, to effectively and efficiently scaffold student learning.

In this chapter, we introduce the power of the integration of varied emerging technologies alongside the SOURCES framework as one aspect of a comprehensive pedagogical and technological approach for supporting active, collaborative, inquiry-based learning. This kind of learning supports extensive and diverse instructional approaches that facilitate interactions with varied primary and secondary sources, as well as tools to support the development of deeper knowledge, critical-thinking, and inquiry skills. More specifically, this chapter focuses on defining Web 2.0 and emerging technological tools that are effective and appropriate in educational settings; differentiating between traditional technological applications and Web 2.0 and other emerging technological tools and their applications in the social studies classroom; the rationale for transitioning from traditional technological applications to the integration of Web 2.0 and other emerging technological applications; and, finally, situating this all within a discussion of the numerous pedagogical affordances of Web 2.0 tools.

As we progress through this portion of the book, we will first examine tools that facilitate student engagement and allow for varied instructional approaches, both student- and teacher-centered, for *Scrutinizing the Fundamental Sources*. Next, we will explore a number of Web 2.0 tools that support *Organizing Thoughts*, primarily through supporting activities that highlight connections and relationships between content and events through visual and other media-supported methods. Next, we will examine tools that support *Understanding the Context* and *Reading Between the Lines*. These will include applications that permit in-depth exploration of complex contexts from multiple perspectives, while also supporting finding, organizing, reviewing, and making sense of information from varied sources and perspectives, thereby facilitating inferences regarding implicit information and content as viewed through multiple lenses. We will then explore tools that facilitate the collection and organization of content and resources, allowing for learners to *Corroborate* (their analyses) *and Refute* (other possibilities) through supporting evidence and documentation. We will provide an extensive discussion of tools that support the final two phases of the *SOURCES* framework, *Establishing a Plausible Narrative* and *Summarizing Final Thoughts*, primarily from a student-centered and experiential learning perspective. Thus, we will focus our attention on collaborative development tools that facilitate multiple forms of student authoring, development, and publishing. The discussion of each tool will (a) be situated within the various phases of the SOURCES framework; (b) provide structured, formal, and coordinated pedagogical implementations of these tools, as well as less structured, informal, and diverse applications; (c) provide supporting examples related to each tool, including screenshots highlighting usability and functionality; and (d) include references to brief videos highlighting basic use of many of the Web 2.0 tools addressed.

The new Web-based applications that have emerged in recent years possess significant potential to improve teaching and learning environments. Rather than using the Web as a tool for accessing information, Web 2.0 tools allow students to create and share information, foster critical and deductive reasoning skills, and increase learner engagement in the educational landscape. In this chapter, we will (a) provide an overview of fundamental differences between traditional and emerging technologies, (b) provide examples of varied categories of traditional and emerging technologies and how they fit into diverse teaching and learning scenarios, and (c) conclude with a discussion of the numerous pedagogical benefits of emerging technologies and their role in social studies education.

WHAT IS WEB 2.0?

The term "Web 2.0" was initially coined by Tim O'Reilly in 2004 in a series of Web conferences, and differs from Web 1.0, or the first generation of the web, in that the primary focus is user contribution, as opposed to user consumption. Web 2.0 tools are dynamic Web-based applications that have a number of guiding tenets: (a) they are user-friendly, (b) they facilitate a participatory culture, (c) they are system/platform/device agnostic, and (d) they focus on the integration of user-generated content. Web 2.0 applications and technologies include blogs (e.g., Blogger), wikis (e.g., Wikipedia), media sharing (e.g., YouTube), social networks (e.g., Facebook), social sharing/curation (e.g., Pinterest), social bookmarking (e.g., Diigo), and collaborative development tools (e.g., G Suite).

TRADITIONAL VERSUS WEB 2.0 TECHNOLOGIES

Although traditional (Web 1.0) and emerging (Web 2.0) technologies possess a number of similarities in functionality, there are a number of pivotal differences. These are evident in a simple examination of a number of terms that are synonymous with Web 2.0, including the "read/write Web," or the "participatory Web," as these terms are quite contrary to the traditional Web or software, which is more consumption-based. Consequently, based on the consumption-based applications, traditional software and Web 1.0 tools are developed with a top-down approach. Conversely, based on the participatory nature of Web 2.0 applications, these tend to be developed with a bottom-up approach, and updates and modifications are largely driven by user input. Although this is changing as emerging technologies become ubiquitous, Web 2.0 tools tend to be less polished and structured in design, functionality, and usability, allowing for user interactions to drive iterations of each, whereas traditional technologies tend to be more edited, produced, and polished, which often limits the input of user interactions in the design and development process. An example of this would be comparing Google Slides, a component of G Suite, to Microsoft PowerPoint, part of the Microsoft Office suite. Animation and other features that can be integrated within a PowerPoint presentation are absent or limited in Google Slides. There are both pros and cons to reduced initial polish and structure in design, functionality, and usability, particularly in an educational context. The lack of certain features can actually direct learners' attention toward a particular task, as distracting functionalities may have been stripped from the tool being used.

Traditional and Web 1.0 technologies tend to be individual sites, whereas Web 2.0 tools tend to be mash-ups, often including constantly evolving data and functionality from a myriad of other sources and tools. A great example of this is the ever-popular social networking site Facebook. Facebook allows for the inclusion of the functionality and integration of a number of external tools, including Pinterest, YouTube, Twitter, and Maps, among others, with an additional series of diverse apps that can be integrated via Facebook's App Center. Next, Web 1.0 tools tend to be more static in nature, primarily serving as hubs of information and possessing limited interactive features, whereas Web 2.0 tools tend to be more dynamic and evolving in nature, as content is constantly being created by various users, alongside interface functionality updates. Examples of this include the myriad of personal website hosts (e.g., GeoCities) that existed at the beginning of the emergence of the Internet (Web 1.0), as opposed to blogs and social profiles (e.g., Blogger, MySpace) that emerged in the early-to-mid-2000s as individuals could more easily develop and publish content that allowed for interactions with others. Lastly, traditional technologies and Web 1.0 tools are more often an individual experience, whereas Web 2.0 experiences are conceived and adapted to be more social.

What does all of this mean for social studies educators? While a number of exemplary traditional (Web 1.0) tools have also been explored in prior chapters of this book, many of the tenets of the historical inquiry process align with the characteristics and functionality of Web 2.0 tools.

WHY INTEGRATE WEB 2.0?

As mobile devices, social networks, and cloud computing applications continue to become ubiquitous, so are the ways in which students are engaging with these tools to support collaborating, communicating, and goal attainment. If we examine the current body of research related to the integration of emerging technologies into the teaching and learning environment, we see that there is a series of emerging themes that are particularly relevant to supporting the SOURCES framework. First, the integration of emerging technology *fosters interactive, self-directed learning* and *higher-order thinking skills,* affording students opportunities to work with tools that more directly support the tasks associated with conducting historical inquiry, as well as other complex tasks that support the SOURCES framework. Second, the inclusion of emerging technology in the teaching and learning environment allows for an *increase in student-centered learning,* affording teachers opportunities to serve in more facilitative roles, and increasing the active role of students in the learning process. Lastly, the integration of emerging technology *improves overall student performance and increases student interest,* issues of critical importance to social studies educators. Although there are many other pedagogical benefits of Web 2.0 tools, these three are most aligned with the empirically based benefits associated with the SOURCES framework, instructional strategies, and methods to engage learners in the historical inquiry process.

A second reason for the thoughtful and consistent integration of Web 2.0 tools into teaching and learning is the fact that *technology is everywhere* and is *constantly evolving,* with ever-increasing functionality and increasing usability. With this increased functionality and improved usability, the capacity to become competent in using a specific tool, or to transfer the skills associated with the use of one tool to a new context or subject area, a new task, or a related tool, is significantly increased.

Lastly, students in K–12 schools today have *grown up with* handheld devices, instant connectivity, and emerging technologies, as part of their everyday lives. Contrary to the experiences and expectations of previous generations of learners, where learning new tools was a much more daunting process, with today's learners using these tools in all aspects of their lives the time required to learn how to use the tools to support educational endeavors is minimal. Furthermore, with the focus on improved usability and better human–computer interactions and experiences, the *compatibility* and *transferability* of skills between tools, platforms, and devices is significant, unlike in the past. As the interactive nature of these tools has allowed for shifts in the educational landscape from more teacher-centered environments, where learners tend to be passive recipients of information, to more student-centered environments, where learners tend to be more actively engaged with the tools, content, and each other, learners will become even more familiar with an ever increasing collection of Web 2.0 tools.

Pedagogical Affordances of Web 2.0 Tools

In addition to the previously discussed affordances, the integration of Web 2.0 tools and other emerging technological applications into the educational landscape offers a variety of educational benefits, including, but not limited, to *continuous connectivity,* the ability to more effectively and efficiently *support collaborative workspaces and interactions, facilitation of deeper knowledge creation,* potential to *engage students in more active instructional settings,* strengthening of the *development of critical and higher-order thinking, increasing learner agency* in the learning environment, providing new opportunities for varied and diverse *methods of sharing information, and more easily facilitating student authoring and publication* (Ajjan & Hartshorne, 2008; Freeman, Adams Becker, Cummins, Davis, & Hall Giesinger, 2017; Li & Pitts, 2009). In the coming chapters, these and other pedagogical affordances will be major drivers of the discussions related to instructional strategies, Web 2.0 and other emerging technologies, and implementing the SOURCES framework.

Benefits of Web 2.0 Tools with Primary Sources and Historical Inquiry

Primary sources are important for numerous reasons, including (a) their ability to engage learners through first-person accounts of events, making events feel more real and helping learners relate to events of the past in a more personal manner; (b) their effectiveness in developing critical-thinking skills; and (c) their facilitation of knowledge construction. Each of these benefits aligns with the primary tenets and many of the functionalities of various Web 2.0 tools. Consequently, merging the use of primary sources and Web 2.0 technologies in the historical inquiry process can help students to facilitate a deeper understanding of history as a series of human events, while also encouraging them to seek additional evidence about a person or event. Furthermore, because primary sources are often incomplete and limited in context, students must use their research skills, prior knowledge, and critical-thinking skills in analyzing other sources to find a pattern, all of which can be encouraged and supported through a structured inquiry-based pedagogical framework and Web 2.0 tools.

Skills such as questioning and making inferences (as opposed to making concrete observations) and considering issues such as bias, purpose, and point of view are enhanced through the use of primary sources and supported by Web 2.0 tools and the historical inquiry process. In utilizing primary sources, students must often reconcile contradictions, compare and weigh the value of multiple resources and perspectives, and deal with complex issues that were timely long ago. As conclusions are reached through analyzing and synthesizing information from a variety of sources, knowledge is constructed, and reconciling this with existing knowledge allows for a deeper understanding.

CONCLUSION

Web 2.0 applications can be effective tools for improving learning outcomes among many populations, including K–12 students. These tools can facilitate more engaging, learner-centered, collaborative, and interactive instructional settings. Further, Web 2.0 applications are particularly useful in social studies and to promote inquiry-based learning, as they support pedagogical approaches that are hands-on, problem-based, student-centered, and both constructivist and constructionist in nature. In the next chapters, we will explore both specific and general ways in which Web 2.0 and other emerging technological applications can be used to establish rich learning environments, citing varied and diverse pedagogical strategies using Web 2.0 and other emerging technological applications to support each of the individual components of the SOURCES framework. Additionally, for many of the Web 2.0 tools discussed, we will provide links to videos highlighting various features and fundamental functionalities of the tools, along with brief snapshots of the tools in action.

A Note About the Web 2.0 Tools Selected for Inclusion

In general, there were four primary criteria for all tools selected to be featured in this book. First, they are cloud- or app-based technologies. Consequently, each tool can be accessed from essentially any Internet-connected computer (provided there are no compatibility/security/blockage issues). Second, the tools are easy to use and easy to learn. Explorations of each tool highlighted began without any prior experience with the tool. If the tool took a significant amount of time to learn how to use, it was omitted from the book. Additionally, if the processes and skills for working with a tool were not transferable to other similar applications, it was removed from consideration. Third, all applications were instructionally flexible, meaning they could be used in a variety of pedagogical approaches. This was important, as a key recommendation of this book is to start with a small collection of tools and then gradually add to them. If a tool can serve only a single function, then it is rather difficult to start with only a small collection of tools and be able to address a wide array of pedagogical approaches. Thus, tools that had more instructional flexibility were highlighted over tools with more focused and limited functionality. Also, although a certain tool may be highlighted for only one particular stage of the SOURCES framework, it is likely that many of the tools highlighted can support pedagogical approaches that align with multiple stages. Finally, as we are well aware of teachers' needs for free resources, all of the applications highlighted in the book have either some level of "free" functionality or are inexpensive. Although some of the items may have somewhat limited functionality in the free version, the price associated with upgrading is typically not substantial.

CHAPTER 7

Using Multimedia-Based Discussion and Polling Tools to Facilitate Scrutinizing the Fundamental Source(s)

In this chapter, we outline ways in which various emerging technologies, including multimedia-based discussion/bulletin boards (e.g., VoiceThread) as well as polling/surveying tools (e.g., Poll Everywhere), can be used by both teachers and students as mechanisms for enabling learners to implement the first stage of the SOURCES framework, *Scrutinizing the Fundamental Source(s)*. As a primary theme of this section, we examine ways in which teachers and students utilize varied emerging technological applications to support initial engagement with primary and secondary sources, focused on simultaneously considering a fundamental question that will guide the inquiry process.

PEDAGOGICAL STRATEGIES FOR SCRUTINIZING FUNDAMENTAL SOURCES

Two elements that are critical to engaging students in the historical inquiry process and properly moving through the *Scrutinizing Fundamental Sources* stage are (a) providing a hook and (b) identifying a fundamental question. Fortunately, there are numerous pedagogical approaches in which these two tasks can be accomplished, as well as a myriad of Web 2.0 tools to support the pedagogical approaches. In this next section, we introduce a variety of both teacher-centered (e.g., Provide a Challenging or Thought-Provoking Question) and student-centered (e.g., Concept Attainment) pedagogical approaches to support providing hooks and identifying fundamental questions, followed by a section in which examples of Web 2.0 tools that support the specific pedagogical approach taken will be discussed.

PROVIDING HOOKS AND IDENTIFYING FUNDAMENTAL QUESTIONS

A hook is simply a tool or strategy used to gain student interest in a topic or an event. This might be an image, a document, or another primary source related to the topic being learned. Although the presence of a hook is a critical aspect of initially engaging learners in the historical inquiry process, identifying fundamental questions is an essential element to properly actuating the historical inquiry process among learners.

When identifying fundamental questions, it is important to follow a few critical guidelines. First, *implement non-dichotomous questions,* those that do not have a simple yes/no, true/false, or rating response. It is imperative that fundamental questions are more open-ended in nature and allow for varied responses. Second, *integrate questions that encourage inquiry.* Lastly, *utilize questions that are personally relevant or those that provide intrigue in authentic ways.* These types of questions will prove to be more useful and intriguing fundamental questions for the students. For example, you might ask, "What was life like on the home front during the Second World War, and how would it compare to life in the United States today?" A question like this will engage students more deeply than a direct yes-or-no question, such as "Was slavery the cause for the American Civil War?" These sorts of questions can be modified by adding "to what extent" to create a question such as "To what extent was slavery the cause of the American Civil War?" Thus, students are required to think more deeply and critically than when asked a dichotomous question.

Questions that require students to examine biases and motives, to synthesize information, to collect and weigh evidence, and then to arrive at source-based conclusions are going to be the most effective fundamental questions to encourage engagement in authentic historical inquiry. Having an effective hook or identifying a fundamental question is a great way to start off a lesson, module, or unit with some positive momentum and to engage learners from the onset. There are a multitude of potential hooks as well as fundamental questioning strategies, as we discuss below.

Embedding in a Story

Engaging learners by embedding a topic or event within the context of a story is an effective instructional approach, as it draws upon emotion, which makes a topic or event more memorable. It is also a great initial strategy for transitioning to one of a myriad of follow-up pedagogical strategies, such as using a K-W-L (Know, Want to Know, Learned) chart (www.nea.org/tools/k-w-l-know-want-to-know-learned.html).

Engaging with Digital Media

Media is particularly useful for facilitating engagement and includes a wide array of options, including images, oral histories, videos, or others. One benefit of media is that there are numerous collections of primary source media that can be utilized as a tool to hook students. This can also be used as an initial tool (teacher-centered) to engage learners, and then later in the lesson/module/unit it can be used again as a student-centered activity, having learners create media as a form of establishing a plausible narrative.

Provide a Challenging or Thought-Provoking Fundamental Question

Offering students a challenging fundamental task or a thought-provoking fundamental question, and allowing them to attempt to solve/answer it using primary sources as supporting evidence or guiding resources, are effective strategies to initiate the inquiry process. A prime benefit of offering an initial fundamental challenge/question is that it is easily accomplished and can be customized for the level of the learners. For example, the amount of introductory information provided can be minimal for advanced learners or can be in-depth for learners who might need more scaffolding, guidance, and structure. At all times when using the Challenging/Thought-Provoking Fundamental Question strategy, it is critical to provide a clear purpose, relevance, and relationship to the topic at hand. Further, specific pedagogical approaches that support providing a challenge/thought-provoking fundamental question (to be discussed in more detail later) are useful in supporting more student-centered approaches, such as Concept Attainment.

Concept Attainment

Concept attainment involves students learning to classify a set of objects or events, much like scientists classify items. When students are classifying objects or events, they are simultaneously determining the rationale for the categorization. This is useful and important as it facilitates and enhances higher-order thinking, affords students opportunities to weigh the contributory value of diverse sources, provides opportunities for learners to make connections among concepts, and has been shown to be useful for increasing learner retention, all of which have significant instructional benefits for other phases of the SOURCES framework, authentic historical inquiry in the social studies classroom, and other content areas.

Summary

These are just a few strategies for providing hooks as well as fundamental questions. The remainder of this chapter discusses a series of Web 2.0 tools that support the pedagogical strategies previously mentioned. In presenting these examples, first, a general category of tools will be discussed, along with functionality and features typically associated with the category of tool being presented, and then a series of specific tool examples will be provided, along with a topic example.

MERGING PEDAGOGICAL STRATEGIES AND EMERGING TECHNOLOGIES FOR SCRUTINIZING FUNDAMENTAL SOURCES

As introduced in the Preface, a primary goal of this book is to illustrate the use of a variety of Web 2.0 tools alongside pedagogical strategies to engage learners in authentic historical inquiry. The time it takes to learn how to implement the various features and functions of these tools is much less than it was in the past, so now the focus is on creating innovative and effective ways to implement them in the social studies classroom and in various instructional settings. Additionally, strategies for utilizing these tools and providing skills that transfer to other tools will be detailed throughout the coming sections.

Engaging Learners with Multimedia-Based Discussion/Bulletin Board Tools

Multimedia-based discussion tools allow users to interact with a discussion thread via multiple formats, such as audio, video, images, drawings/annotations, or text. As with traditional discussion tools, a prompt or initial comment might be provided, and learners may respond based on various guidelines. Although prompts, threads, replies, and feedback can be accomplished via a traditional text-based discussion forum, integrating additional forms of media engenders richer student-driven discussions, deeper and more comprehensive discussion interactions, and improvement of learners' social presence. Added functionality of tools such as VoiceThread and Padlet, which allow users to add multimedia-based contributions in a variety of ways, as well as easily integrate external web resources, allows for additional benefits to learners.

VoiceThread. VoiceThread (voicethread.com) is one of the most popular multimedia-based discussion tools. Like other multimedia-based discussion tools, VoiceThread is a cloud-based presentation application that allows anyone to remotely share audio, video, images, documents, or other media, and then learners can respond using audio (via internal microphone, phone, or audio file), text, video (via webcam or external video file), or images/annotations, or a combination of media. As a cloud-based tool, VoiceThread allows for additional benefits. As content/data is stored and managed on remote servers, rather than on local or personal devices, minimal computing power is necessary to experience the capabilities of such tools. Further, VoiceThread can be shared with others, with commenting functionality restricted by the administrator (i.e., teacher). Another feature of VoiceThread is that the skills necessary to use the tool are often transferable to other tools, so the process of responding to a slide/thread via audio, video, or text in VoiceThread is similar to that process in other tools.

VoiceThread facilitates multiple strategies to hook students, including *Embedding in a Story* and *Engaging with Media*. For example, in Figure 7.1, a

Figure 7.1. Whole Class Hide and Seek Using VoiceThread

See *VoiceThread* in action using the QR code shown.

strategy known as *Whole Class Hide and Seek* is being used. In this activity, the teacher (notated by *1* on the screen) has recorded audio providing some context for the image displayed, and prompted students to highlight specific items of note (related to the lesson objectives) and engage in a discussion about the item and why it was highlighted, using the various response options (notated by 2 on the screen). In this example, the images are embedded in a story, and the learners are both interacting with and creating media throughout the lesson.

Padlet. Digital bulletin board applications are similar to multimedia-based discussion boards, but possess a number of differences. Primarily, digital bulletin board applications allow users to curate, post, and manage content in a single web browser–based location. Padlet (padlet.com) is one example of a digital bulletin board application, and although it is similar to VoiceThread, it has different features and functionality. For example, Padlet allows teachers to pose fundamental questions, prompts, resources, or challenges using text, audio, video, images, or Web resources (Figure 7.2). Padlet promotes collaboration and interactivity by permitting learners to respond by posting to either their own Padlet wall or by annotating the teacher's or another student's existing wall. These Padlet walls can be either individually developed or created in collaboration with others, and are shareable with either the general public or a focused group of individuals. The teacher can use Padlet to support various levels of user control and can moderate annotation functionality. Padlet is an excellent tool to facilitate concept attainment or to provide a challenge or thought-provoking question. Additionally, as a hook for students, collections of primary sources could be provided to learners via Padlet in a disorganized manner, with the goal of ultimately reconciling the meaning and connections between the primary source items. For example, as illustrated in Figure 7.2, learners could be asked, perhaps in a collaborative setting, to categorize (Concept Attainment) the importance of the men in the images as their roles relate to the Battle of Antietam, as well as provide a rationale for the ranking developed. This could then transition into subsequent phases of the SOURCES framework, such as *Organizing Thoughts.*

Alternatively, learners might be provided a series of resources and asked to determine which resource (e.g., image) does not fit with the others. Instructors could use one of the features highlighted in Figure 7.2 to provide a challenge or thought-provoking question using one or more of the resources available, including adding text and linking to a specific Web resource, recording an audio clip, recording the screen and providing narration highlighting specific tasks, annotating the images or content on the Padlet canvas, integrating a map, or linking to other Padlet canvases. Padlet's interface and user-friendly features, such as adding various content, moving content, editing content, or even copying content from one Padlet to another, are simple and intuitive. Finally, if too advanced to utilize as hooks with your learners, these tools might be appropriate for use in culminating activities. An alternative option for a digital bulletin board tool is Webjets (www.webjets.io).

Figure 7.2. Concept Attainment Using Padlet

See *Padlet* in action using the QR code shown.

POLLING AND SURVEY TOOLS FOR FACILITATING ENGAGEMENT AND FUNDAMENTAL QUESTIONING INSIDE AND OUTSIDE OF THE CLASSROOM

Activities designed to hook students and engage them with a fundamental topic or question are not limited to tools that are used only in the classroom. There are a variety of Web 2.0 tools that, although possessing in-class applications, are also useful for promoting engagement outside the classroom, which can be facilitated through the development of asynchronous surveys/polls that can serve to guide in-class instruction in a more informed manner. These include a myriad of polling/surveying tools, such as Poll Everywhere (www.polleverywhere.com; Figures 7.3–7.4), Crowdsignal (formerly Polldaddy; crowdsignal.com; Figures 7.5–7.6), or QuestionAir (getquestionair.com; Figures 7.7–7.8), that are useful in encouraging discussion and collaboration between students while also aggregating learner feedback to inform a comparative analysis of a fundamental question, concept, or collection of primary sources.

Poll Everywhere/Crowdsignal/Socrative

Using digital polls and surveys in the classroom has a number of pedagogical benefits that align with the historical inquiry process espoused throughout the SOURCES framework. For example, polls are useful in promoting engagement, increasing active learning, exploring learner understanding of concepts, and providing learners with agency in the learning process, all of which can promote richer learning environments and promote deeper learning. Additionally, there are a number of surveying/polling tools that have direct instructional applications in the social studies classroom and that can support the historical inquiry process in particular. One such example is Poll Everywhere, which is an extremely flexible and easy-to-use polling/surveying mobile app and/or Web-based audience response tool that permits an instructor to collect responses to a multitude of question/poll/survey types via text messaging, laptop/desktop/tablet, or even Twitter. Poll Everywhere implements a simple user interface, allows for a variety of open-ended or dichotomous question formats and representations of data, and integrates diverse methods of data collection, including text messaging from phones, submissions via Twitter, or laptops/desktops, with the ability to export and integrate poll items into PowerPoint, Keynote, or Google Slides presentations, with live responses visible and able to be shared and published in a number of formats. Poll Everywhere provides a series of guides for developing live polls, a blog providing news and features, and case studies that highlight diverse uses of Poll Everywhere.

Crowdsignal, similar to Poll Everywhere, is an extremely easy-to-use polling/surveying/quizzing/ratings tool that allows an instructor to collect responses to an assortment of questions/polls/surveys via mobile devices and

Figure 7.3. Poll Everywhere Interface

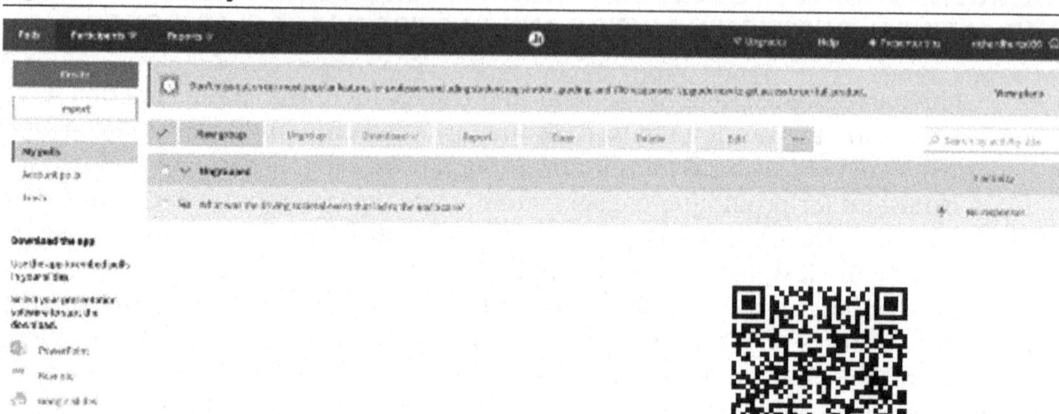

Figure 7.4. Poll Everywhere Example

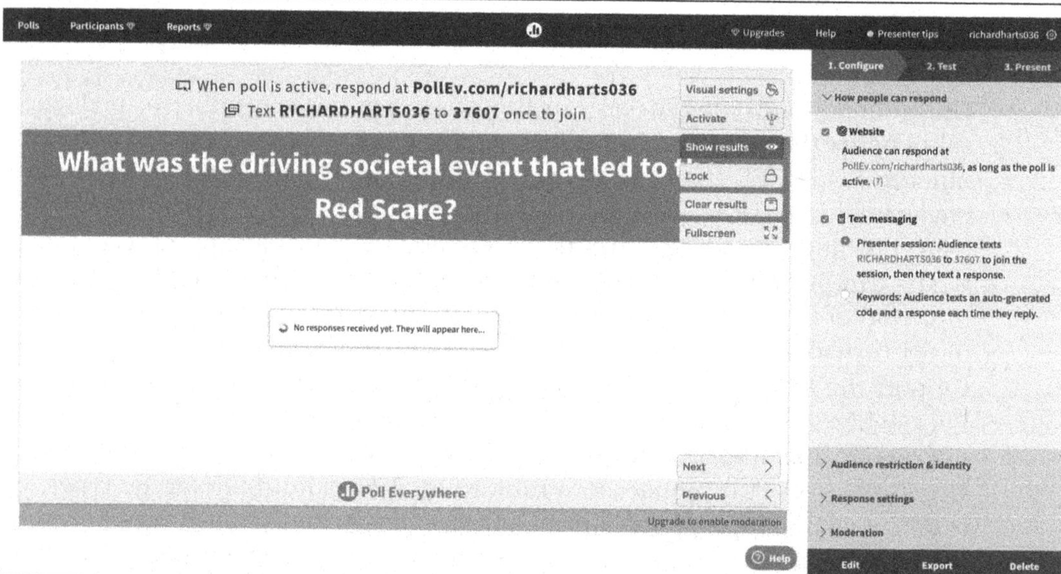

See *Poll Everywhere* in action using the QR code shown.

multiple social media applications. Crowdsignal provides a dashboard that facilitates the organization, copying, editing, and management of multiple surveys, polls, quizzes, or ratings. As with Poll Everywhere, Crowdsignal allows for text and visual representations of data, including completion date trends, participant location data, time-to-complete responses, and attrition rates. Crowdsignal surveys, polls, quizzes, or ratings can be shared via a direct link; embedded into a website as a pop-up slider, banner, button, or QR code; or shared via social media applications. An alternative option to both Poll Everywhere and Crowdsignal, and a tool that includes added classroom functionality, is Socrative (socrative.com). Although this tool is not addressed in this book, it is one that we have found some teachers prefer to Poll Everywhere, Crowdsignal, or other such tools.

Figure 7.5. Crowdsignal Interface

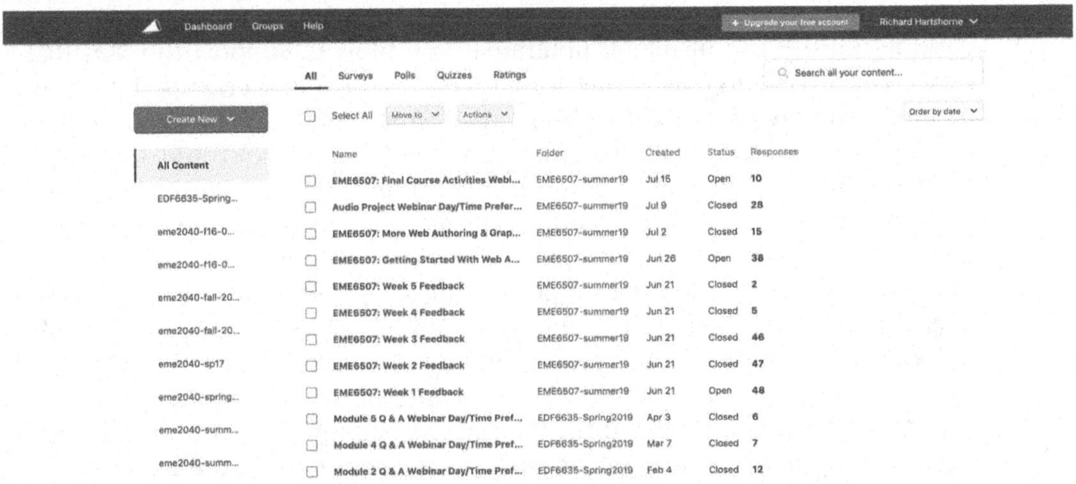

Figure 7.6. Crowdsignal Example

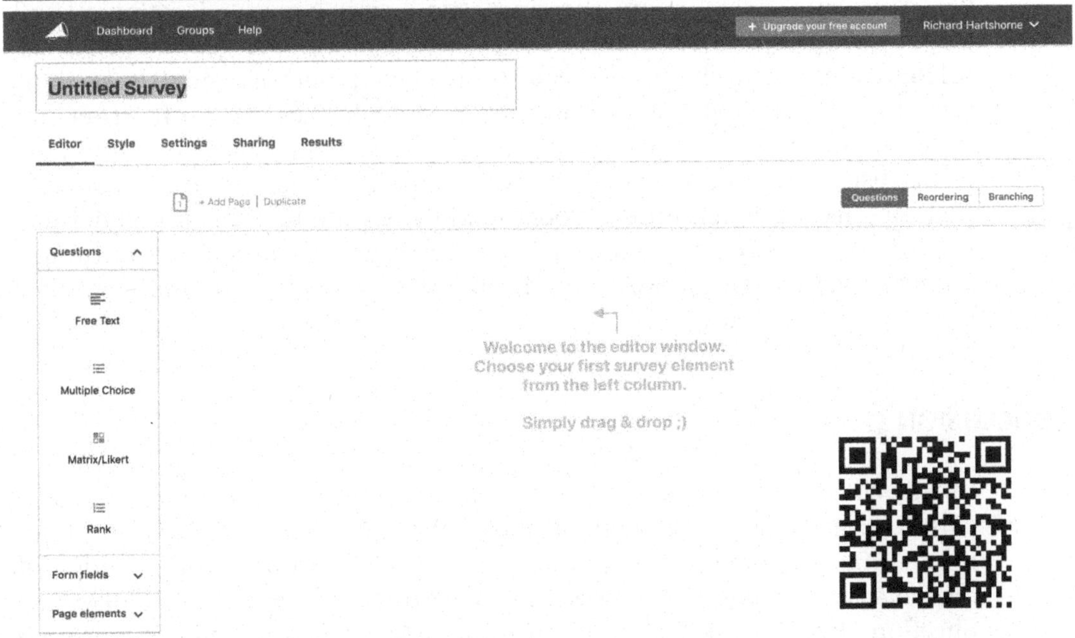

See *Crowdsignal* in action using the QR code shown.

QuestionAir

When transitioning from previous or traditional pedagogical approaches and technological applications, it is easy to become overwhelmed not only with the sheer magnitude of available tools, but also the functionality and usability of what is available. If one is new to integrating specific types of technological applications in the classroom, it is often useful to select a tool with a focused collection of applications and features that promotes ease of use. If considering the use of digital polling/survey tools to support the SOURCES framework, QuestionAir is one mobile app for live audience polling that is flexible and easy to use, with an adequate number of back-end and end-user interfaces (Figure 7.7). A presenter can easily create polls and share them with an audience through the app using a mobile device. Within the mobile platform, questions, answers, and results flow between the presenter and audience members like text messaging, but with a polling interface. Unlike the previously discussed Web-based polling apps, only the polling data are sent over the network. Because the app uses a mobile platform, delays (regardless of location) are reduced, and presenters can use features such as push notifications to alert audience members of new questions and results.

QuestionAir is different from Web-based polling tools in that there is no need for plug-ins or extensions to display information to the audience through the app. This can be particularly helpful in school settings with networks and firewalls that limit installation of such plug-ins or extensions. Audience members can be in the same room, the same school, or in a remote location, so polls can be conducted with a multitude of audiences simultaneously, which is useful for examining multiple perspectives on a given topic or event. Users simply need to have the app installed on their mobile devices and an Internet connection, and they can participate in single-choice list (Figure 7.8), multiple-choice list, ratings, ranking/ordered lists, word cloud, text entry, or statement polls or surveys, by entering a code provided by the teacher or poll designer (Figure 7.7). Lastly, the communication between the presenter and the poll audience via the QuestionAir app is anonymous, if desired, and encrypted, which provides security.

CONCLUSION

In this chapter, we highlighted both teacher-centered and student-centered pedagogical strategies—providing hooks and identifying fundamental questions—that support the first phase of the SOURCES framework, *Scrutinizing the Fundamental Sources*. We presented a series of emerging technological applications (multimedia-based discussion boards, digital bulletin boards, polling/surveying tools) that scaffold and extend these instructional approaches

Figure 7.7. QuestionAir Interface

Figure 7.8. QuestionAir Example

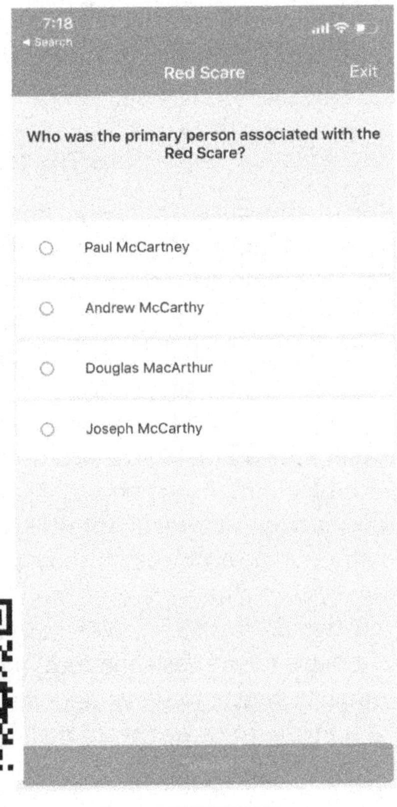

See *QuestionAir* in action using the QR code shown.

to promoting initial interest in a topic or event. Further, we introduced the importance of implementing nondichotomous and open-ended questioning, examining questions that encourage inquiry, and utilizing questions that are personally relevant or those that make a topic intriguing in authentic ways. We described just a few examples of the various tools that can be used as hooks for students and as ways to approach fundamental and secondary questions. The pedagogical strategies associated with these tools can be merged, and the tools themselves can support and facilitate other aspects of the SOURCES framework, which you will see in the coming chapters. We have demonstrated that these methods are easily integrated with existing pedagogical practices to make the learning environment more effective, efficient, and engaging. Finally, the accessibility of these tools via mobile and desktop devices allows for implementation both inside and outside the classroom, making it easier to extend the classroom outside the brick-and-mortar school walls. As we move through the remaining chapters, we will revisit some of these instructional strategies and emerging technological applications and how they can serve to more comprehensively support the SOURCES framework and, more specifically, the historical inquiry process.

Pro Tip 1: Managing Passwords

Does this tool require a minimum character count for passwords? Do I need to use a symbol? What about capital letters? Numbers? Can I use words in the password? Do I have to change the password with any specific frequency? I want a unique and secure password, but how will I remember it? Where did I put that sticky note with all of my passwords on it? (Don't do this.) All of these issues, and others, make managing password collections a daunting task. Fortunately, there are password managers, which will permit you to store your passwords, synchronize your passwords across devices, and create single-click log-ins for all your username/password combinations. Some password managers have more advanced features, including two-factor authentication, the ability to create secure notes for specific sites, automatic form-filling, browser plug-ins for ease of use, and password generators. Some allow you to share passwords with others, or secure other sensitive information. Password managers are more than just a cloud-based location to store user names and passwords. LastPass (www.lastpass.com; Figure 7.9), 1Password (1password.com), and Dashlane (www.dashlane.com) are among the most popular password managers. As your toolbox begins to grow, and you have multiple passwords for a variety of resources that you utilize, these password managers will save you time and, possibly, frustration.

Figure 7.9. LastPass Interface

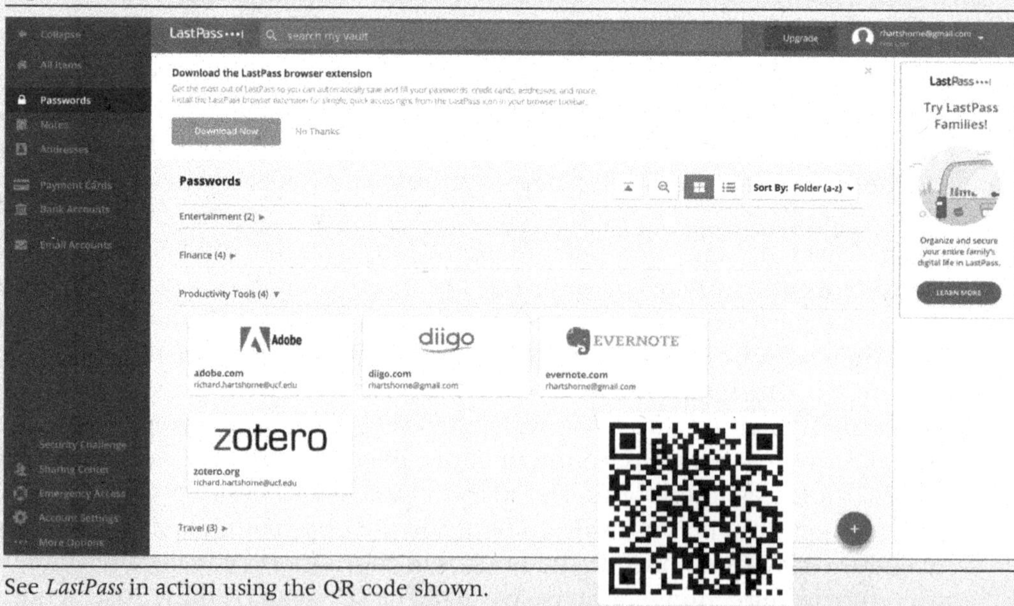

See *LastPass* in action using the QR code shown.

CHAPTER 8

Using Collection, Categorization, Storage, and Annotation Tools to Facilitate Organizing Thoughts

During the second stage (*Organizing Thoughts*) of the SOURCES framework, students reflect on what they know at this point and what questions they have, and begin considering the sources needed to supplement what they already know so they can begin answering the fundamental question. In this chapter, we outline this stage of the framework and demonstrate how emerging technologies can facilitate and support the organization process. More specifically, we will explore tools that facilitate the organization of learner thoughts through organizing and categorizing primary and secondary sources (e.g., Tizmos), and annotating and sharing primary and secondary sources (e.g., Evernote). These tools can be used by both teachers and students as mechanisms for enabling learners to implement the second stage of the SOURCES framework, *Organizing Thoughts*. As a primary theme of this section, we examine ways in which teachers and students utilize innovative instructional strategies alongside these tools to support collection, curation, categorization, management, and sharing of sources, and begin making sense of primary and secondary sources that will further guide the inquiry process.

PEDAGOGICAL STRATEGIES FOR FACILITATING ORGANIZING THOUGHTS

A critical aspect of historical inquiry is a clear distinction between primary and secondary sources. It is important to understand that the fundamental question being explored is a driving determinant in the differentiation between primary and secondary sources. As mentioned in Chapter 1, if the source is from the time period being examined or if it is directly related to the topic, then it is likely a primary source. Alternatively, if modification, analysis, or commentary has been applied to the source, or if the author is removed from the events or time period being explored, then it is likely a secondary source. Although these are not novel concepts, we are highlighting them because students often have a difficult time conceptualizing them. Once students have a clear understanding of primary and secondary sources, it is important that they be provided with varied and sustained opportunities to engage with diverse types of sources. Also, reading, analyzing, classifying, and organizing primary and secondary sources is often a new and difficult process for many students. Thus, it is important to provide various *scaffolding* activities to facilitate processes associated with organizing thoughts. For example, when given a letter, students might read the letter as they would read a typical letter, starting in the upper left-hand corner, reading left to right, from top to bottom. However, when analyzing primary and secondary sources, information other than the content of the narrative is critical to gaining a comprehensive understanding of the context, the purpose, and any mitigating issues or circumstances related to the source. Consequently, it is critical to provide students with strategies for comprehensively analyzing sources. One way to do this is through the use of analysis tools and sheets (examples were provided in Chapter 1 and can also be found at www.archives.gov/education/lessons/worksheets, www.loc.gov/teachers/usingprimarysources/guides.html, and www.mdhs.org/education/teachers/primary-source-worksheets). These can serve as effective scaffolding tools for the historical inquiry process, and can be extended using the emerging technologies presented in this chapter.

As we discuss the tools in this chapter, it will be important to consider how you might use them in your own instructional setting. Also, many of the tools will support you in using various items that are typically considered primary sources, and as examples are illustrated, note that most of the tools will allow for easy integration of digitized materials, including books, pamphlets, government documents, diaries, photographs, maps, audio recordings, video recordings, and other digital representations. Keep this in mind as we move through this chapter, and consider how this might work in conjunction with the analysis tools and sheets provided. Further, the emerging technological tools will focus on scaffolding strategies that will facilitate learners' organizing, categorizing, annotating, sharing sources, and collaborating with others. This is important because later in the SOURCES framework, such organization, categorization, annotation, and sharing will provide the structure for the last three steps: *Corroborating and Refuting, Establishing a Plausible Narrative,* and *Summarizing Final Thoughts.*

MERGING PEDAGOGICAL STRATEGIES AND EMERGING TECHNOLOGIES FOR FACILITATING ORGANIZING THOUGHTS

The emerging technological applications explored in this section provide a great deal of instructional flexibility, as they can be used by both teachers and students to organize, categorize, annotate, and share a variety of primary and secondary sources, as well as any additional digital resources. They give the user numerous and varied opportunities for engagement activities with primary and secondary sources and allow for a great deal of scaffolding, as teachers can provide a targeted and intentional set of sources that students can engage with, as well as additional supportive annotations and notes. Any instructional activity can be started with a great deal of structure, annotation, and notes (teacher-centered), depending on the level of the students, and then gradually reducing, or fading, the amount of structure and ultimately putting the tools entirely in the hands of the students (student-centered). We first focus on ways that teachers and students can organize sources, annotate sources, make various notes on sources, create reminders, share sources, and collaborate. One of the main reasons for this is that later in the book, we discuss tools that allow students to work with the sources and accomplish more specific tasks.

Organizing and Categorizing Primary and Secondary Sources

It is important to consider the level of guidance and support (scaffolding) needed, and the manner in which primary and secondary sources are organized and categorized within the context of historical inquiry activities, as well as the perspective from which the organization and categorization is occurring (teacher-centered or student-centered), and the experience and level of the learners. Activities designed to scaffold the historical inquiry process and interactions with primary and secondary sources, which facilitate the organization of learner thoughts, can be supported by a variety of Web 2.0 tools with varying features and functionality. These include social bookmarking tools such as Tizmos, cloud-based storage sites such as Dropbox and Google Drive, and cloud-based bibliographic tools such as Zotero.

Tizmos. The social bookmarking tool Tizmos (www.tizmos.com) allows you to share a collection of visual Web resources, including sites, videos, images, audio, and maps (Figure 8.1). With a free Tizmos account, you are provided with three folders, which can hold up to 50 web-based bookmarks/resources. You can also integrate one video-based, rather than still-image-based, Tizmo, and two custom photographs. This is useful from a teacher's perspective in that it allows control over the resources that are accessed by students. Also, the visual nature of the Tizmos interface is more engaging to learners, while providing a visual preview of resources provided. Furthermore, the content can be organized by topic, specific project, date range, or whatever schema that is selected by the teacher or student. Finally, the user interface for Tizmos is easy to use, which makes it appealing for learners who are new to interacting with technology, or are interacting with content that is new to them.

One of the benefits of such a tool, from a scaffolding perspective, is that Tizmos supports intentionality in the learning process and helps keep students

Figure 8.1. Tizmos Interface

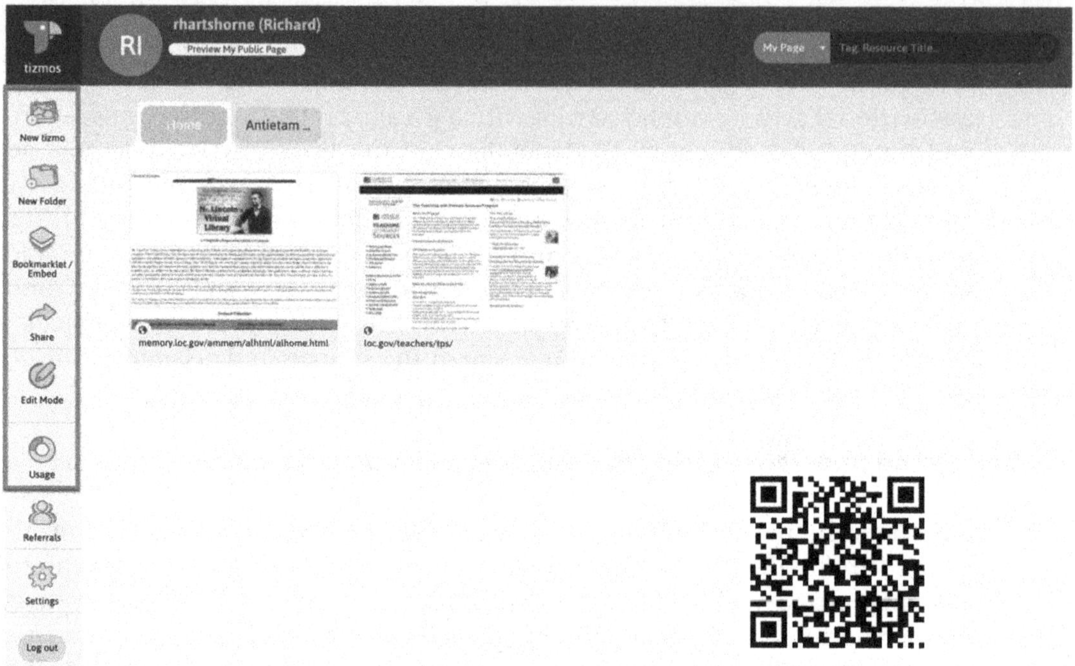

See *Tizmos* in action using the QR code shown.

focused on the topic and resources at hand, unlike what might occur if learners are conducting a search of their own. If students are less experienced with the content, or have limited experience conducting Internet searches, the instructor could provide a structured set of resources with a Tizmos collection, guiding them toward the specific resources with which they would like them to interact. Tizmos also has a number of privacy tools that allow control over who sees what resources. These can be used to provide different resource collections to various courses, the public, parents, or other stakeholders. From a learner-centered perspective, students can create, tag, and share their own Tizmos collections, and then utilize them in appropriate tasks associated with historical inquiry, such as referencing resources for piecing together a plausible narrative. Other social bookmarking sites with functionality related to that of Tizmos include Dropmark (www.dropmark.com) and Pinboard (pinboard.in).

Dropbox and Google Drive. While social bookmarks such as Tizmos allow for the individual or collaborative collection, organization, and sharing of websites, cloud-based storage sites such as Dropbox and Google Drive allow for individual or collaborative collection, organization, and sharing of a wide array of digital media, such as text, images, audio, and video. In this section, we will highlight the similarities and differences between these two cloud-based storage sites.

Dropbox (www.dropbox.com; Figures 8.2–8.3) is a cloud-based storage service that permits the user to store video, audio, documents, images, PDFs, and other file types. Although the basic plan (free) allows for only 2 GB of storage, one can obtain more free storage by recommending users, taking a usability survey, and other activities. As illustrated in Figure 8.3, Dropbox provides extensive options for organizing and sharing files and folders (Item 1); downloading, rating, pinning, and transferring files and folders (Item 2); and interacting with files and folders shared with others (Item 3). Google Drive (drive.google.com; Figures 8.4–8.5) has similar storage functionality to Dropbox but provides a larger amount of free storage (15 GB vs. 2 GB). As highlighted in Figure 8.5, Google Drive has various browser extensions. This gives the user the chance to get a great deal of work done directly from the browser (Item 1); works seamlessly with the Google productivity tools, G Suite, including Google Docs, Sheets, Slides, Forms, Drawings, and Sites (Items 2–3); and allows for ease in searching, sharing, tagging, and organizing files, folders, and projects (Item 4).

Both Dropbox and Google Drive are useful for collecting and hosting a vast amount of primary and secondary resources, provided you are cognizant of specific copyright limitations of resources collected, and then sharing those resources with others. Within Dropbox and Drive, there is flexibility in creating as many folders as you like, as well as a great deal of control over whom you share various sources with, as well as the type of control you give in interacting with the sources (read-only, editing, etc.). Additionally, Dropbox and Drive can be installed on any laptop, desktop, or mobile device, and then they can be synced to a particular account, allowing for access to any Dropbox and Drive resources from any device. From a learner perspective, students can create content, sources, drafts of narratives, or anything else, which could then be shared with anyone else, including peers, parents, instructors, or others. Dropbox and Drive can also be used as submission tools. For example, if an instructor had learners create videos, podcasts, papers, or image edits providing a discussion of the analysis of a particular challenge or question and how sources were used to develop an answer, this artifact could simply be uploaded to Dropbox or Drive, and a link could be provided directly to the teacher. The teacher could then create an archived collection of student-created videos for a variety of future uses (exemplars for future courses, content resources for future courses, etc.). Lastly, there are a number of other tools, such as Box (www.box.com) and OneDrive (onedrive.live.com), that offer similar functionality to Dropbox and Google Drive. An added benefit is that many of these tools work seamlessly with learning management systems (LMSs) such as Canvas and Google Classroom; this is critical, as use of these tools continues to increase in K–12 settings.

Figure 8.2. Dropbox Interface

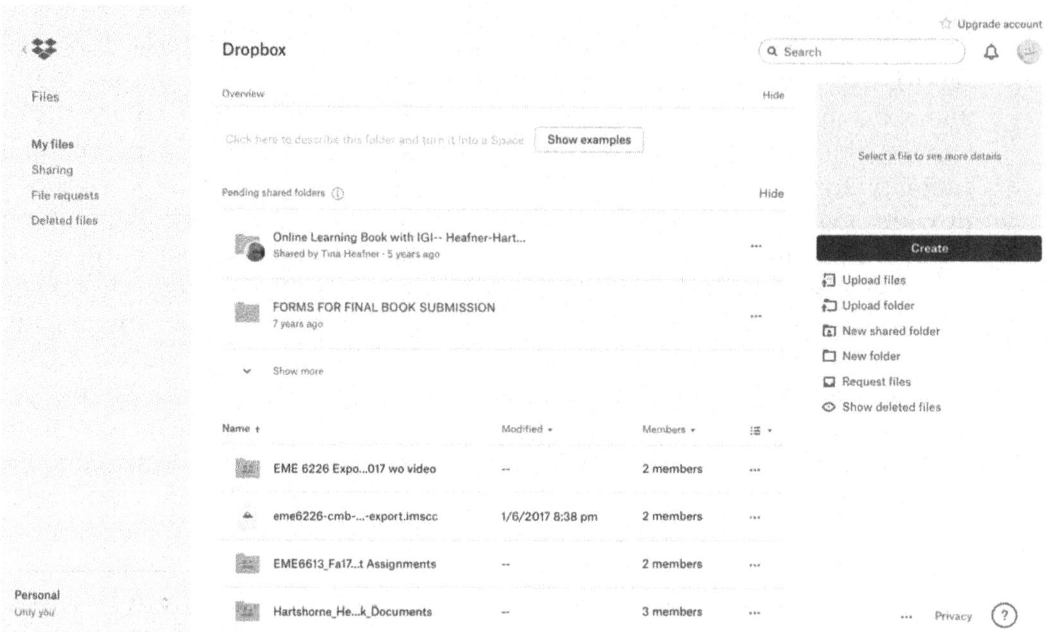

Figure 8.3. Dropbox Functionality

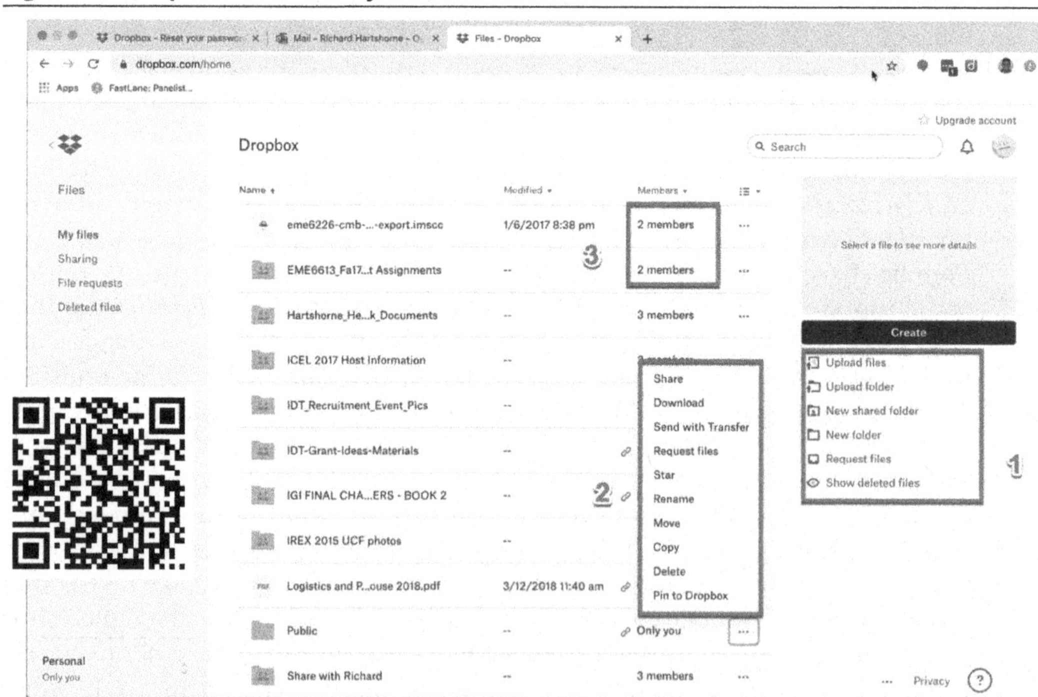

See *Dropbox* in action using the QR code shown.

Figure 8.4. Google Drive Interface

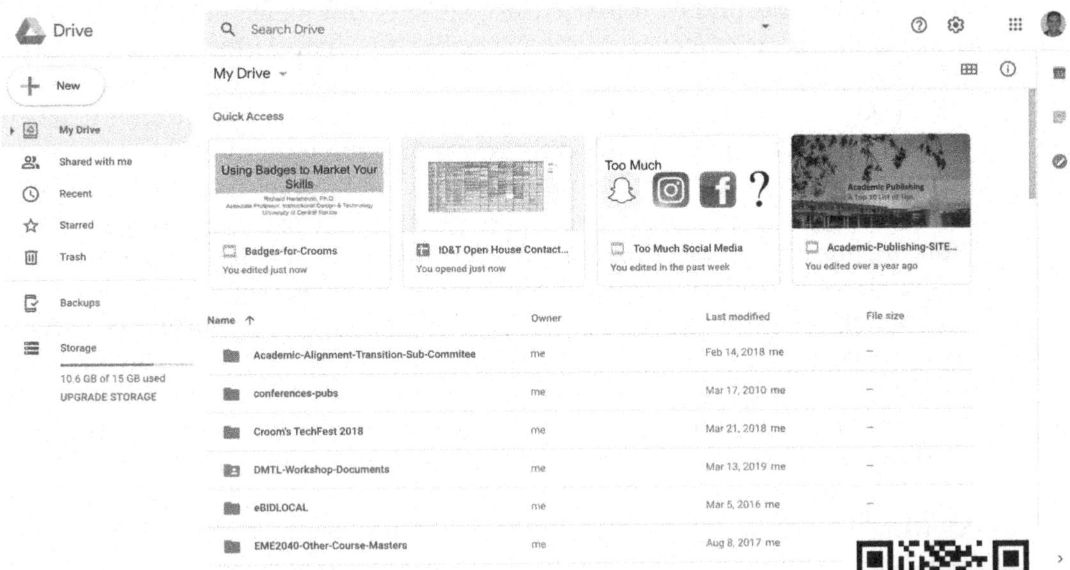

Figure 8.5. Google Drive Functionality

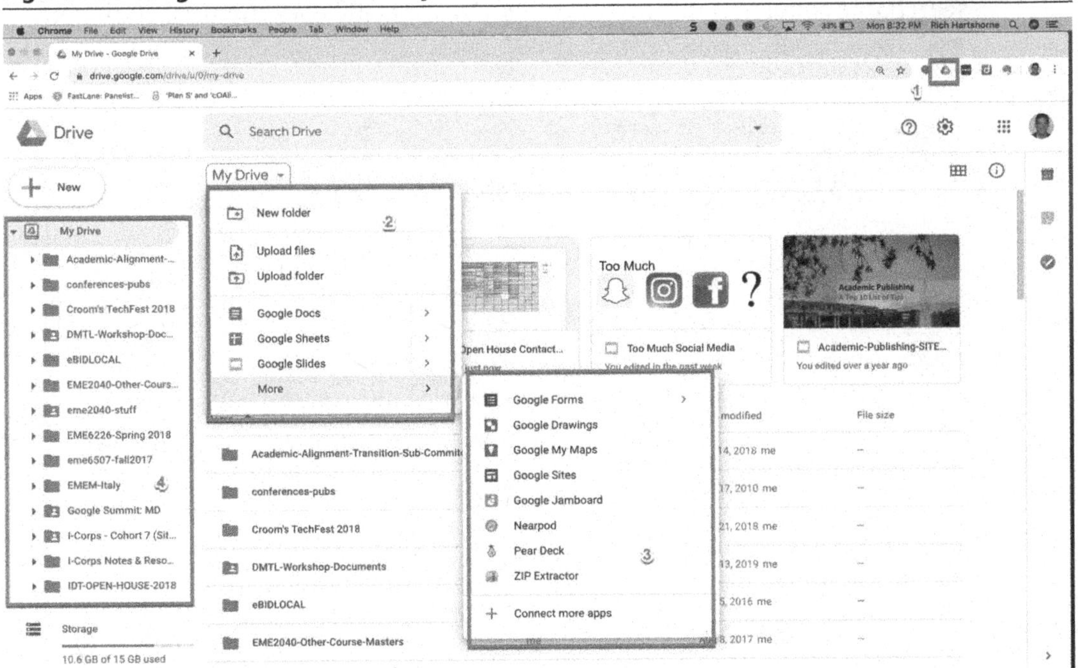

See *Google Drive* in action using the QR code shown.

Zotero. Cloud-based bibliographic organization tools are similar to both social bookmarks and cloud-based storage sites but focus more on individual and collaborative collection of bibliographic information for digital resources of all sorts. Zotero (www.zotero.org; Figures 8.6–8.8) is such a tool similar to the desktop software EndNote (endnote.com) and is useful for both teachers and students as a tool for collecting research, sources, and other documents, and then organizing, citing, and sharing the collections as needed. Zotero synchronizes collections across devices and platforms, allowing for ease of collection organization, exporting, and sharing resources (Figure 8.7, Item 1) and citing via web browser (Figure 8.8, Items 1–2). As highlighted in Figure 8.7, additional helpful features of Zotero include automatic importing of content associated with a resource into the Zotero collection (Item 2), the option to include additional notes and attachments for particular resources (Item 3), and the ability to tag and notate collections and individual resources (Item 4).

The robust functionality of Zotero allows for a multitude of uses in varied contexts that support the historical inquiry process. For example, if a user is viewing a source on the Library of Congress website, with the click of a button Zotero will import the resource and associated metadata into the user's collection. For multimedia resources, imported metadata includes item type, title, author, date, URL, tags, notes, and actual images. If a manuscript is added, Zotero will include the title, author(s), abstract, other citation information, tags, and a PDF of the manuscript (if available). This creates a full-text searchable collection of sources related to a specific content area, challenge, or

Figure 8.6. Zotero Interface

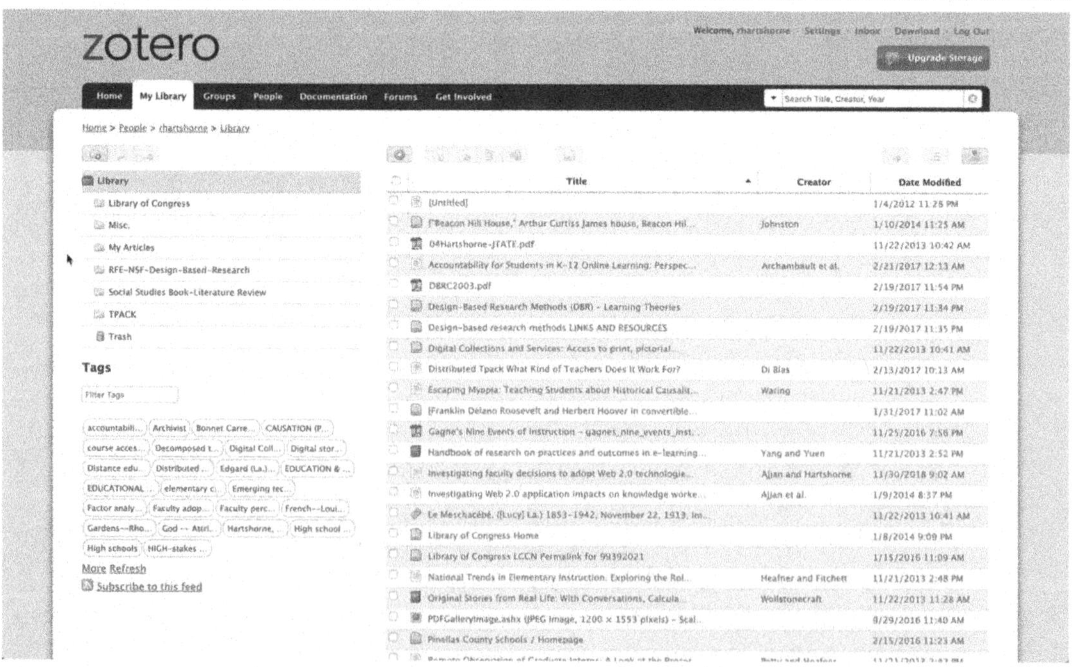

fundamental question. Then it is up to the learner to identify relevant sources and utilize them in effective and appropriate ways for supporting responding to the challenge or fundamental question. Lastly, Zotero, via a word processing plug-in, can add citations and automatically create a bibliography based on citations used in APA, MLA, Chicago, or other publication styles (Figure 8.8). Like other tools highlighted in this chapter, Zotero is versatile: It allows teachers to scaffold the learning environment and engage learners with primary and secondary sources, and learners can take greater control over their interactions with sources within the historical inquiry process.

Figure 8.7. Zotero Functionality

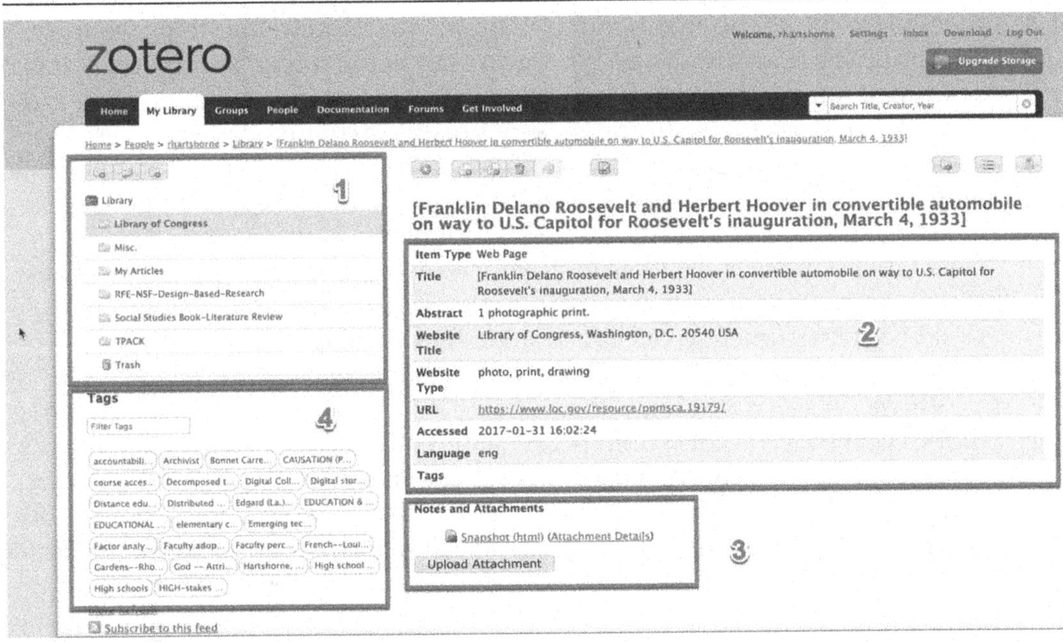

Figure 8.8. Zotero Citation Functionality

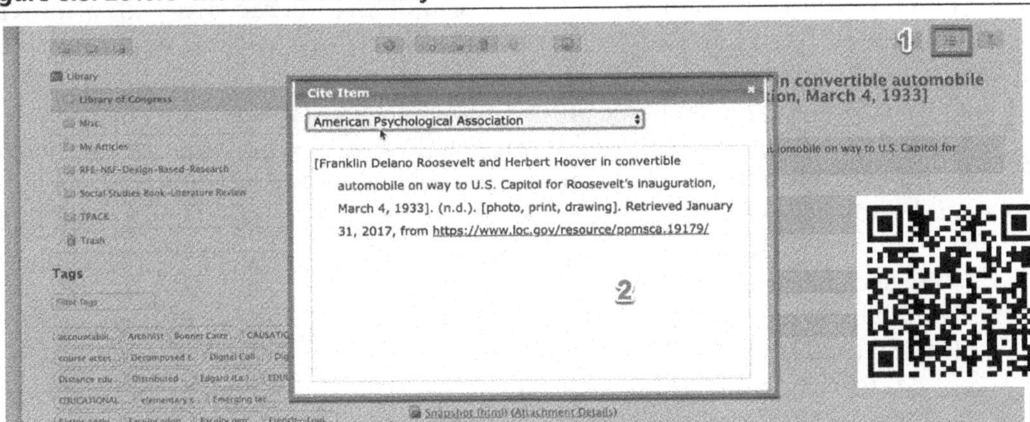

See *Zotero* in action using the QR code shown.

Annotating and Sharing Primary and Secondary Sources

Another way in which the level of guidance, support (scaffolding), and facilitation of the organization of learner thoughts is enhanced is by annotating various artifacts and collections of artifacts that will be used by students in the historical inquiry process. With such annotations instructors can provide additional commentary on a source, highlight various aspects of a source, or identify associated sources that may provide additional support for a task, challenge, or fundamental question. From a learner's perspective, annotation functionality affords the opportunity to organize thoughts through highlighting and notating seemingly important aspects of a source, sharing thoughts and comments related to a source with collaborators, or noting questions, concerns, or curiosities related to a specific source—thus providing an additional level of learner interaction with a primary source, secondary source, or other artifact that supports the historical inquiry process. Activities designed to scaffold the historical inquiry process, organization of thoughts, and other interactions with primary and secondary sources, using teacher- or student-centered sharing of annotated primary and secondary sources, can be supported by a number of different Web 2.0 tools with varying features and functionality. These include annotatable social bookmarking tools such as Diigo, and annotatable cloud-based document collection/storage sites such as Evernote.

Diigo. Diigo (www.diigo.com; Figures 8.9–8.10) is a social bookmarking tool that allows for collecting, organizing, curating, and sharing of sources. Additional functionalities include cropping, annotating, and printing of resources (Figure 8.9, Item 1), adding a comment or "sticky note" to a resource (Figure 8.9, Item 2), and highlighting selected portions of a resource (Figure 8.9, Item 3). A social bookmarking tool is similar to the Bookmarks or Favorites tool in your web browser but is accessible from any computer in which the application is installed, rather than a single desktop or laptop. Diigo's functionality can be extremely helpful for scaffolding interactions with a source, or providing additional intentionality, guidance, and structure associated with the use of a particular source. Other helpful features of Diigo include developing a collection of searchable groups and/or tags for a bookmark (Figure 8.10, Item 1), sharing and dissemination of either an unannotated or annotated source (Figure 8.10, Item 2), the ability to easily embed additional active links and resources, such as images, PDFs, or notes, to a source (Figure 8.10, Item 3), and the Diigolet applet (Figure 8.10, Item 4), which is a browser plug-in that permits users to highlight, tag, annotate, share, and read sources at a later date, in addition to simple bookmarking. All of this can be done without leaving the web browser environment.

A teacher could share a specified collection of sources, provide highlights or notes associated with a collection, and/or share either annotated or

Figure 8.9. Diigo Interface: Article Example

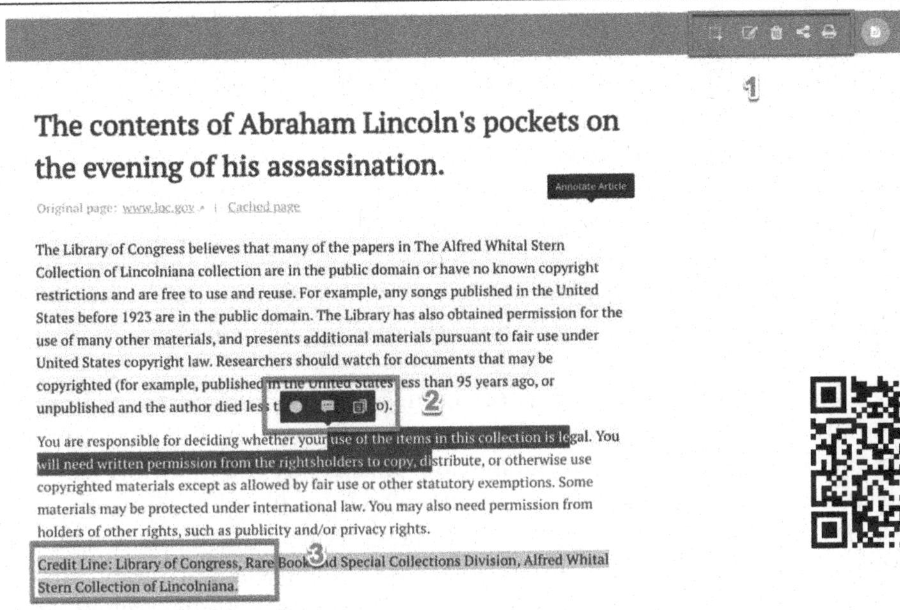

Figure 8.10. Diigo Interface: Article Library

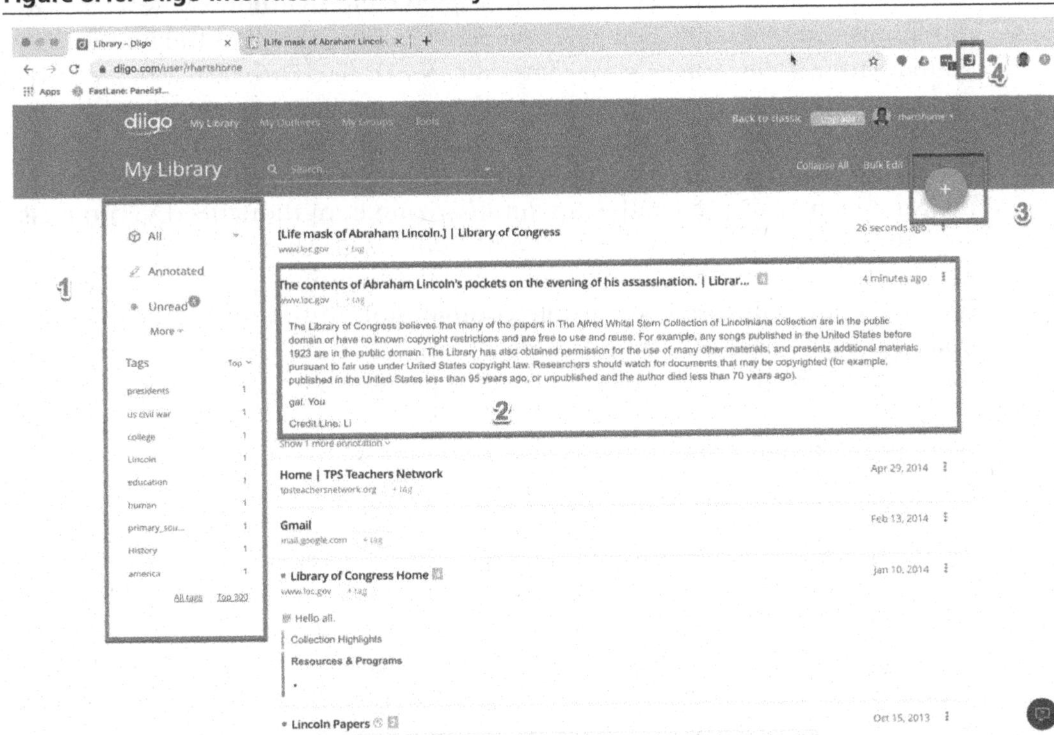

See *Diigo* in action using the QR code shown.

unannotated works related to a source. This allows for greater control in the level of guidance and structure needed for individual or groups of students. Students can also work with the sources, highlight certain aspects, collect sources for future tasks, and share with collaborators. A classroom collection of sources and support materials (analysis tools/sheets) could also be provided to support structured and intentional interactions with a variety of sources. Another aspect of Diigo is its classroom-friendly design allowing for educational application, which is not the case with many Web 2.0 tools. Diigo is one of many social bookmarking and related tools for consideration, including Pocket (getpocket.com) and the previously mentioned Tizmos , all of which allow for the collecting, curating, organizing, annotating, and sharing of varied sources.

Evernote. Evernote (evernote.com; Figure 8.11) functions like a combination of Dropbox or other cloud-based storage sites and Diigo or other annotatable social bookmarking/sharing tools, with the addition of some other useful features. Specifically, Evernote is a cloud-based application that allows users to take notes (Item 1), set reminders, collect and annotate various documents (Items 2–4), and clip items from the web via a browser plug-in (Item 6). Then clips or documents can be placed into collections, tagged, annotated, or shared (Item 5). Additionally, web searches for content related to a clip can be conducted, and those clips can be viewed in Evernote. Notes, lists, and reminders can be established and organized in Evernote and then easily integrated with a collection of class materials. Much like Dropbox, Google Drive, Tizmos, or Diigo, Evernote can be useful as a scaffolding tool. Teachers can provide structured and intentional sources for learners, and learners can use this tool in the process of corroborating and refuting sources and events, establishing a plausible narrative, or summarizing final thoughts. Evernote also facilitates interactions with teachers and students via sharing and note-taking/highlighting. There are active communities of Evernote users in various sectors, including education (evernote.com/community), and they continually update various uses of the tool. With Evernote's popularity among teachers, the user community has a heavy educator presence.

CONCLUSION

In this chapter, we highlighted both teacher-centered and student-centered pedagogical strategies that support the second phase of the SOURCES framework, *Organizing Thoughts*. We presented a series of emerging technological applications (social bookmarks, cloud-based storage sites, cloud-based bibliographic tools, and annotating and sharing tools) that scaffold and extend the instructional approaches to enable collecting, curating, categorizing, annotating, and sharing primary and secondary resources and can serve as tools to

Figure 8.11. Evernote Interface

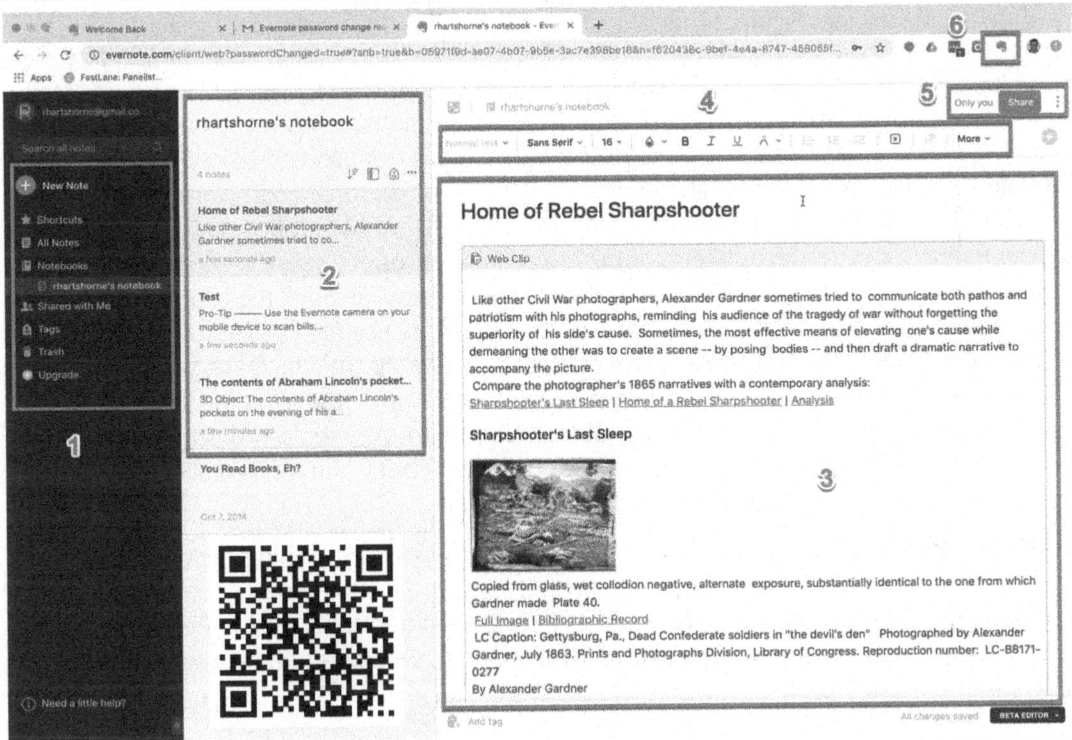

See *Evernote* in action using the QR code shown.

support learners in the early phases of the historical inquiry process. Further, we introduced the importance of affording learners opportunities to consider what they know versus what they do not know at a point in time, to examine what questions they have related to the fundamental question, and to begin considering the sources needed to move forward in the inquiry process.

These are just a few examples of the tools that can be used for both scaffolding learner interactions with primary and secondary sources in the historical inquiry process and facilitating the organization of their thoughts. We also examined emerging technological applications and pedagogical approaches that can support *Organizing Thoughts,* while simultaneously establishing a foundation for transition to the third phase of the SOURCES framework, *Understanding the Context*. We will explore that phase in the next chapter, as it is important to consider how these tools can work in conjunction with other tools and pedagogical processes to support the SOURCES framework in its entirety. As it becomes easier to integrate these tools seamlessly into existing pedagogical practices—or slightly modified variations of existing pedagogical practices—the learning environment will become more effective, efficient, engaging, and supportive of the historical inquiry process.

Pro Tip 2: Email Management

In this book you will learn of a multitude of technological tools that you can add to your toolbox. As the vast majority of these tools are cloud-based tools that will require an email address (and username/password) for registration, it might be useful to create a unique email address to organize and manage communications from your instructional tools, and avoid intermingling other email addresses, such as your personal or school emails. Due to ease of organization and integration with the Google Drive suite (benefits to be discussed later in the book), we recommend obtaining a Gmail account (mail.google.com). Then, as you add new tools to your Web 2.0 toolbox, create a new label for the tool and organize communications from the tool accordingly (you can even use filters to automatically label incoming emails from particular services). This will significantly increase your efficiency when using these tools, as well as decrease intrusions from these tools into your personal and other email accounts. Also, many of the applications and tools in this book integrate with Gmail and Facebook accounts, so having either or both of these will allow for simplified log-ins as additional tools are added to your toolbox.

NOTE: Many tools now support log-in through association with third-party applications, such as Google, Facebook, or LinkedIn. Beware: They may also request access to personal data related to the account being used to log-in. It is important to examine the types of access and types of data being accessed by these tools when determining whether or not to use the log-in via a third-party platform option.

CHAPTER 9

Using Collaborative and Discussion Tools to Facilitate Understanding the Context

In this stage (*Understanding the Context*), students bolster their content knowledge by reading and engaging with various sources of children's literature and trade books, websites, and primary and secondary sources. They reflect on what they know at this point and on what questions they have, and begin considering the sources needed to supplement what they already know and sources that can aid them in answering the fundamental question. In this chapter, we outline this stage of the framework and demonstrate how emerging technologies can facilitate and support the organization process. More specifically, we will explore tools that facilitate learner thoughts through organization and categorization of primary and secondary sources (e.g., Tizmos) and annotating and sharing primary and secondary sources (e.g., Evernote). These tools can be used by both teachers and students as mechanisms for enabling learners to successfully move through and beyond the second stage of the SOURCES framework, *Organizing Thoughts*. As a primary theme of this section, we examine ways in which teachers and students utilize innovative instructional strategies alongside these tools to support collection, curation, categorization, management, and sharing of sources, and begin making sense of primary and secondary sources that will further guide the inquiry process.

FACILITATING UNDERSTANDING THE CONTEXT

Especially when utilizing sources found in primary source repositories, there is a great deal of useful information (author, publisher, abstract, date of creation, and more) that can be gained from the bibliographic information alone and the opportunity to find other sources from the same creator or within the same collection, often supporting additional mechanisms for understanding the context. Luckily, historians and archivists working with these sources often provide their own narratives around the subject or even short video clips outlining their thoughts.

PEDAGOGICAL STRATEGIES FOR FACILITATING UNDERSTANDING THE CONTEXT

In order to gain a comprehensive understanding of historical context, there are a number of prominent issues to consider with regard to historical inquiry. These include the lack of multiple perspectives, that is, viewing and examining historical events from a single perspective (Waring, 2010). These myopic ways of thinking result in a very limited view of the context associated with historical events—mono-causal history, or the suggestion that there is a single cause to a particular historical event. This is an issue that is proliferated through the use of standardized tests, as test questions tend to oversimplify complex events throughout history (e.g., cause of the American Civil War), and encourages historical presentism, or viewing historical events through present morals, values, and understanding. In order to have a thorough understanding of the context of historical events, it is important to consider these issues. To do this, it is critical to provide students with opportunities to interact with a variety of sources, presented from multiple perspectives, to address the complexity of events, and for the context related to events to emerge during the historical inquiry process.

In considering pedagogical practices to facilitate the understanding of context, it is useful to implement tools that *promote collaboration, communication,* and *discussion* of historical events and context. The previously discussed tools promoted collection, annotation, and engagement with primary and secondary sources, whereas this collection of tools will *promote discussions* of the collections, *analyses,* and *interpretations* of the sources. Thus, as tools that facilitate understanding the context are addressed, it is important to consider how the tools in this chapter can be integrated with tools addressed in previous and future chapters to facilitate historical inquiry via the SOURCES framework.

MERGING PEDAGOGICAL STRATEGIES AND EMERGING TECHNOLOGIES FOR FACILITATING UNDERSTANDING THE CONTEXT

The tools described in this section provide a great deal of opportunity for collaboration, communication, and discussion, supporting previously collected or annotated sources, in varied settings, structures, and contexts. The tools can be used to facilitate student–student, student–instructor, or student–other collaborations and communications, while allowing diverse input and insight from multiple and diverse sources. They support many varied engagement activities with primary and secondary sources and open opportunities for pedagogical approaches to examining historical events from multiple perspectives, exploring the multicausality of historical events, and situating events and themes in their historical context. These supports include collaboration tools such as Edmodo, and backchannel platforms such as YoTeach!, Backchannel Chat, and GoSoapBox.

Collaboration and Discussion with Primary and Secondary Sources

In the previous chapter, there was an introduction to a collection of tools that support both teacher- and student-centered organization, categorization, annotation, and sharing of primary and secondary sources to facilitate historical inquiry, in order to enhance the *Organization of Thoughts*. To support the next phase of the SOURCES framework, it is important to complement those tools with applications that facilitate *Understanding the Context* of historical events. Thus, to extend organization, categorization, annotation, and sharing tools and activities, it is necessary to provide support and opportunities for collaboration, communication, and discussion, all of which are core functionalities of many Web 2.0 tools, such as social networks. In this section, we will discuss a social network for educational settings, Edmodo, which is effective for facilitating collaboration and communication among students, teachers, parents, and other stakeholders in the educational environment. As previously mentioned, collaboration and communication are fundamental to Web 2.0 tools. Therefore, it is important to note that although Edmodo is the main tool being discussed in this section, almost every other tool addressed in this book has some collaboration or communication functionality that can be utilized in a variety of pedagogical approaches in various stages of the SOURCES framework and historical inquiry process.

Edmodo. Edmodo (www.edmodo.com; Figure 9.1) is a social networking site, much like Facebook, but serves as an educational technology platform for schools and other educational settings. It is a robust, highly functional environment that allows users to share resources with teachers or students and post content such as primary and secondary sources or prompts to load challenges or fundamental questions, or provide quizzes or polls (Figure 9.1, Item 1); send alerts or notifications (Figure 9.1, Item 2); and join and create a variety of teacher- or student-centered groups (Figure 9.1, Item 3), all within this single entity. Another benefit of Edmodo is the ability to create and differentiate between specific classes (Figure 9.1, Item 4). Fostering specific types of environments, examining sources or questions from multiple perspectives, or other communicative and collaborative activities can be facilitated through the creation of structured and intentional groups/classes, and by providing the group/class with a collection of sources or other materials via folders or other group/class settings. It is also possible to search the entire Edmodo network for various applications that have a series of existing resources, lessons, activities, and challenges that support collaborative and communicative events. These can support all phases of the SOURCES framework and historical inquiry, but most prominently the *Understanding the Context* phase.

Figure 9.1. Edmodo Interface

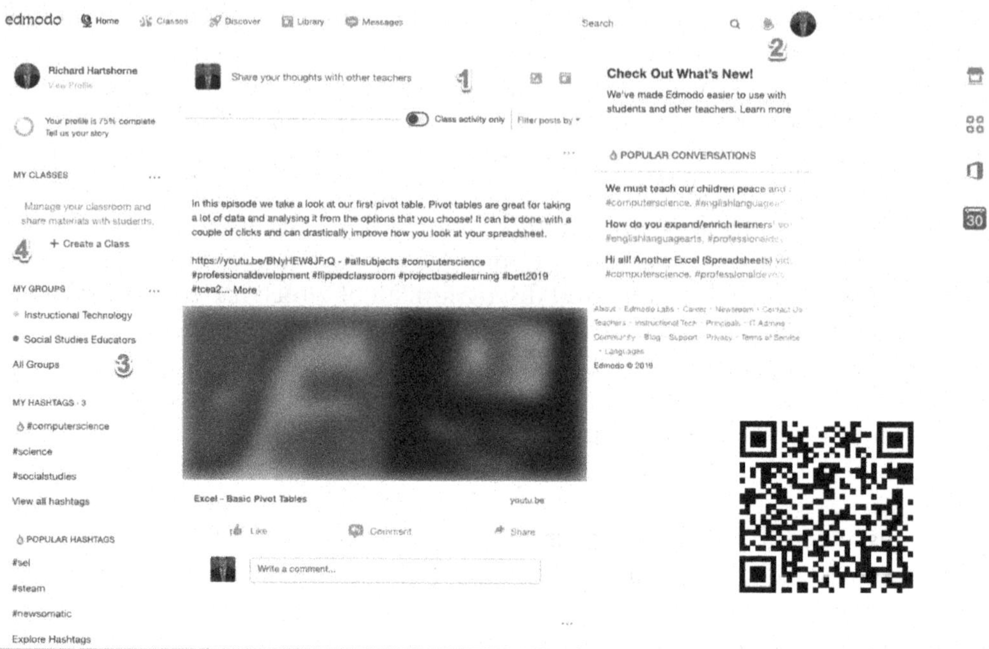

See *Edmodo* in action using the QR code shown.

Flipgrid. In recent years, other social media tools with applications primarily in educational settings, particularly K–12 schools, have emerged. Flipgrid (info.flipgrid.com; Figure 9.2) is one such example, allowing for teachers to post question/prompts and then share a URL/QR-code (Figure 9.3) to help students share responses via video, images, or other modes.

Backchannel Tools for Interacting with Primary and Secondary Sources

Backchannel platforms are easy-to-use single-stream discussion platforms that allow instructors to gather input regarding a topic, identify potential misconceptions among learners, or address potential points "voiced" from learners who typically might not speak up in the traditional face-to-face classroom setting. Backchannels can serve as a secondary discussion and create a venue for students to clarify any concerns without fear of embarrassment, shyness, or other reasons. They also permit learners to provide feedback during a lecture or discussion, such as asking for additional guidance, structure, or clarification. In the context of the SOURCES framework, backchannel platforms allow for acquisition and reconciling of multiple perspectives regarding an event, source, or concept; facilitate discussion of varied causes and factors associated

Figure 9.2. Flipgrid Interface

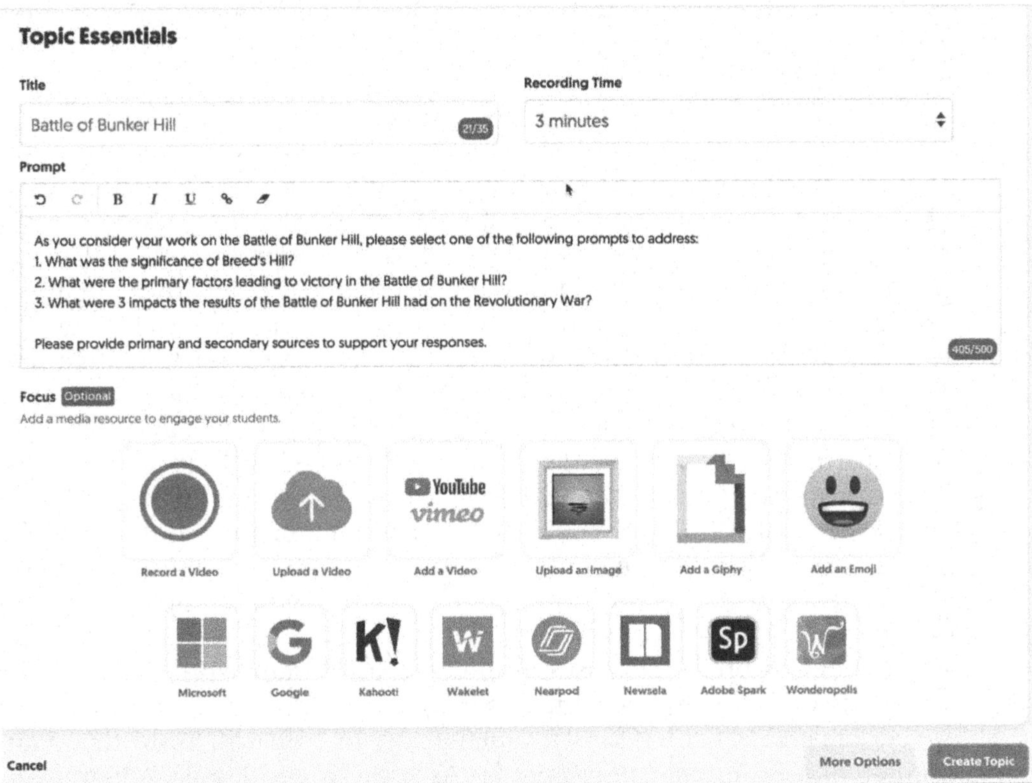

Figure 9.3. Sharing a Flipgrid with Students

with an event, source, or concept; and provide venues for addressing issues such as the morals, values, and understandings of the time in which an event, source, or concept occurred or emerged.

YoTeach!/Backchannel Chat/GoSoapBox. YoTeach! (yoteachapp.com), Backchannel Chat (backchannelchat.com), and GoSoapBox (www.gosoapbox.com) are three backchannel platforms that provide for varied discussions for classes. Each of the tools provides venues for either synchronous (i.e., during class) or asynchronous (i.e., outside of class) communications, and can be useful in gaining participation from learners less likely to participate in typical class discussions, and allowing for students to provide feedback and request additional clarification during a lecture or discussion. All three have similar functionality and interfaces that are user-friendly. A backchannel using YoTeach! (Figure 9.4) can be set up in under a minute, and allows the instructor to enable various administrative features, such as accessing student participation statistics, integrating a learner comment button, facilitating course votes, establishing a room password, and hiding the room from search engines, which can limit access to a particular room. Students can interact within the room via texting, posting an image, drawing, or uploading a file. For example, teacher- or student-created documents that were collected and/or annotated in previous phases of the SOURCES framework can be shared and discussed in the YoTeach! environment.

Backchannel Chat has similar functionality to YoTeach!, but with a slightly different user interface (Figure 9.5). As with YoTeach!, a backchannel discussion can be set up within a minute and has an intuitive interface for all

Figure 9.4. YoTeach! Interface

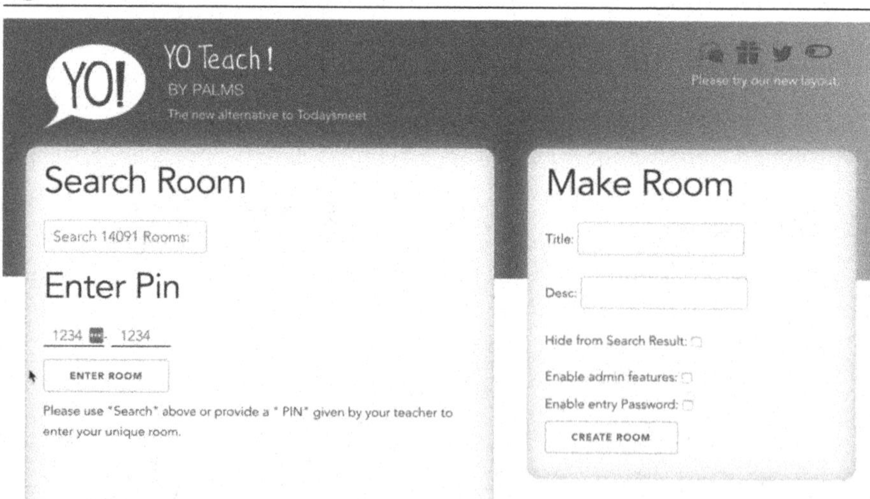

See *YoTeach!* in action using the QR code shown.

Figure 9.5. Backchannel Chat Interface

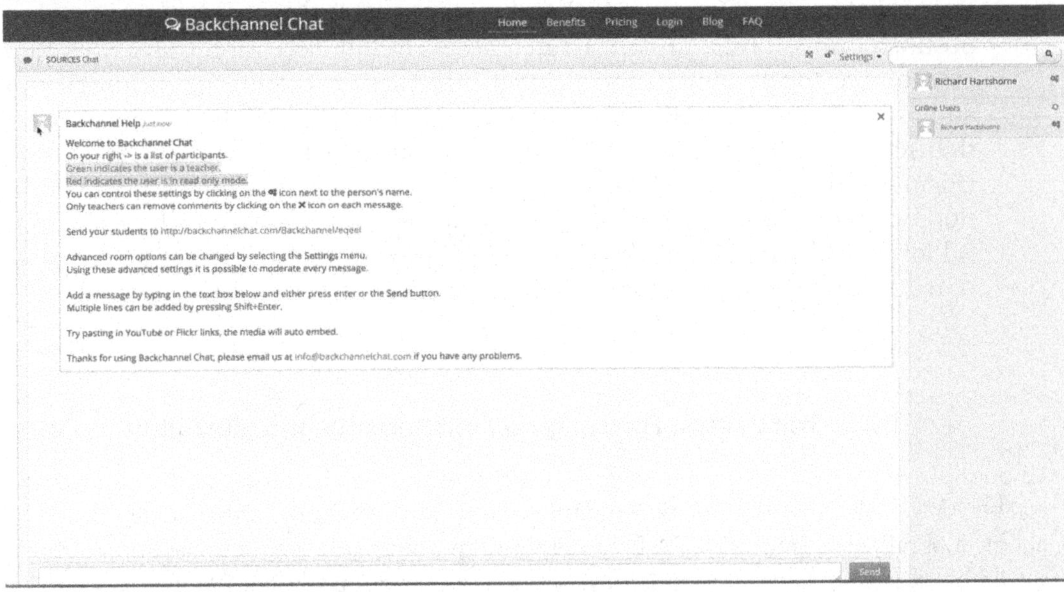

Figure 9.6. GoSoapBox Interface

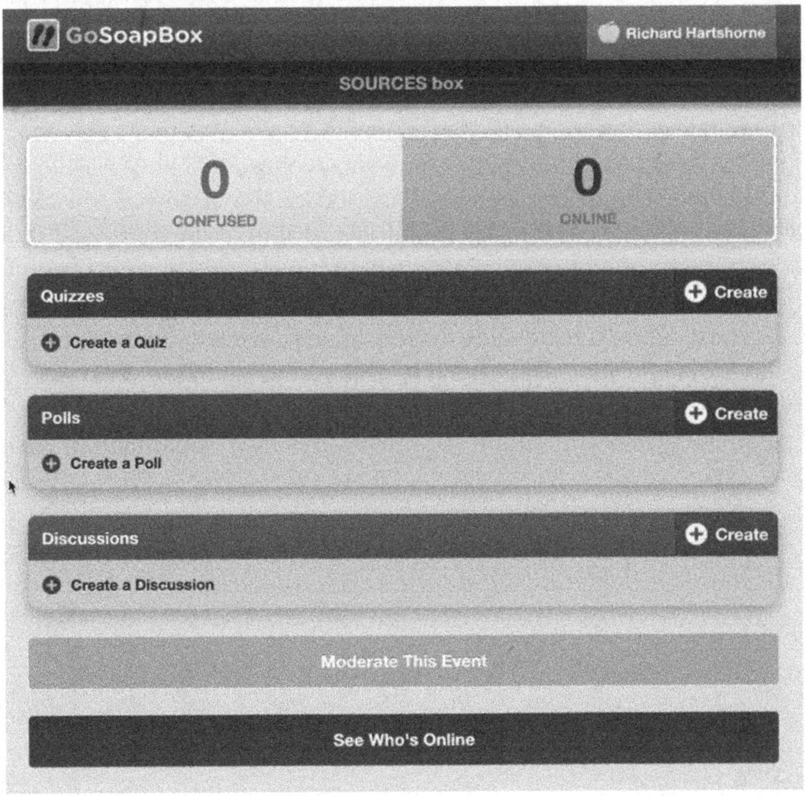

participants (students and teacher). It allows for moderation and control of the backchannel discussion, including message deletion, updating control of posting permissions, a profanity filter, access to full discussion transcripts, and ease of use for students (no personal information required). Although not addressed here in detail, Etherpad (etherpad.org) is another useful option that features similar functionality to Backchannel Chat. Finally, GoSoapBox (Figure 9.6) is similar to YoTeach! and Backchannel Chat but provides additional quizzing, polling, and discussion features to an event, which can be useful for identifying misconceptions as well as for supporting other pedagogical practices that facilitate *Understanding the Context.*

Pro Tip 3: Start Small, Focusing on Functionality and Flexibility

Throughout this book, many technological applications are being presented and discussed. Obviously, it would not be prudent to take all of the tools and associated pedagogical approaches and immediately integrate them into your existing classroom. This would be overwhelming, and would result in a less efficient and effective learning environment. Therefore, it is suggested that you start with a small collection of tools, perhaps one tool for one pedagogical approach that supports each of the phases of the SOURCES framework. How might you do this? Recall that two guiding tenets for the selection of the technological applications presented throughout this book are multifunctionality and instructional flexibility. Essentially, the tools selected possess extensive features and functionality that are relevant in the K–12 classroom, and have uses that apply to a multitude of pedagogical approaches, often supporting various phases of the SOURCES framework. As you consider refining your classroom and instructional approaches, it would be useful to start with only a small collection of multifunctional and instructionally flexible tools, and then add to those tools as your comfort level with Web 2.0 and emerging technological tools and associated instructional approaches increases. As you select tools, choose those with the most varied functionality for your specific context, as well as tools that support instructional goals in your classroom. Then, as you begin to see what works and what does not work, modify your tools and instructional approaches, but also use that information to guide the selection of future tools, as well as their application in the classroom.

CONCLUSION

In this chapter, we highlighted both teacher-centered and student-centered pedagogical strategies that support the third phase of the *SOURCES* framework, *Understanding the Context.* We presented a series of emerging technological applications (social collaboration tools and backchannel platforms) that extend the instructional approaches that facilitate diverse interactivity, collaboration, and communication among students, teachers, parents, and other stakeholders to support learners as they transition through the historical inquiry process. We also introduced the importance of affording learners with opportunities to interact, communicate, and collaborate both synchronously and asynchronously, as well as in face-to-face or remote/virtual settings, each of which can be useful in promoting critical examination of concepts and events, as well as deeper reflection on interactions, topics, and events, which provides a particularly useful foundation for the later phases of the historical inquiry process.

These are just a few examples of the multitude of Web 2.0 tools that can be used to support and promote communications, collaborations, and discussions, allowing for learners to examine concepts from multiple perspectives and avoiding mono-causal views of historical events. As highlighted throughout this book, these collaborative and multimedia-based discussion tools are most effective when used in conjunction with other tools and pedagogical processes to support the SOURCES framework in its entirety. These tools all have diverse and flexible instructional features and functionality, and can be seamlessly integrated into traditional pedagogical approaches, thereby fostering a communicative, collaborative, discursive, efficient, and engaging learning environment. Further, we examined emerging technological applications and pedagogical approaches that can support *Understanding the Context,* while simultaneously establishing a foundation for transition to the fourth phase of the SOURCES framework, *Reading Between the Lines,* which will be explored in the next chapter, as it is important to consider how these tools can work in conjunction with other tools and pedagogical processes to support the SOURCES framework in its entirety. As it becomes easier to integrate these tools seamlessly into existing pedagogical practices—or slightly modified variations of existing pedagogical practices—the learning environment will become more effective, efficient, engaging, and supportive of the historical inquiry process.

CHAPTER 10

Reading Between the Lines and Corroborating and Refuting

Using Scaffolding Tools for Source Sets

With a more deeply constructed understanding of the topic, students are asked to revisit the fundamental source in this fourth stage (*Reading Between the Lines*) to gain a better understanding of the source, the topic, and where the inquiry may take them. In the fifth stage (*Corroborating and Refuting*), students are asked to carefully examine a set of primary and secondary sources to help them corroborate and refute current understandings about the topic and fundamental question, which will help them to develop a narrative defending their thoughts on the subject at hand. Higher-level students should be expected to construct the set of sources themselves and progress through the stages in a more independent manner. These two stages are very closely connected, are supported through similar overlapping pedagogical strategies, and can be facilitated through the implementation of the same types of emerging technological tools. In this chapter, we will explore tools that facilitate *Reading Between the Lines* and *Corroborating and Refuting* through teacher-centered scaffolding/prompting tools (e.g., Pear Deck) to allow for deeper exploration of primary and secondary sources and multiple and diverse perspectives related to specific topics and events. Additionally, we will explore collaborative productivity and organizational tools (e.g., Slack) that enable learners to seamlessly collaborate, share thoughts and resources, and debate diverse viewpoints with supporting evidence. We will outline how these types of emerging technologies can facilitate these two stages of the SOURCES framework together.

PEDAGOGICAL STRATEGIES FOR FACILITATING READING BETWEEN THE LINES AND CORROBORATING AND REFUTING

A foundational idea of the pedagogical strategies that support the SOURCES framework is that it is important to provide learners with numerous, sustained, and varied methods of engaging with primary and secondary sources throughout the inquiry process. This is no different for the *Reading Between the Lines* and *Corroborating and Refuting* phases of the SOURCES framework.

However, opportunities such as reading, analyzing, classifying, and interpreting primary sources, which are critical elements of the *Reading Between the Lines* and *Corroborating and Refuting* phases, are new and difficult for many students. Thus, it is important to provide various scaffolding resources to support these processes. In previous chapters, a number of resources for scaffolding, including analysis sheets, were provided. This chapter will add an examination of Web 2.0 and emerging technology tools that can be used in conjunction with those scaffolding resources as well as primary and secondary source materials, to facilitate the *Reading Between the Lines* and *Corroborating and Refuting* phases. Further, the tools addressed in this chapter will allow for integration of various source items such as digitized books and letters, government documents, maps, audio recordings, videos, and other types of primary and secondary source documentation. We consider how these primary and secondary sources, Web 2.0 tools, and analysis sheets and resources can deepen students' experiences of reading between the lines and corroborating and refuting information.

MERGING PEDAGOGICAL STRATEGIES AND EMERGING TECHNOLOGIES FOR READING BETWEEN THE LINES AND CORROBORATING AND REFUTING

As *Reading Between the Lines* and *Corroborating and Refuting* are logical extensions of the *Understanding the Context* phase of the SOURCES framework, many of the previously described tools are also useful in these phases. For example, tools that enhance collaboration, communication, and discussion (e.g., Backchannel Chat, YoTeach!), as well as tools that facilitate student–student, student–instructor, and student–other interactions and engagement (e.g., Diigo, Edmodo, Zotero) can also support *Reading Between the Lines* and *Corroborating and Refuting*. The tools explored in this section, however, will focus on supporting and extending the functionality of the previously addressed traditional and emerging technological applications, as well as emerging technological applications that support curation of source materials while simultaneously supporting enhanced pedagogical prompts and initial instructor guidance and scaffolding, collaborations, communications, and engagement. As previously mentioned, three prominent issues as students begin historical inquiry are: (a) viewing and examining particular events from a single perspective, resulting in a very limited idea of the complexity of those events; (b) having a mono-causal view of history (suggesting that there is only a single cause of a particular historical event); and (c) historical presentism (narrowly viewing historical events through present morals, values, and understanding rather than considering the zeitgeist). To address these, it is important to provide students with opportunities to view a variety of primary and secondary sources to facilitate deeper explorations of events, allow for complex analyses of historical events, and promote the emergence of evidence-based inferences during the inquiry process. Many of the previously addressed tools and pedagogical approaches are useful in these endeavors and can be supportive in promoting *Reading Between the Lines* and *Corroborating and Refuting*. To extend the functionality of these tools, we will explore pedagogical tools that support enhanced collaboration, communication, and discussion of historical events, while also supporting deeper engagement with primary and secondary sources, alongside an enhanced focus on discussion of the collections, analysis, and interpretations of primary and secondary sources addressed via pedagogical approaches supporting earlier phases of the SOURCES framework. These tools will include teacher-centered scaffolding/prompting tools, collaborative productivity and organization tools, and digital curation tools.

Teacher-Centered Scaffolding/Prompting Tools

Many of the skills associated with *Reading Between the Lines* and *Corroborating and Refuting* are new to students and consequently require additional support or scaffolding. In this section, we will examine tools that can be merged with previously discussed scaffolding and support resources to promote complex and holistic analyses of resources and sound inferences from deep analysis of sources. We will start with these teacher-centered tools to provide scaffolding and prompts for learners to assist in guiding explorations: Pear Deck, Nearpod, and Biteable.

Pear Deck. The versatile tool Pear Deck (www.peardeck.com; Figure 10.1) gives the user the power to create presentations (e.g., with PowerPoint, Google Slides) to be converted into interactive resources for learners. It allows teachers or students to post and respond to content such as primary and secondary sources or prompts, display content to a controlled group, or manage a large collection of material, all within this single entity. PowerPoint presentations can be uploaded to the Pear Deck sites, or Google Slides presentations can be altered via the Pear Deck add-on, allowing for seamless integration with the tool. Pear Deck presentations give the learner opportunities for interactivity with the presentations, including responding to questions via text, dragging-and-dropping, drawing, or interacting with live Web content (Figure 10.2). Pear Deck maintains a library of activities and templates that serve varying instructional goals (Figure 10.2) and cover diverse subject areas (Figure 10.3). For example, teachers can choose from a variety of beginning lesson tools such as "bell ringers," mid-lesson supports such as assessments or transition prompts, or end-of-lesson items such as reflections or exit tickets. Specific tasks such as critical thinking can be supported via a series of interactive slides, including slides that facilitate making connections and considering different viewpoints or interpretations (Figure 10.4), all of which support various aspects of the SOURCES framework. Further, Pear Deck provides drag-and-drop Fact/Opinion, Cause/Effect, What Kind of Source Is This?, and other formats of slides that, with instructor questioning and prompts, can support instructional approaches to *Reading Between*

Figure 10.1 Pear Deck Google Slides: Interactive Questions

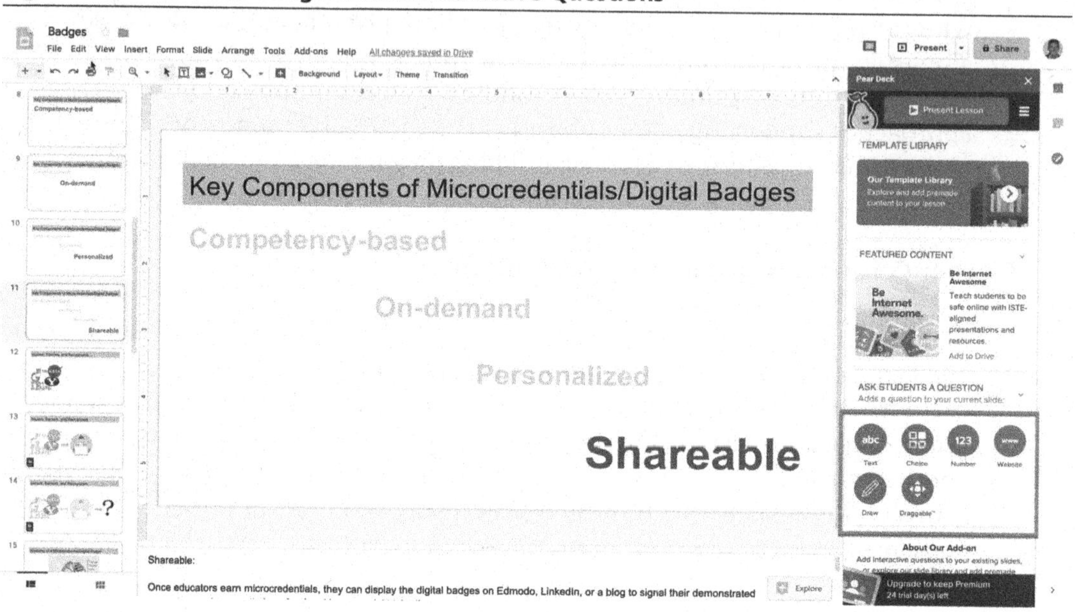

Figure 10.2. Pear Deck Google Slides Add-On: Template Library

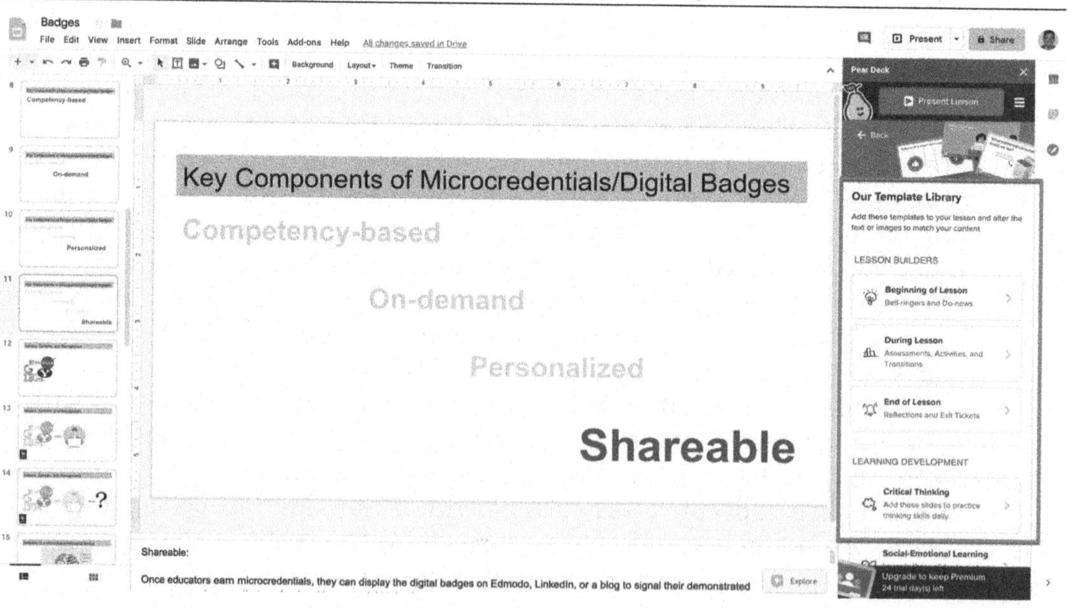

the Lines and *Corroborating and Refuting.* Once a Pear Deck is created, it can be shared with any relevant stakeholders (Figure 10.5). Pear Deck sessions can be opened and closed multiple times, archived, and modified multiple times (Figure 10.6).

Figure 10.3. Pear Deck Google Slides: Critical Thinking

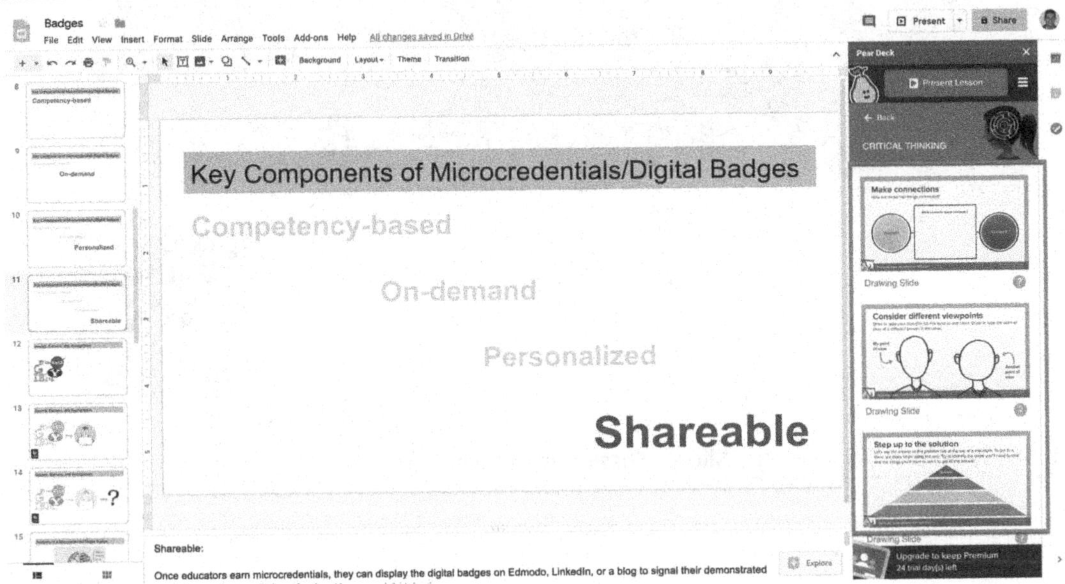

Figure 10.4. Pear Deck Google Slides: Social Studies/Inquiry

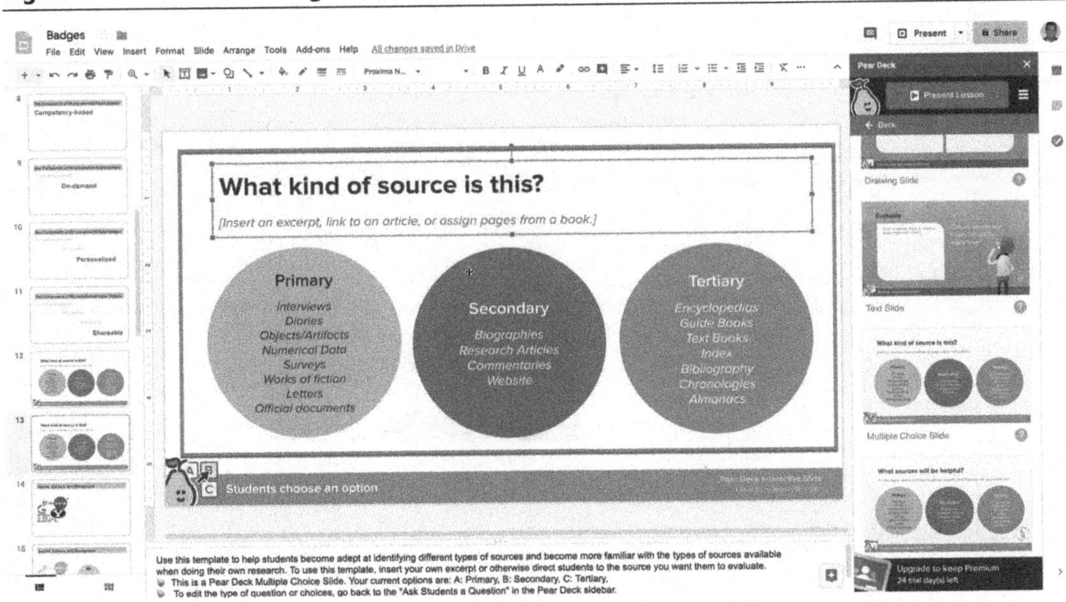

Figure 10.5. Pear Deck Google Slides: Invitation to Join

Figure 10.6. Pear Deck Google Slides: Session Interface

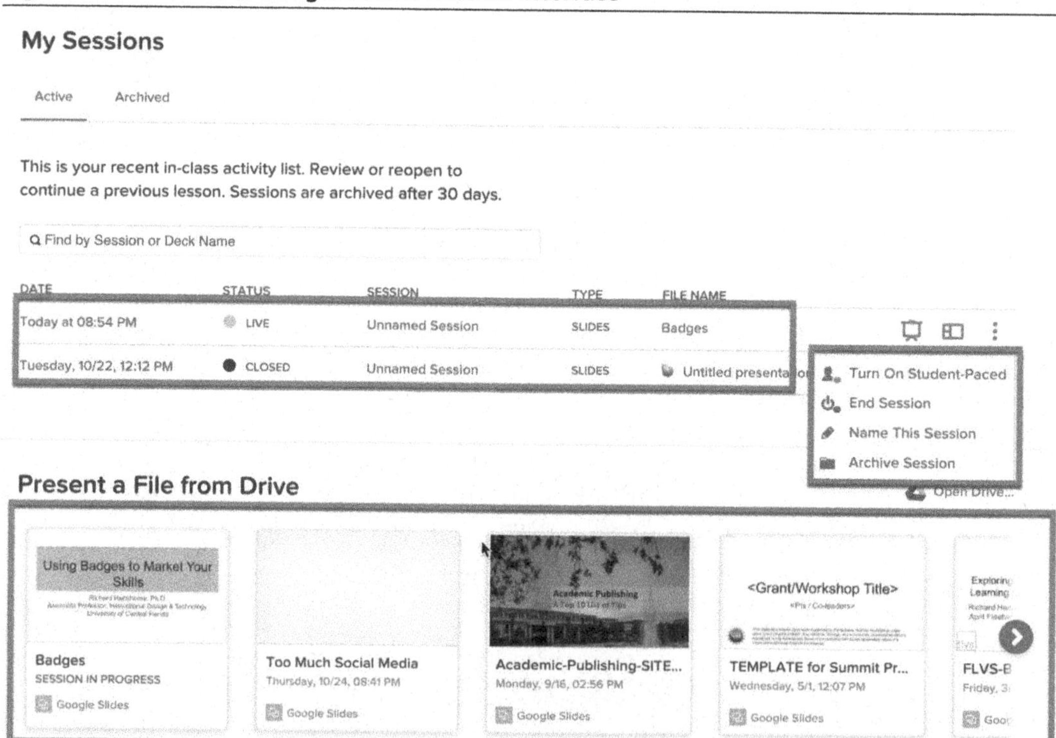

See *Pear Deck* in action using the QR code shown.

Another benefit of Pear Deck is that because it is integrated with Google Slides, the amount of support provided to specific learners can be customized through immediate copying and sharing of different types of presentations; the content can be adapted so it is pedagogically appropriate for specific groups of learners. Thus, instruction can be personalized and individualized, based on a number of parameters, allowing for targeted instructional approaches and effective facilitation of *Reading Between the Lines* and *Corroborating and Refuting*.

Nearpod. Similar to Pear Deck, Nearpod (nearpod.com; Figure 10.7) is a tool that converts presentations (e.g., PowerPoint, Google Slides) into interactive resources for learners, but works seamlessly with mobile operating systems, integrates formative assessment functionality into lessons, and has more extensive integration with cloud storage tools such as Dropbox and Box. Lessons can be created directly in Nearpod, or in Google Slides via a Google Slides add-on. Nearpod allows for teacher scaffolding and learner interactivity through the inclusion of audio, drawings, collaborative posts (images and text), three-dimensional elements, open-ended questions, polls, quizzes, embedded slideshows, Microsoft Sway elements (sway.office.com), or video elements (Figure 10.8). These can be imported or embedded directly from Internet repositories such as YouTube, or personal repositories such as Google Drive or Dropbox. Lessons can be enabled as live lessons or as student-paced lessons, and students can interact with lessons on desktop or mobile devices. As with Pear Deck, Nearpod maintains a continually expanding library

Figure 10.7. Nearpod Interface

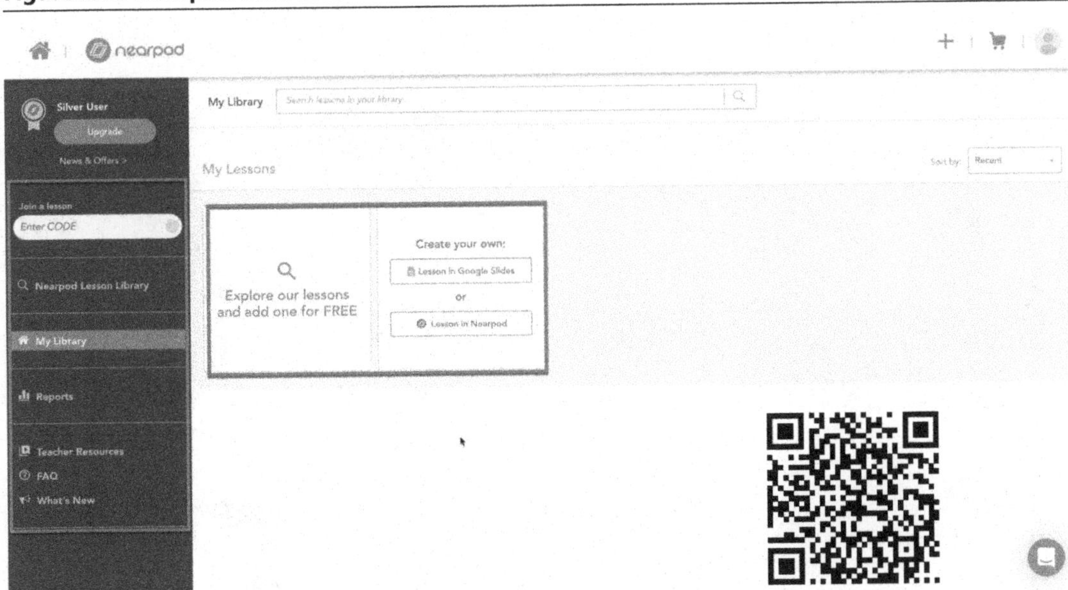

of lessons in a variety of social studies areas, including U.S. History, World History, Landmarks and Geography, Civics, Economics, and Social Studies, searchable by grade level and by specific content area (Figure 10.9). These lessons can be imported into a personal library and edited in a manner to support instructional goals. As in Pear Deck, specific tasks such as critical thinking can be supported via a series of interactive slides, including slides that facilitate organization of resources, consideration of fundamental questions, interacting with sources, contributing thoughts, examining multiple sources, and providing interpretations, all of which support the *Reading Between the Lines* and *Corroborating and Refuting* phases of the SOURCES framework.

Nearpod lessons and slides can be shared with any relevant stakeholders via a user code; sessions can be opened and closed multiple times, archived, and modified multiple times; teachers or students can post and respond to content and prompts; and content can be displayed to a controlled group. As Nearpod integrates with Google Slides (as well as with the Google Classroom LMS), there is a great deal of flexibility for easily modifying and customizing instructional content and interactions for various learners or learner groups, allowing for targeted instructional approaches and effective facilitation of the *Reading Between the Lines* and *Corroborating and Refuting* phases of the SOURCES framework.

Figure 10.8. Nearpod Google Slides Add-On: Functionality

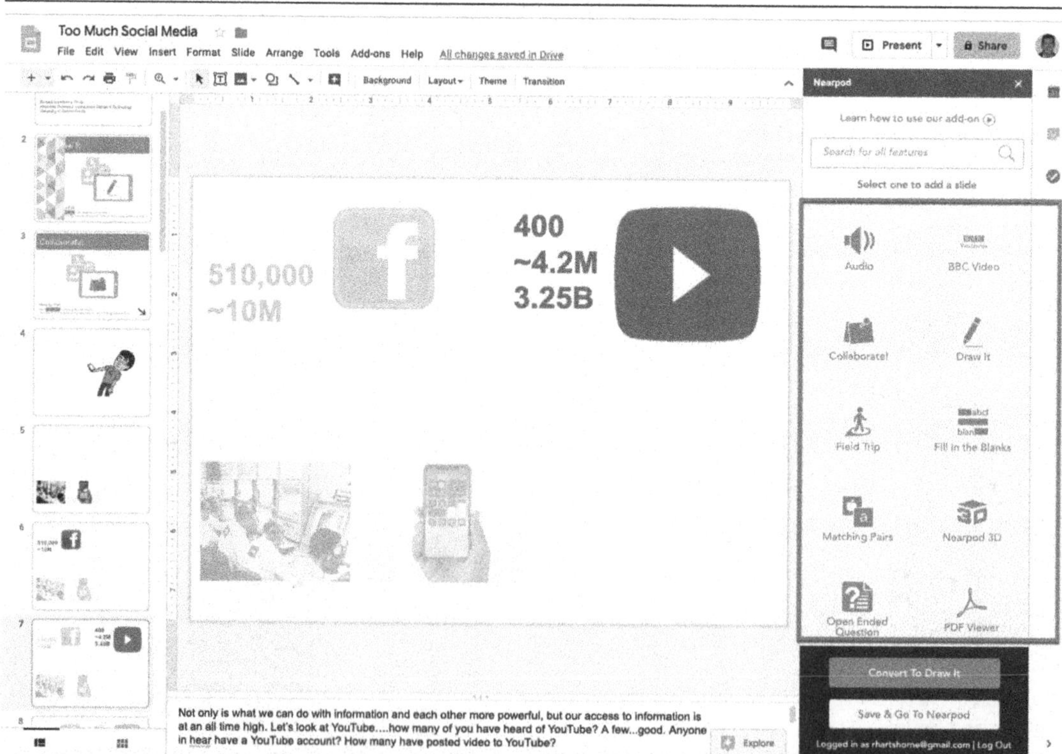

Figure 10.9. Nearpod Social Studies Library

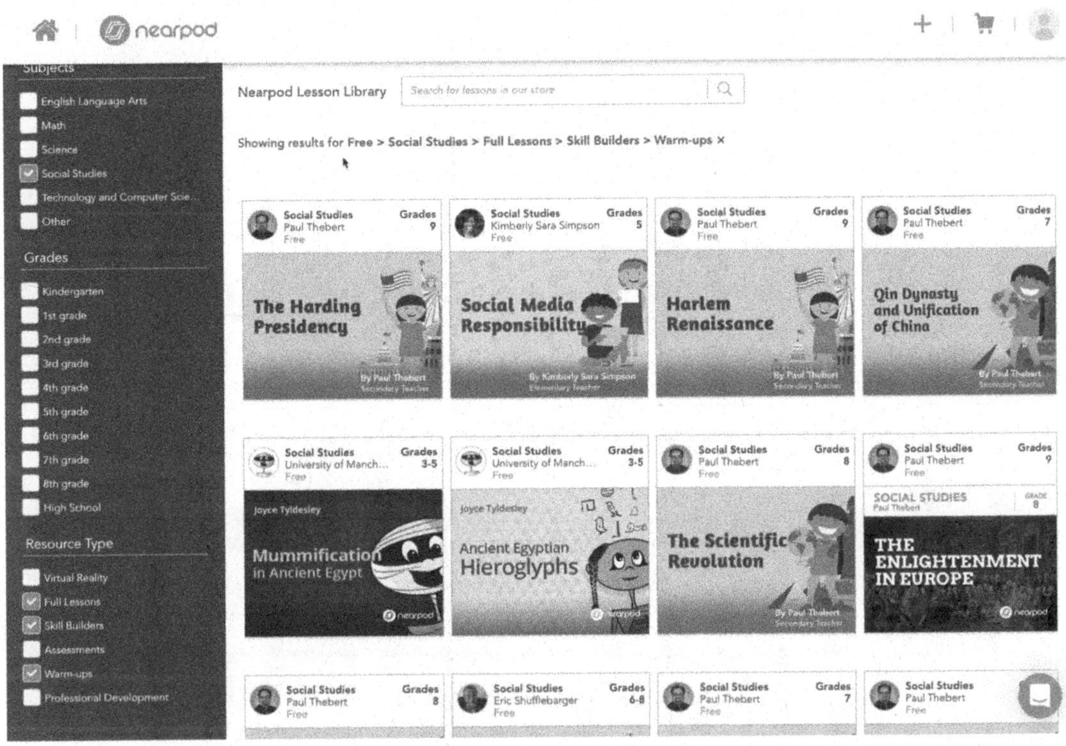

See *Nearpod* in action using the QR code shown in Figure 10.7.

Biteable. A tool for creating brief "explainer" videos, Biteable (app.biteable.com; Figure 10.10) can be used by teachers to provide specific instruction or scaffolding; or it can be an assessment tool, as it allows learners to make videos illustrating their level of understanding of a fundamental question or other prompt. The easy-to-use interface supports creating videos from scratch (Figure 10.11), and permits quick text editing, inclusion of images and other resources, selection of basic scenes from a library of options, selection of audio from a library (or by uploading a file), and compiling all content into an easily shared video.

Biteable has a series of templates (Figure 10.12) related to promoting a course, event, product, sale, service or business; explaining a concept, or instructions on how to do something, presenting at an event, a pitch, or to a team; or sharing an announcement, update, quote, or testimonial. Although some of these are not directly related to instructional goals, many enable significant creativity and flexibility for integration into the historical inquiry process. Biteable provides automated rendering of videos, and resultant products can be shared instantaneously. Further, combining Biteable videos

Figure 10.10. Biteable Starter Interface

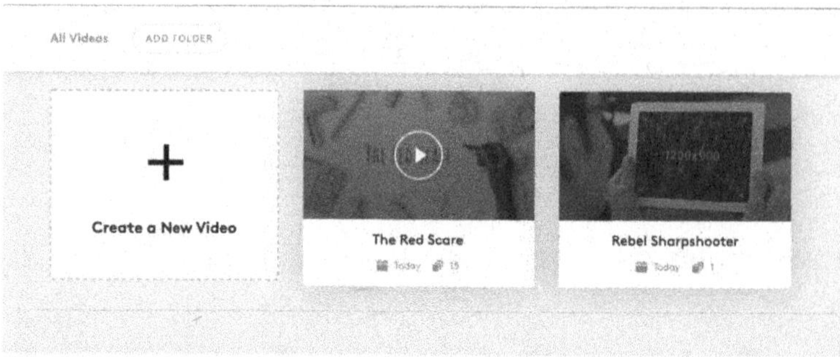

Figure 10.11. Biteable Video from Scratch Interface

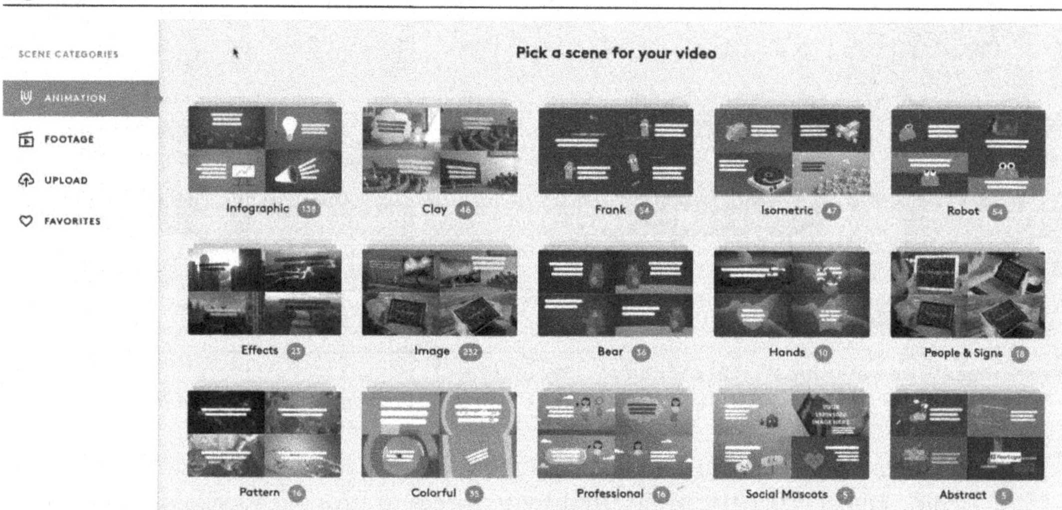

with other Web 2.0 tools can allow for rich and deep teacher-centered or learner-centered educational settings, as the video can seamlessly incorporate instructional support and learner scaffolding, organizing content, examining primary and secondary sources from varied perspectives, or facilitating the development of cases to support a particular viewpoint or understanding related to a concept or event—all critical aspects of the *Reading Between the Lines* and *Corroborating and Refuting* phases of the SOURCES framework.

Collaborative Productivity and Organization Tools

A core goal of *Reading Between the Lines* is a thorough understanding of the time period and the myriad of variables that might influence a specific event. To

Figure 10.12. Biteable Video from Template Interface

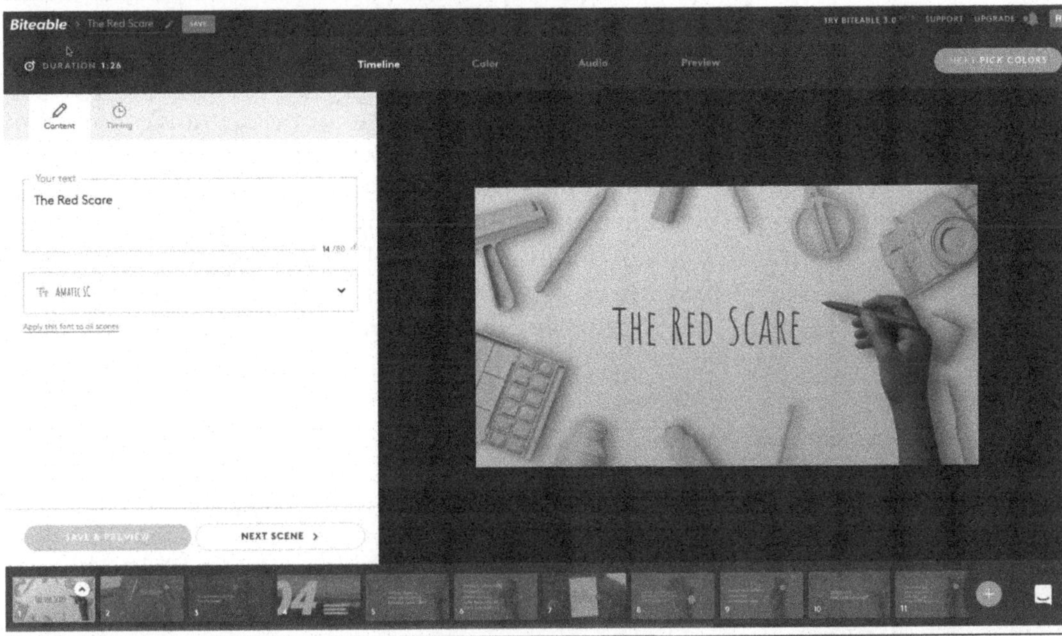

See *Biteable* in action using the QR code shown in Figure 10.10.

achieve this, it is necessary to collect, organize, and examine various sources associated with a particular event, and then make inferences based on an analysis of the relevant documents. Following *Reading Between the Lines*, *Corroborating and Refuting* is the next phase. To do this effectively, students must conduct a deeper examination of the sources and associated events and collect and organize sources and information that corroborate a particular perspective, as well as sources and information that allow them to refute other perspectives, and this must be done in an exhaustive manner. In this section, we will explore tools that support collaborative productivity, discussion, and organization of primary and secondary sources to promote complex and holistic analyses of resources, as well as the development of sound inferences. These tools, including Slack, Dropbox Paper, and Coggle, are useful in facilitating student-centered learning environments, as they provide instructional experiences driven by learner agency, needs, and interactions. While these tools also have a place in more teacher-driven learning scenarios, their focus on providing easy-to-use collaborative environments for seamless communication, sharing of files, tracking of communication and participation, and other organizational functions makes them particularly useful in supporting student-centered pedagogical approaches that align with the *Reading Between the Lines* and *Corroborating and Refuting* phases of the SOURCES framework.

Slack. Slack (slack.com; Figure 10.13) is a real-time, synchronous/asynchronous application that can be used in either a browser-based environment or as a desktop- or mobile-downloadable application. It is a communication hub for various types of collaborations, permitting creation of specific groups and channels of communication with a great deal of collaborative control of the settings. Slack allows for: (a) sharing, archiving, and searching of documents of all types; (b) creating, organizing, and tracking communication and participation in conversations; and (c) supporting either extremely simple or very complex interactions. Working in "channels," which are similar to chat rooms but can be classwide or organized around small groups, users have increased instructor and learner flexibility in the collaborative setting. Slack

Figure 10.13. Slack Interface/Channel

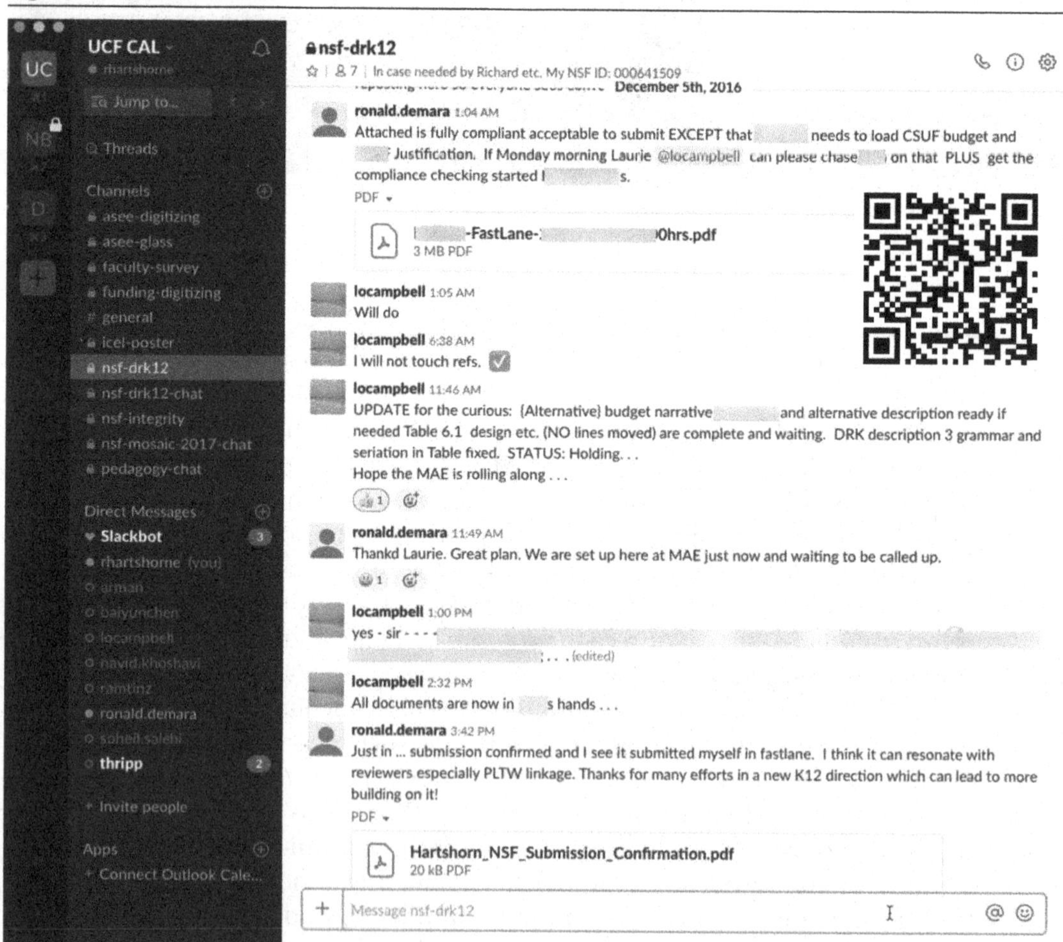

See *Slack* in action using the QR code shown.

offers notification alerts, as well as the creation of polls to collect perspectives on a given topic or event. For the teacher, documents can be shared with carefully selected groups, prompts and tasks can be aligned with the documents provided, and all interactions, participation, and sharing of documents can be archived for teacher review. From a learner perspective, as with other collaborative tools addressed, students can participate in collaborative brainstorming, discussion, and debate sessions, and can accumulate collections of resources to either provide a more comprehensive view of a particular topic or event, or to corroborate or refute a particular perspective. Learners can create content, organize and curate sources, and develop drafts of narratives, which can all be used to support complex discussions associated with *Reading Between the Lines* and *Corroborating and Refuting*.

Dropbox Paper. The collaborative workspace Dropbox Paper (www.dropbox.com/paper; Figure 10.14) is a document-editing tool that supports real-time synchronous or asynchronous collaborative writing and can be used as either a browser-based tool or via a desktop/mobile downloadable application. Although possessing much of the functionality of other collaborative document editors (e.g., Google Docs), Dropbox Paper also permits content sharing, creating tasks and assigning tasks to specific team members through the use of @mentions, support for robust interactive media elements, and

Figure 10.14. Dropbox Paper Interface

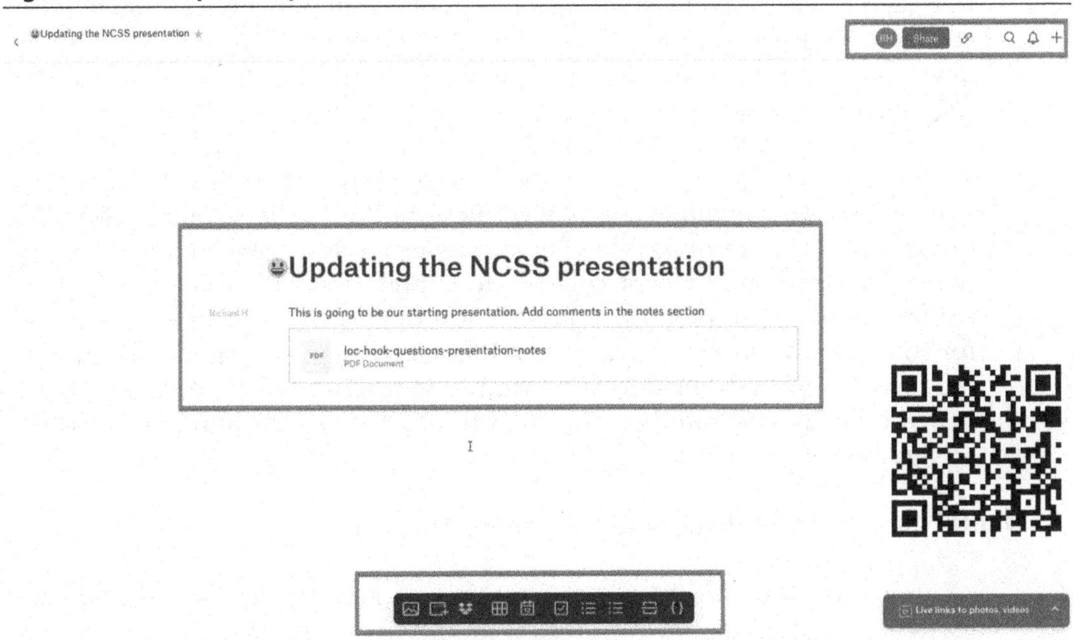

See *Dropbox Paper* in action using the QR code shown.

seamless integration with the Dropbox features and functionality. Dropbox Paper is an excellent workspace for collecting, organizing, sharing, discussing, and analyzing primary and secondary sources, which is critical to supporting instructional approaches and tasks associated with the *Reading Between the Lines* and *Corroborating and Refuting* phases of the SOURCES framework. Yet Dropbox Paper has a relatively simple user interface, with limited formatting functionality, which can be useful in minimizing distractions and in maintaining learner focus on a specific task or goal: users don't have to use all the bells and whistles of a selected tool.

Dropbox Paper does have all the basic functionality of a typical word processing application, as it presents varied levels and controls for sharing, editing, and commenting; and supports participation and attribution tracking and version tracking—that is, viewing or reverting to prior versions of a document. As with Slack, teachers can share documents and tasks with specific groups or even individuals, and can track interactions and participation from group members. Learners can participate in robust collaborative discussions or debates; create, collect, organize, curate, and share primary and secondary sources; and easily manage input from different collaborators. All of this functionality makes Dropbox Paper an excellent tool for supporting instructional approaches for the *Reading Between the Lines* and *Corroborating and Refuting* phases of the SOURCES framework.

Coggle. The collaborative, visual concept mapping application Coggle (coggle.it; Figure 10.15) is an intuitive tool to support either individual or collaborative brainstorming and student organization of thoughts through the development of visual connections and disconnections between content, topics, individuals, and events. Coggle allows for easy content creation beyond text-based concept maps, including drag-and-drop functionality with media from the Web. Concept maps can be shared easily either via a public or private URL or by downloading as PDF files. As with other cloud-based tools, Coggle allows for intuitive viewing and reverting to past versions of concept maps, seamless inclusion of collaborators, and efficient examination of the contributions of various collaborators. Although Coggle is an excellent tool for educators, a number of other cloud-based concept mapping tools that you may wish to explore include MindMup (www.mindmup.com), Bubbl (bubbl.us), iMindQ (www.imindq.com), and MindMeister (www.mindmeister.com), all functionally similar to Coggle.

Digital Curation of Primary and Secondary Sources

As previously mentioned, a core purpose of *Reading Between the Lines* and *Corroborating and Refuting* in historical inquiry is to help students gain a thorough understanding of the time period and the myriad variables that might

Figure10.15. Coggle Interface and Visual Concept Mapping Sample

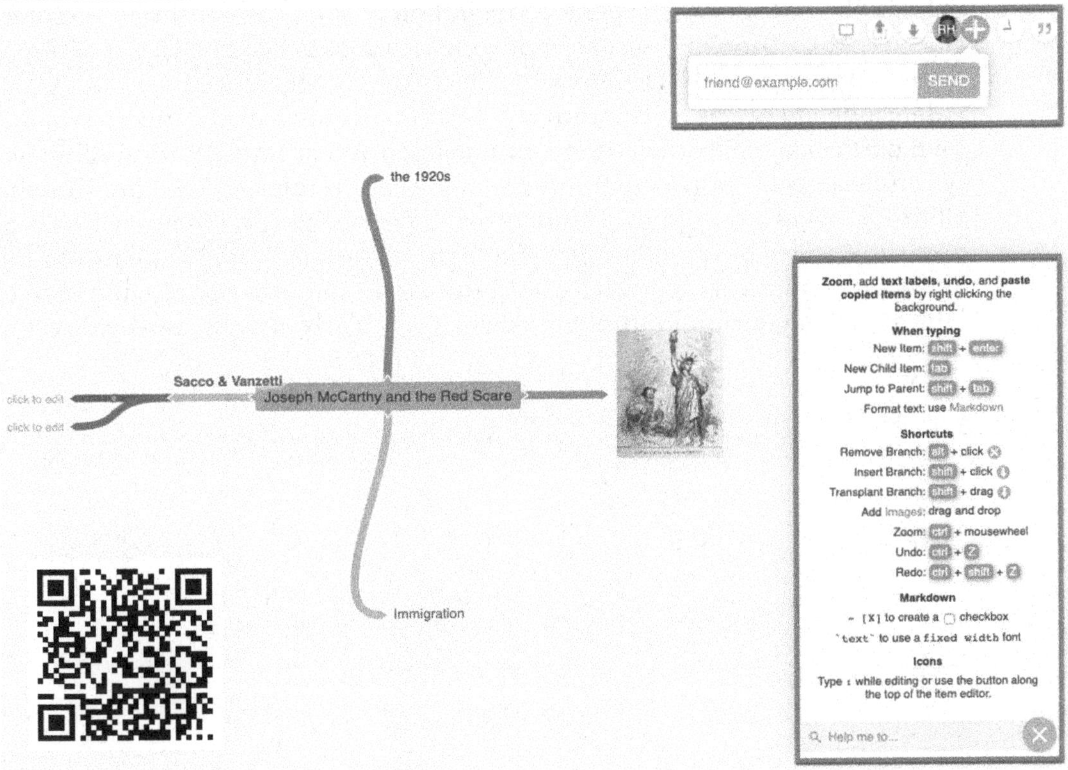

See *Coggle* in action using the QR code shown.

have influenced a specific event. Engaging learners in the digital curation process is an effective pedagogical approach for providing opportunities for deeper examination of primary and secondary sources and associated events, as it involves the conceptualization, appraisal, collection, organization, storage, access, use, and transformation of source materials, all important to *Reading Between the Lines* and *Corroborating and Refuting*. In this section, we will explore a tool that supports digital curation to promote complex analyses of resources as well as facilitating the development of inferences from this deep analysis of sources. This tool, Tes Teach with Blendspace, can be used in both teacher- and student-centered instructional approaches.

Tes Teach with Blendspace (www.tes.com/lessons; Figure 10.16) is a browser-based curation tool for educators analogous to Pinterest. From a teacher-centered perspective, Tes Teach with Blendspace allows for the sharing of collections of sources with learners, the development of innovative and engaging lessons, tracking of learner engagement with a lesson, alignment of standards with a specific lesson, inclusion of prompts or activities for individual or collected sources, and easy integration of Web content from YouTube, Google Drive, Dropbox, or externally created media (Figure 10.17). From a learner perspective, collections of artifacts can be developed and modified, either individually or collaboratively, as inferences are made and viewpoints on a particular topic or event are either supported or refuted, until ultimately a collection of sources that either supports or refutes an idea are present. Utilizing digital curation as a student-centered pedagogical approach to support the *Reading Between the Lines* and *Corroborating and Refuting* phases of the SOURCES framework is engaging to learners and supports the development of critical- and higher-order thinking skills—particularly analysis and evaluation.

Figure 10.16. Tes Teach with Blendspace Interface

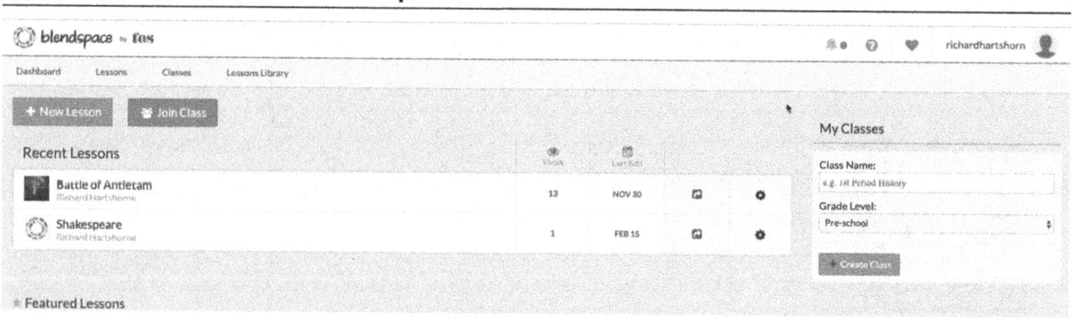

Figure 10.17. Tes Teach with Blendspace Example

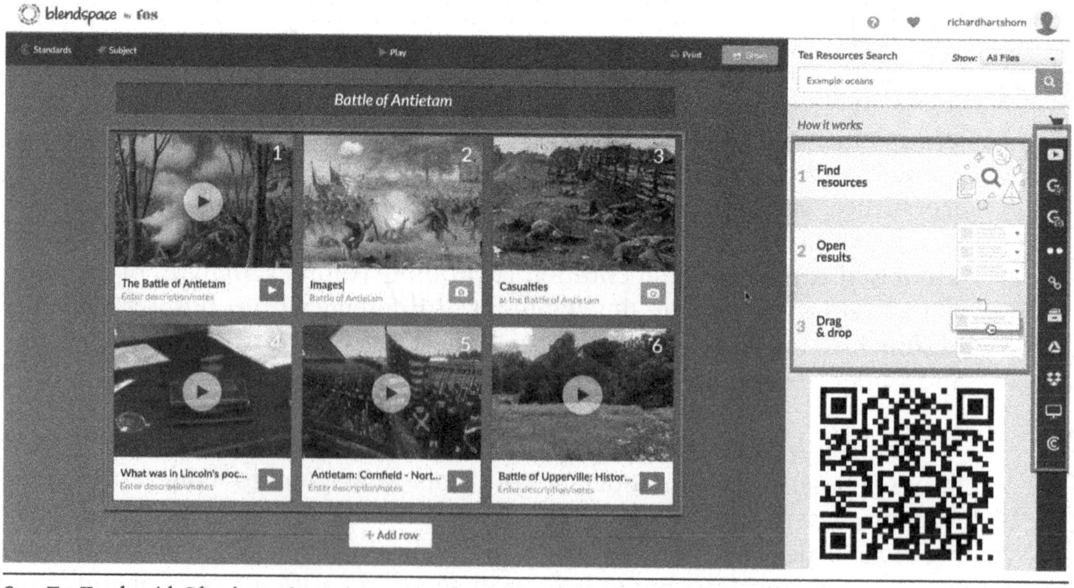

See *Tes Teach with Blendspace* in action using the QR code shown.

CONCLUSION

In this chapter, we highlighted both teacher-centered and student-centered pedagogical strategies that support the fourth and fifth phases of the *SOURCES* framework, *Reading Between the Lines* and *Corroborating and Refuting*. We presented a series of emerging technological applications (teacher-centered scaffolding/prompting tools, collaborative productivity and organizational tools) that frame and extend the instructional approaches that support scaffolding, as well as collecting, categorizing, sharing, discussing, and enhancing individual and collaborative meaning-making. Further, we provided ways in which these tools support transitioning into the final phases of the SOURCES framework, *Establishing a Plausible Narrative* and *Summarizing Final Thoughts*, which will be explored in the next chapters.

Pro Tip 4: Join a Professional Organization/Attend a Conference

So many tools, so little time. How it is possible to keep up? One strategy that we have found useful over the years is to join a professional organization with a focus on the integration of technology into the classroom, such as the International Society for Technology in Education (www.iste.org), or join a special interest group (SIG) or community within a content-area professional organization, such as the Technology Community of the National Council for the Social Studies (www.socialstudies.org) or the National Council of History Education (www.nche.net). Interacting with professional organizations, SIGs, or communities can keep you engaged year-round. We have also found it useful and inspiring to attend a professional conference that has a focus on the integration of technology into the classroom. These might include the conference associated with a professional organization of which we are a member, or one in which we do not have an affiliation, such as the Future of Education Technology Conference (www.fetc.org) or SXSW EDU (www.sxswedu.com). Some of these conferences have virtual presentations and allow for virtual attendance, which may be less costly. Lastly, these organizations provide a plethora of instructional resources and opportunities, such as access to useful reports, teacher lessons and support materials, and professional development experiences.

CHAPTER 11

Developing and Publishing Tools to Facilitate Establishing a Plausible Narrative

In order to assess the depth of student understanding of a series of events, concepts, or timelines during the sixth stage (*Establishing a Plausible Narrative*), students construct a narrative based on the sources with which they have engaged, to argue a position in answer to the fundamental question posed at the beginning of the inquiry process. This narrative could be in the form of a written paper, documentary video, website, diorama, skit or play, or whatever other form deemed most appropriate by the teacher to assess the knowledge gained and the quality of the argument. In this chapter, we outline this stage of the framework and show how emerging technologies can facilitate and support the process of establishing a plausible narrative.

PEDAGOGICAL STRATEGIES FOR FACILITATING ESTABLISHING A PLAUSIBLE NARRATIVE

As students engage with primary and secondary sources and properly analyze them, they should work toward establishing a plausible narrative, utilizing the available evidence that most accurately and effectively supports answering the initial fundamental question or challenges provided. As students work on their narratives, they should seek evidence from a variety of sources that might contradict or corroborate their thesis, and then reconcile those sources. Typically, at the K–12 level, the analysis of sources is not exhaustive. However, learners should be encouraged to explore and provide a sufficient number of sources to confidently present a plausible narrative for a fundamental question or questions. Based on the fundamental question(s), the number and types of sources will vary from one investigation to the next. Consequently, it is critical to provide students with a degree of agency, allowing them to explore and select a variety of ways to establish, design, construct, and present their plausible narrative. They should be given opportunities to design, construct, and present their narratives verbally, symbolically, graphically, or in another visual manner. Students might opt to do a simple written report, or they may choose to develop a website, create a museum-like exhibit, design and perform a dramatic performance, or even produce a multimedia documentary. It is important to note that the format of the established plausible narrative is not critical; the important thing is that the plausible narrative include various sources and perspectives that are not mono-causal, and are not mired in historical presentism. It is also important for students to remember that when creating these narratives, they need a sufficient amount of evidence, and should consider sources that contradict their narrative, as well as sources that corroborate it. Sources must be sought, examined, and considered throughout the process of establishing the narrative. The goal should be to construct the most plausible narrative for the historical topic or question of study, based on the available evidence.

MERGING PEDAGOGICAL STRATEGIES AND EMERGING TECHNOLOGIES FOR ESTABLISHING A PLAUSIBLE NARRATIVE

In this section, we will address tools to support the establishment of a plausible narrative, specifically ones that enable analysis, design, development, and dissemination of text, audio, video, hypermedia, and other multimedia. These tools also help package these digital elements into meaningful products for sharing with varied audiences. Essentially, these tools allow students to tell what they know about a specific topic in a way not possible via a traditional assessment (i.e., paper–pencil test). Although some tools do not directly allow students to illustrate their knowledge or narrative, they help develop a plausible narrative more fully. Included are student publication and authoring tools such as Weebly and Canva; collaborative multimedia productivity suites and tools such as ThingLink, Animoto, and Explain Everything Whiteboard; and online writing tools such as Google Docs, Penzu, and Draft.

Student Publication and Authoring

Weebly. The cloud-based web editing site Weebly (www.weebly.com; Figure 11.1) gives users the power to create websites from a variety of templates. Weebly supports free hosting of Weebly-developed sites and allows exporting for hosting on a personal web server or other external host. The user can create 10 sites for free, and the Weebly platform provides an analytics dashboard for examining the number of unique website visitors, form entry content (if applicable), and notifications of new tips and updates to the platform.

Figure 11.1. Weebly Dashboard Interface

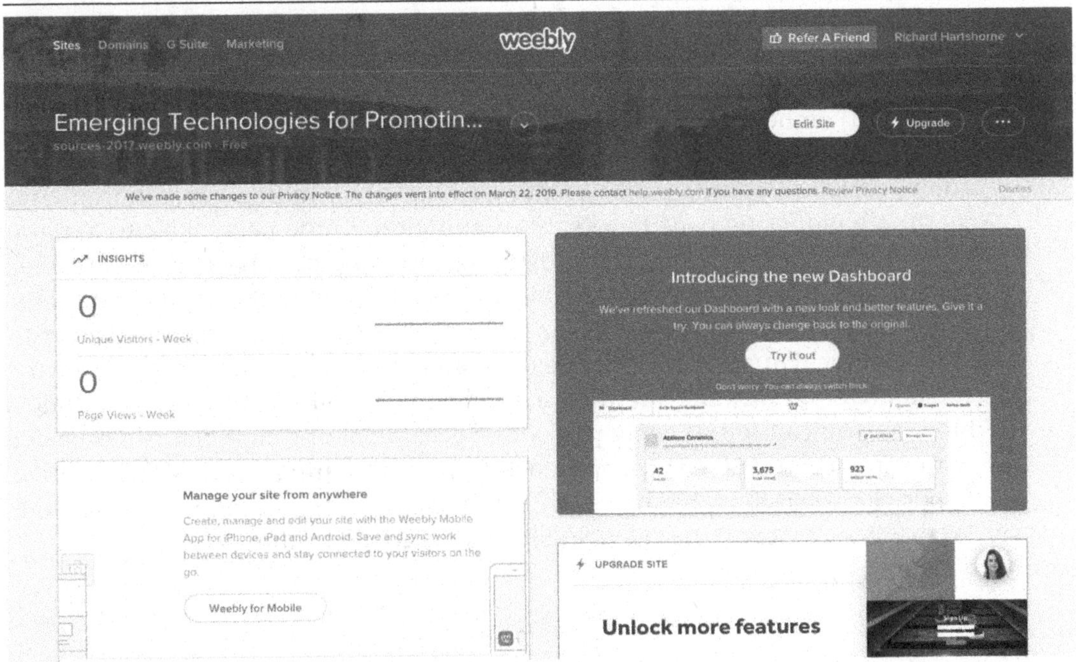

Figure 11.2. Weebly Build Tab

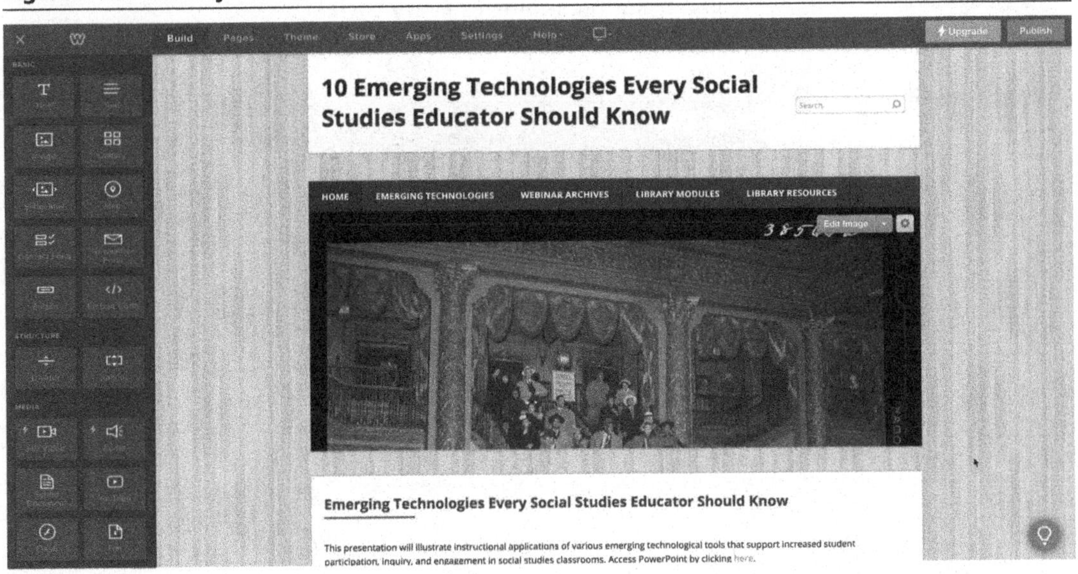

In exploring the *Build* tab of Weebly (Figure 11.2), basic functionality includes: (a) titles and varying levels of text; (b) single images, galleries of images, and slideshows; (c) maps; (d) contact forms, surveys, RSVP forms, and newsletter forms; (e) web buttons, embedded HTML items, dividers, and spacers; (f) embedding of Scribd and YouTube content, Adobe Flash, and files; and (g) block quotes and social icons. The *Pages* tab (Figure 11.3) allows for adding/deleting/editing pages, creating nested or cascading navigation menus by simply indenting page blocks, reassigning the home page of a site, renaming or changing the header style of a page, or copying a page. The *Theme* tab (Figure 11.4) gives the user the ability to easily change the entire site theme or to change specifics such as color schemes, font styles, interactive elements, and captions. Finally, under the *Settings* tab (Figure 11.5), one can change the site address, modify the site title, add or remove collaborators, and include a blog. As you can see, Weebly provides a great deal of functionality associated with supporting pedagogical approaches for establishing a plausible narrative. Other cloud-based web editors with similar but distinct functionality include Wix (www.wix.com) and Google Sites (sites.google.com).

Figure 11.3. Weebly Pages Tab

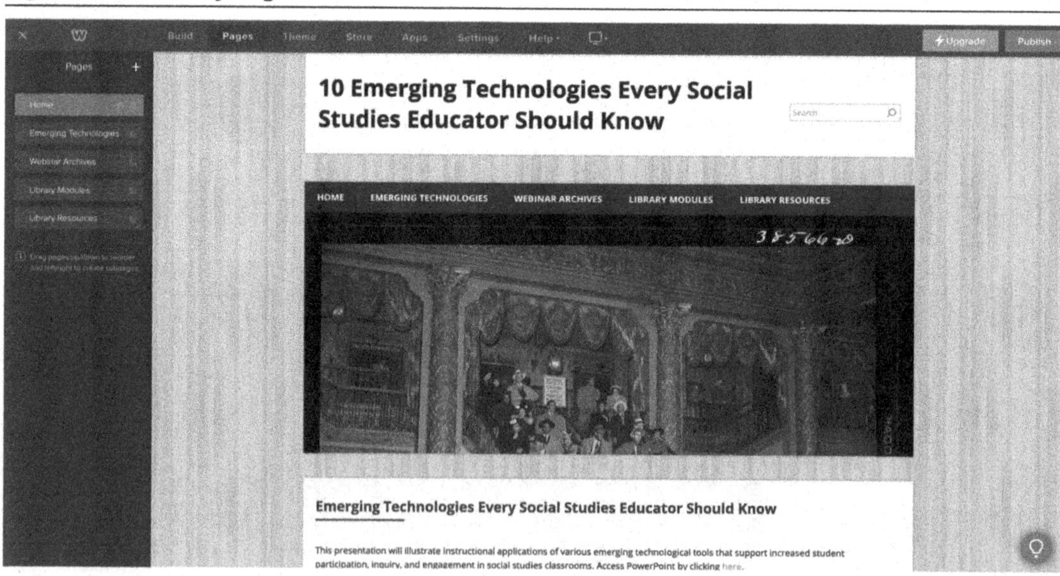

Figure 11.4. Weebly Theme Tab

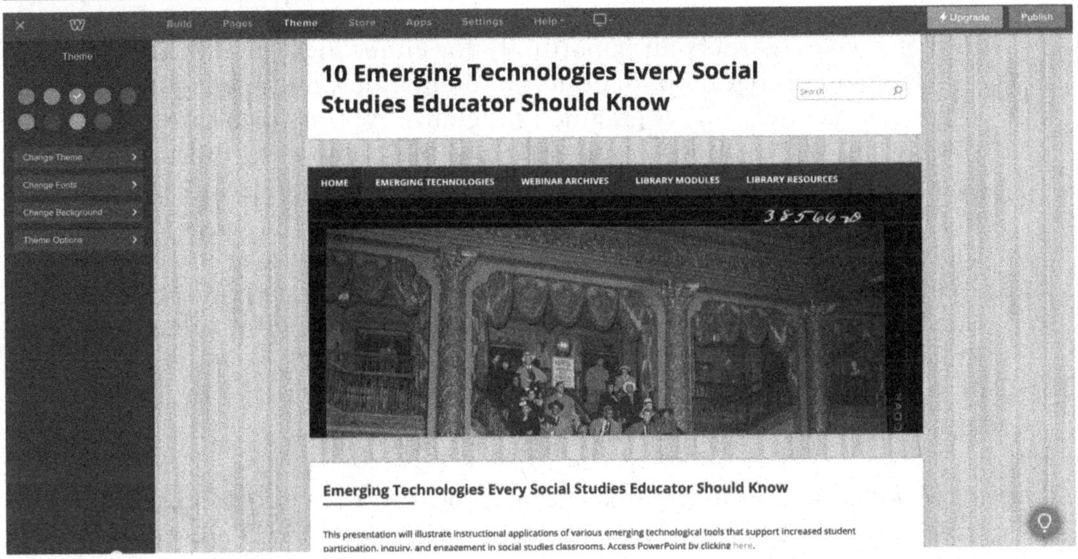

Figure 11.5. Weebly Settings Tab

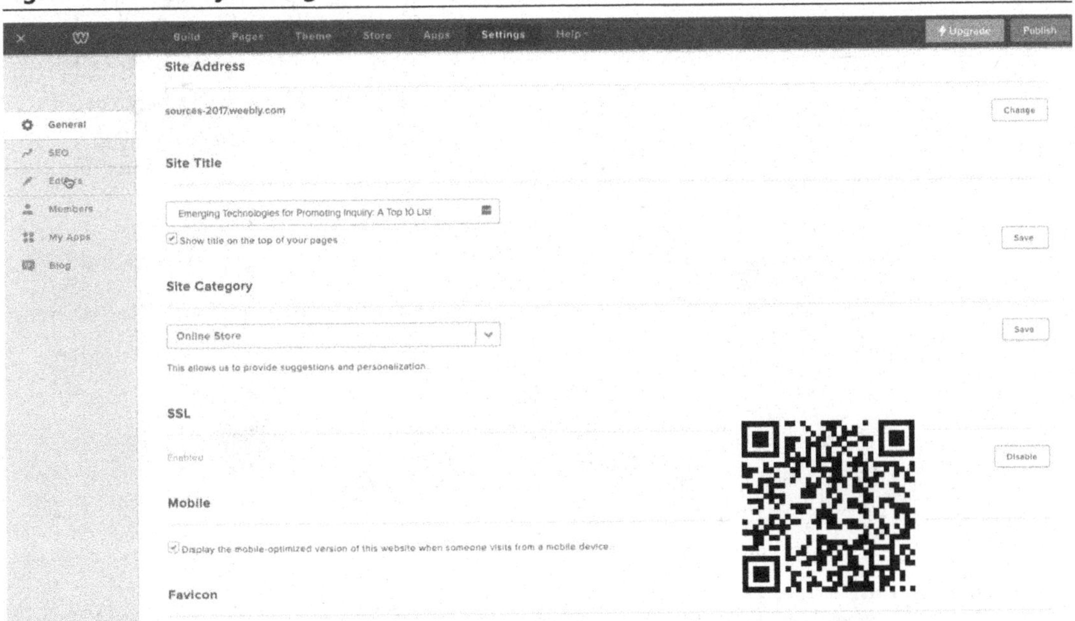

See *Weebly* in action using the QR code shown.

Canva. Canva (canva.com, Figure 11.6) is an excellent tool for supporting the *Establishing a Plausible Narrative* phase of the SOURCES framework in that it gives learners an opportunity for either individual or collaborative development of collections of posters, presentations, flyers, infographics, book covers, newsletters, social graphics, programs, reports, media kits, and more (Figure 11.7). This allows students to develop and present their understanding of the topic. In addition to the creation of digital artifacts, Canva supports the development of print and physical artifacts. As with other collaborative tools, Canva allows for easy inclusion and organization of group members, as well as sharing of final products with individuals or larger populations. Canva handles varied forms of media, helps in organizing content and modifying products, and has robust formatting features (Figure 11.7).

Collaborative Multimedia Productivity

ThingLink. The education technology platform ThingLink (www.thinglink.com; Figure 11.8) is a browser-based or app-based tool that allows both teachers and students to easily insert "hot spots," or visible or invisible buttons that trigger interactive action, into images, converting images into robust teaching and learning tools. ThingLink can be used for sharing courses and folders, which facilitates collaborative design and development. In addition to

Figure 11.6. Canva Dashboard Interface

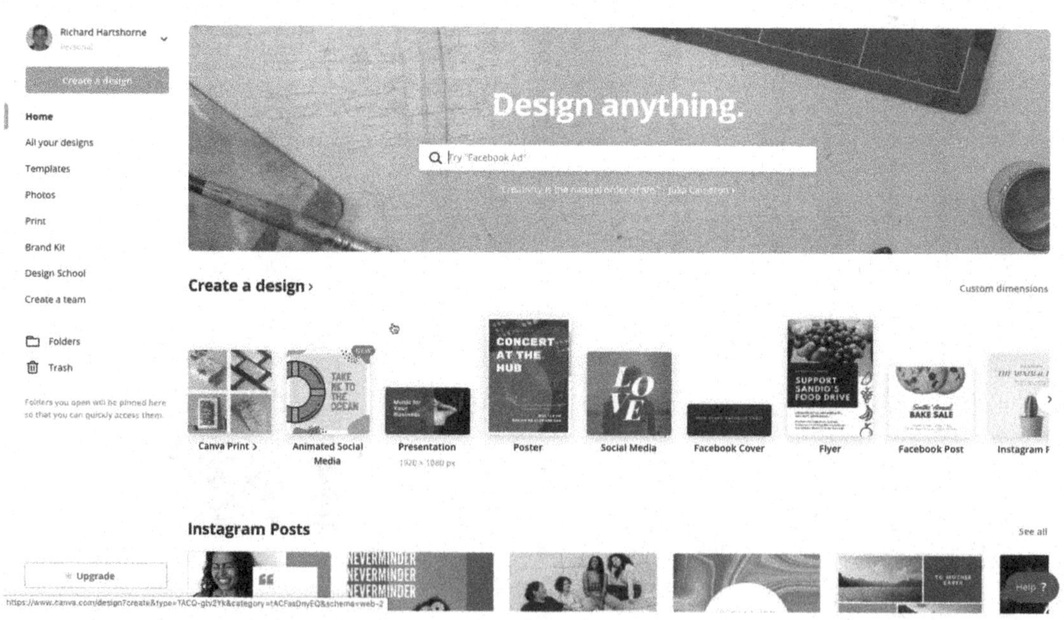

Figure 11.7. Canva Magazine Cover Sample

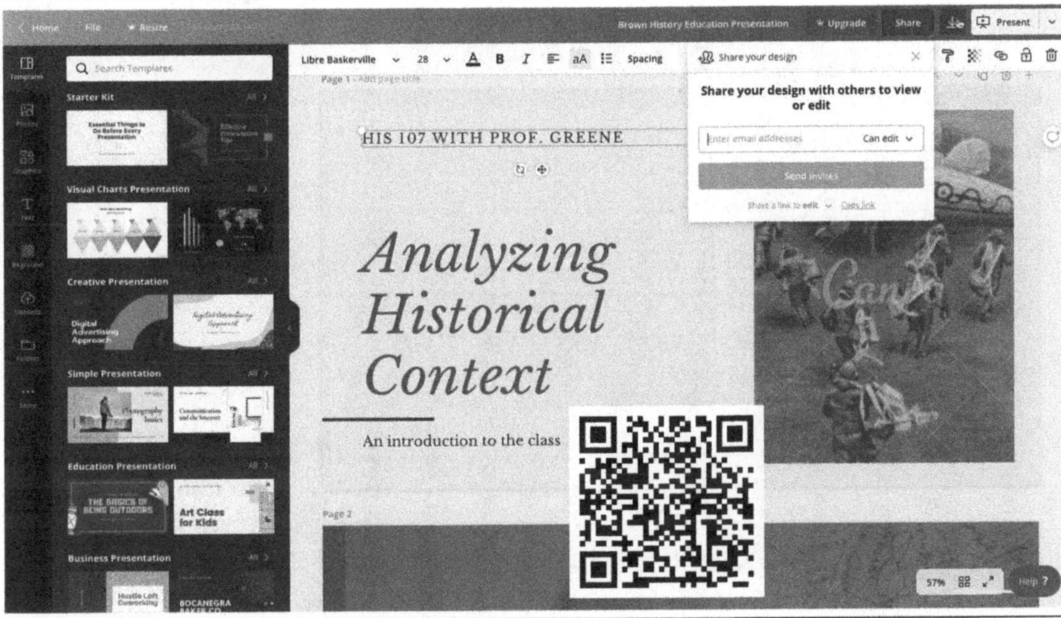

See *Canva* in action using the QR code shown.

Figure 11.8. ThingLink User Dashboard Interface

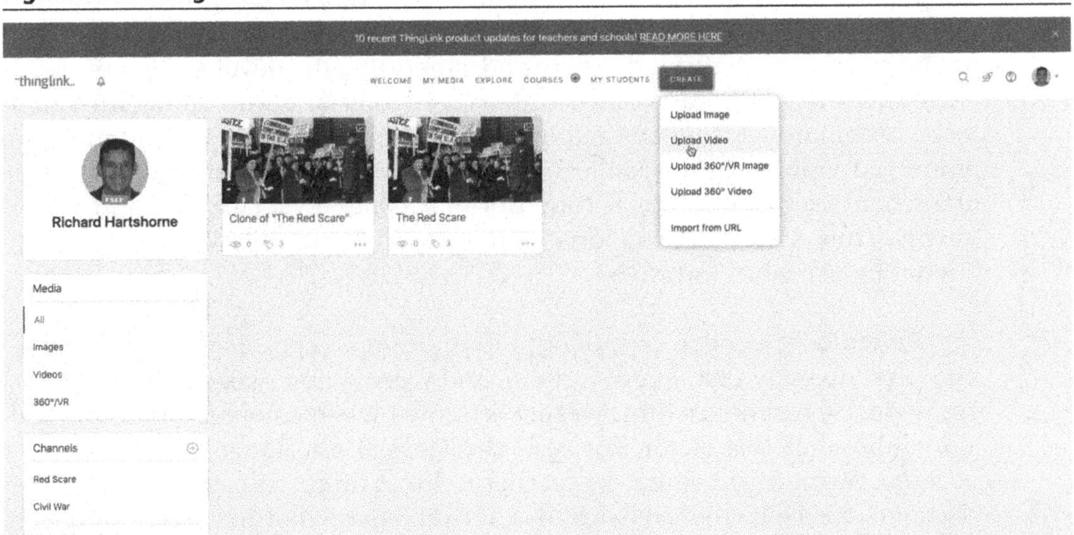

Figure 11.9. ThingLink Sample

See *ThingLink* in action using the QR code shown.

text-based image annotations, learners can integrate audio or video notes and annotations on images, embed content from a website, or create a tour from multiple images and interactions (Figure 11.9). Web content such as YouTube or Flipgrid can be integrated easily with ThingLink, which is useful for facilitating creative and critical thinking and supporting the development of simple or complex narratives associated with a given topic or event. ThingLink can be used for offline viewing and editing, tagging animations and annotations for improved visibility, and seamless integration with Microsoft Teams—helpful if a school uses Office 365, as content can be shared via channels and assignments. Thus, ThingLink supports both individual and collaborative establishment of a plausible narrative.

Animoto. The video creator Animoto (animoto.com; Figure 11.10) helps the user integrate text, images, audio, and video when making short (30-second) videos. Animoto's functionality is limited when compared to robust video editors, but this factor can be a pedagogical advantage in *Establishing a Plausible Narrative*; it allows the learner to focus on the subject at hand rather than on the bells and whistles of a technological tool for a more efficient

Figure 11.10. Animoto Interface and Functionality

See *Animoto* in action using the QR code shown.

development of a plausible narrative. Specifically, Animoto users can insert audio, place media in a particular order, provide supporting text for images and other media, and then assemble the video automatically once all content is laid out, as one would with a storyboard. With Animoto, learners log in, select a video style, and then incorporate media from a variety of web-based resources including Dropbox, Flickr, Facebook, Instagram, and SmugMug, or directly upload an image or media library. Text or captions can be added to images and integrated into the video. Final videos can be shared via a variety of social media outlets (e.g., Facebook, Instagram, YouTube, Twitter), or a direct link or email, or uploaded to and embedded in an existing website. Although not collaborative, Animoto is a powerful tool for providing students with agency in presenting a plausible narrative.

Explain Everything Whiteboard. The online story creator Explain Everything Whiteboard (whiteboard.explaineverything.com; Figure 11.11) allows for the inclusion of audio, video, web resources, and more. Its simple interface has a great deal of functionality. Projects can be started from blank documents or from a series of easily editable templates such as timelines (Figure 11.11, Item 1), Venn diagrams, cause and effect diagrams, storyboards, meetings, and notepads. Explain Everything Whiteboard has a number of drawing tools (Figure 11.11, Item 2), and also can be used for the recording and integration of audio. Users can invite collaborators for draft versions, share drafts and final versions with a targeted audience, or share them with a larger audience via a code or URL (Figure 11.11, Item 3). Multiple resources can be integrated into a single project for more complex and comprehensive narratives.

Figure 11.11. Explain Everything Interface: Timeline Example

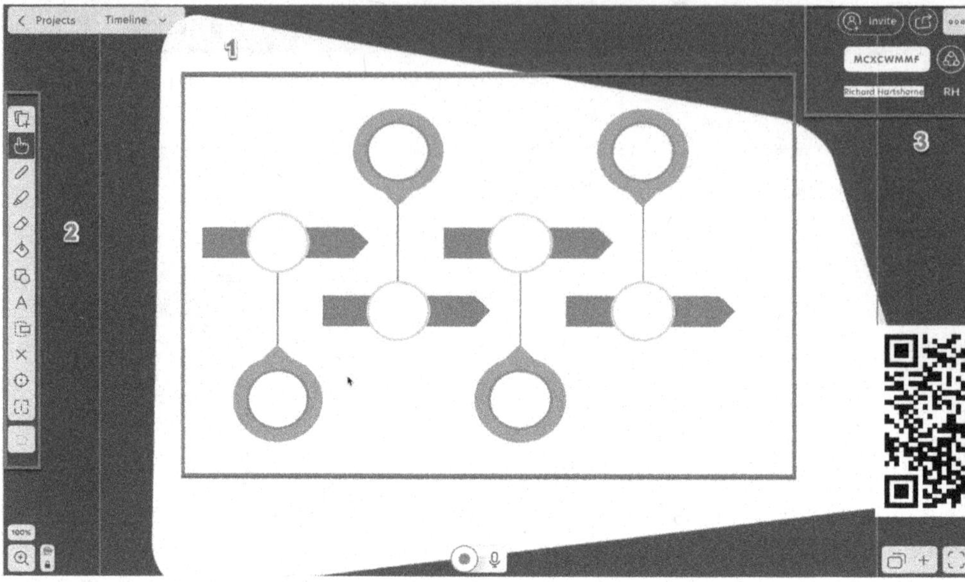

See *Explain Everything Whiteboard* in action using the QR code shown.

Online Collaborative Writing Tools

Google Docs. A component of the G Suite, Google Docs (docs.google.com; Figure 11.12) integrates seamlessly with a number of tools previously mentioned in this book. Google Docs is a robust tool for facilitating the design and development of collaboratively developed narratives. It has wide-ranging functionality and permits students to create media-enhanced text documents together. Google Docs has all of the basic functionality of a typical word processing application such as Microsoft Word (Figure 11.12, Item 1), and it enables varied levels of sharing, editing, and commenting via a simple sharing user functionality (Figure 11.12, Item 2) that includes sharing with specific individuals or groups of individuals via email, as well as making narratives accessible to a public audience.

When shared, interaction with a Google Doc can be constrained by the author. For example, a document might be shared as a view-only document for some collaborators, whereas other collaborators may have access to fully edit the document. Additional features, such as commenting, making suggestions, resolving suggestions, tracking participation, tracking individual edits by different collaborators, and viewing various historical versions of a document, all make Google Docs a powerful tool for *Establishing Plausible Narratives* both individually and collaboratively.

Figure 11.12. Google Docs: Document Interface

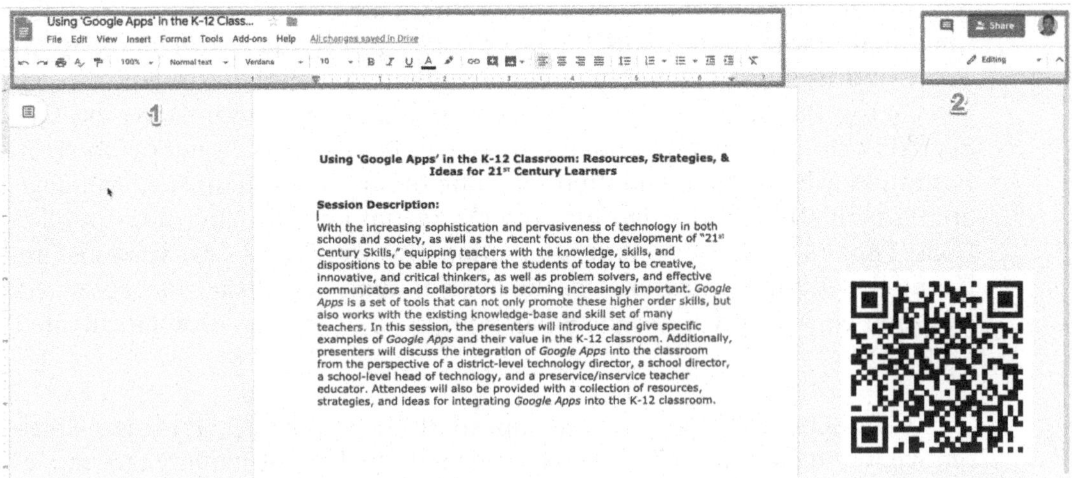

See *Google Docs* in action using the QR code shown.

Penzu. The blogging platform Penzu (penzu.com; Figure 11.13) markets itself as the anti-blog and acts more as an online diary or personal journal than something to be shared with the world. This is helpful in educational settings, as it addresses privacy issues and concerns that might not be addressed with

Figure 11.13. Penzu Interface

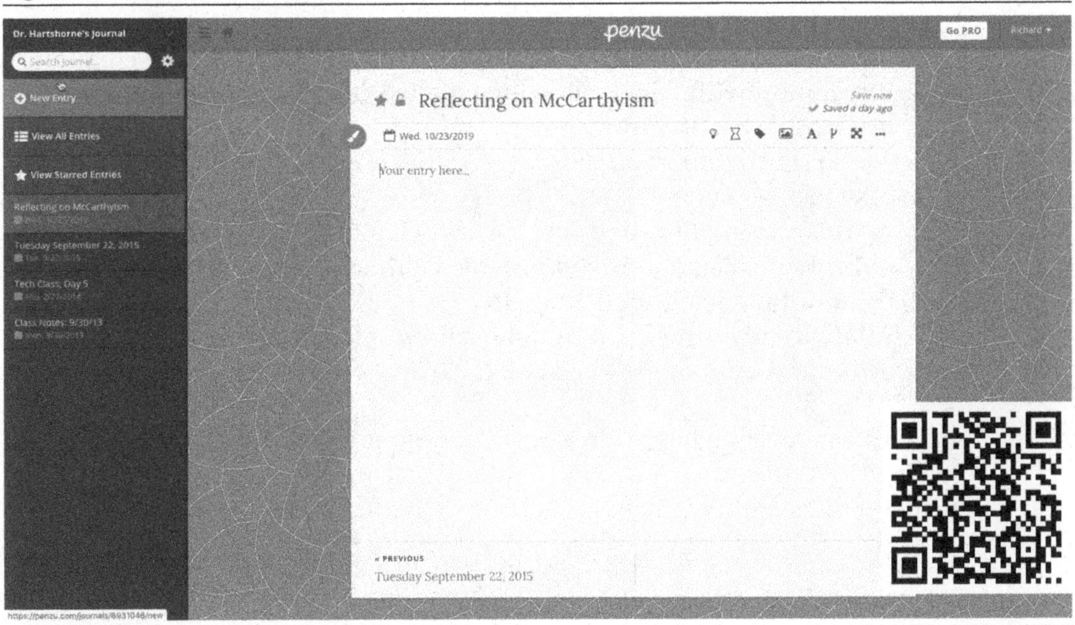

See *Penzu* in action using the QR code shown.

other blogging sites: For example, some blogging sites limit the audiences with which a blog may be shared, but may contain advertisements for other blogs that might not be appropriate for K–12 students. Penzu is particularly appropriate and useful for elementary-aged students, as it teaches them, through piecing together a plausible narrative, netiquette and other information literacy skills. From an instructional perspective, Penzu allows students to create narratives from scratch, and then integrate other web content such as images and limited audio and video into their personal journals and other publications. Penzu facilitates content integration and viewing of past versions, and has other multimedia features for the development of plausible narratives that can then be shared via specific email addresses, or via an automatically generated URL.

Draft. Similar to Google Docs, Draft (draftin.com; Figure 11.14) is a collaborative writing tool useful for developing individual or collaborative narratives. In addition to many of the features of Google Docs and other collaborative writing tools, Draft has unique features, including:

1. Streamlined document version control, providing a master copy as well as individual collaborator copies. This allows for the document owner to ignore or accept individual comments, and also for individual collaborators to have their own versions based on comments and suggestions they have made to the master document.
2. "Ask a professional" copyediting, in which suggested edits can be made by a professional reviewer.
3. Simplified presentation functionality, focusing on easy slide creation.
4. Integration with email, allowing emailed content to be automatically inserted into a draft document.
5. Audio transcription, making converting audio to a draft document an easy process.
6. A "robotic simplification tool," in which a draft robot will become a document collaborator and provide comments in an effort to simplify the wording of a draft document.
7. Analytics reporting of draft publications, blogging/publication of draft documents, and more (Figure 11.15).

Draft's streamlined user interface is excellent for keeping learners focused on *Establishing Plausible Narratives,* rather than on formatting and other less impactful tasks, either collaboratively or individually.

Figure 11.14. Draft Dashboard Interface

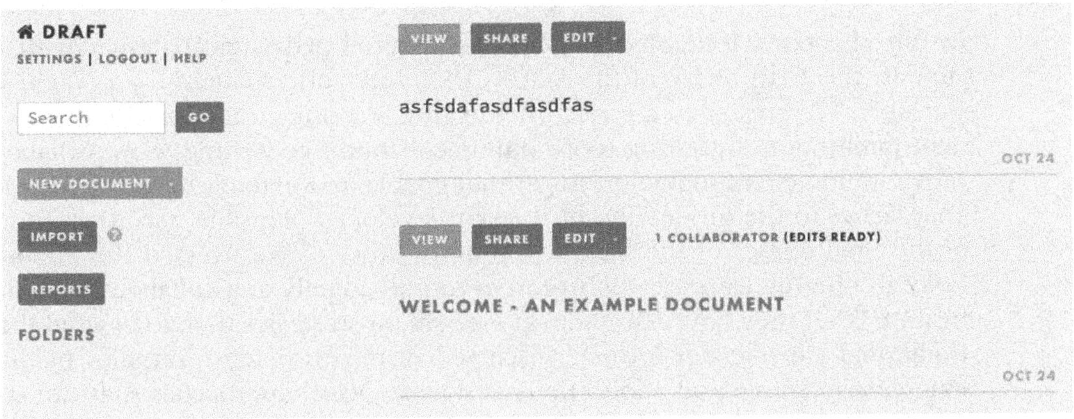

Figure 11.15. Draft Editing Interface

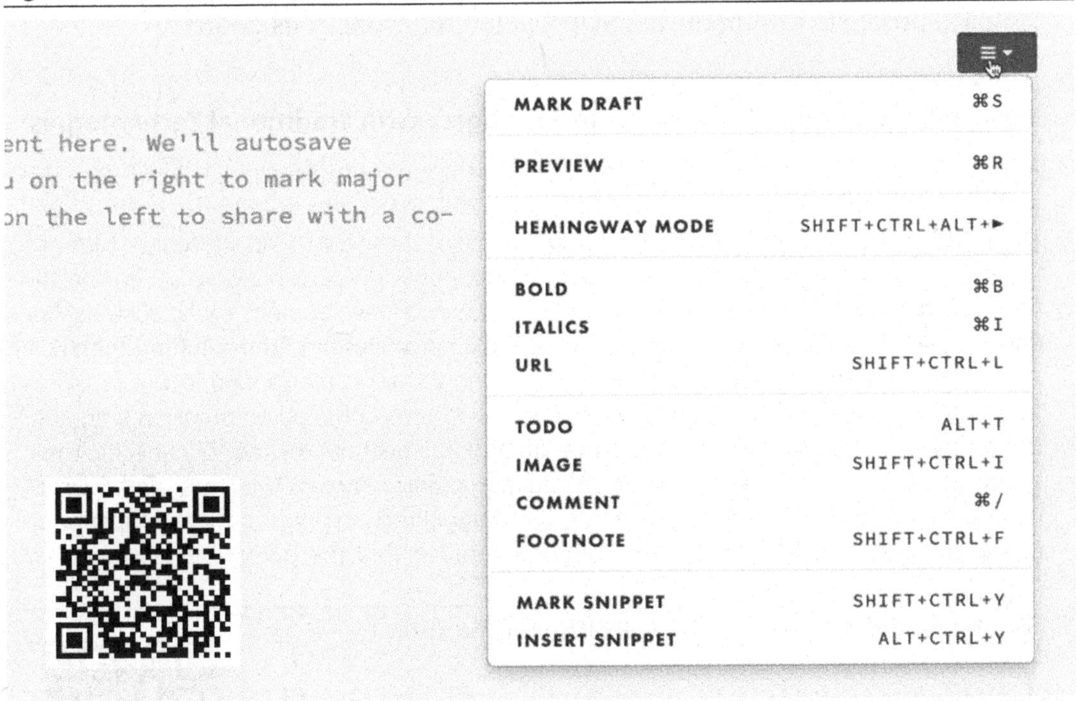

See *Draft* in action using the QR code shown.

CONCLUSION

In this chapter, we highlighted student-centered pedagogical strategies that support the sixth phase of the SOURCES framework, *Establishing a Plausible Narrative*. We presented a series of emerging technological applications (student publication/authoring tools, online collaborative writing tools, collaborative multimedia production tools) that enable and extend the instructional approaches to the production of student-developed plausible narratives, one of the final phases of the historical inquiry process. We stressed the importance of offering learners opportunities to individually and collaboratively illustrate what they have learned, via assessment strategies that go beyond the traditional paper/exam format. Discussed were just a few examples of the emerging technological applications and pedagogical approaches that can simultaneously scaffold such learning. In the next chapter, we will explore the final phase of the SOURCES framework, *Summarizing Final Thoughts*, looking at instructional strategies that facilitate this phase, and at emerging technological applications that can work in conjunction with other tools and pedagogical processes to support the SOURCES framework in its entirety.

Pro Tip 5: Supplement Emerging Technologies with Traditional Technologies

Although the pedagogical approaches presented throughout this text align well with the participatory and interoperative environment of Web 2.0, many traditional technologies are useful in supplementing and supporting the use of these tools and strategies. Many of these tools would be useful if, for example, school networks prohibited access to specific Web 2.0 sites or applications. Open-source multimedia development tools, such as Audacity or GIMP, can be used in producing plausible narratives, and the resulting materials can be easily integrated into a number of the Web 2.0 tools mentioned in this book, as they are simply external media files. A tool like Wolfram Alpha, a computational engine, can be used to provide additional information and perspectives related to a specific topic or event, to inform *Understanding the Context*, *Reading Between the Lines*, and *Corroborating and Refuting*. Below, we have listed traditional technologies that have functionalities useful in supplementing the tools discussed throughout this book.

Wolfram Alpha **wolframalpha.com**

Extensive computational engine that stores and retrieves expertise and knowledge via answers, analyses, and reports. Also provides an extensive collection of resources with applications in the social studies classroom and beyond.

GIMP **gimp.org**

A free, easy-to-use, open-source image editor usable across multiple operating systems (e.g., Windows, macOS, Linux).

Audacity **audacityteam.org**

A free, easy-to-use, open-source audio editor usable across multiple operating systems (e.g., Windows, macOS, Linux).

Shotcut **shotcut.org**

A free, easy-to-use, open-source video editor usable across multiple operating systems (e.g., Windows, macOS, Linux).

Blue Griffon **bluegriffon.org**

A free, easy-to-use, open-source Web editor usable across multiple operating systems (e.g., Windows, macOS, Linux).

Jing **techsmith.com/jing-tool.html**

A free, easy-to-use screen-casting program that allows for capture, storage (using screencast.com), and sharing of still images or video of a user's computer screen.

Apache OpenOffice **openoffice.org**

An easy-to-use open-source office productivity suite, including a word processing tool, presentation tool, spreadsheet tool, and more.

CHAPTER 12

Creating a Digital Portfolio to Facilitate Summarizing Final Thoughts

In this final phase of the SOURCES framework *(Summarizing Final Thoughts)*, students are asked to revisit and reflect upon the entire inquiry process and the fundamental questions that were posed at the beginning of the investigation, and determine if the process worked well for them. In doing so, learners consider what elements they would modify, reflect on the content acquired, and identify questions that are left lingering. As previously outlined, some questions that learners should consider might include, "How do I know what I know?," "What questions still exist?," and "How might I answer questions that still exist?" In this chapter, we will outline this final stage of the framework and how emerging technologies can facilitate and support the numerous processes associated with summarizing final thoughts.

PEDAGOGICAL STRATEGIES FOR FACILITATING SUMMARIZING FINAL THOUGHTS

The last thing that the student should do in the inquiry process and via the SOURCES framework is reflect on his or her experience. Learners should ask themselves, "What actions and decisions were particularly useful for deriving my plausible narrative?," "What actions and decisions were less useful?," and "What would I do differently the next time I perform a historical investigation?" Possibly the most important questions a student should answer at the end of their inquiry are, "What did I learn from the experience?" and "What else do I want to know?," as no good historical investigation is ever truly finished, and new questions worthy of inquiry often arise from an investigation. The beauty of approaching the teaching of history in this manner is that the interest in and retention of historical content is increased. Authentic historical inquiry, as conducted via the SOURCES framework, also facilitates the development of necessary daily life skills, including critical thinking, analyzing various types of corroborating and contradictory sources, constructing narratives, and seeking multiple perspectives. To extend the benefits of this approach, it is critical to provide learners with instructional activities that support reflection, including journals, audio notes, summaries, self-quizzes, presentations, and others.

MERGING PEDAGOGICAL STRATEGIES AND EMERGING TECHNOLOGIES FOR SUMMARIZING FINAL THOUGHTS

As with other emerging technological applications addressed throughout the book, the tools used to support learner reflection are dependent upon the pedagogical strategy implemented. For example, if the instructor wants to have a large-group discussion, some of the tools previously mentioned that support this strategy can be implemented. For example, YoTeach! or Backchannel Chat can encourage those who might not normally participate in the reflective discussion to get involved. Also, polling and surveying tools such as Poll Everywhere, QuestionAir, or Crowdsignal can be used to address any questions that remain or to help students arrive at consensus. Additionally, any of the individual or collaborative writing tools, such as Google Docs, Dropbox Paper, Penzu, or Draft, can facilitate self-reflection via document entries, which can be utilized throughout the SOURCES framework. This is important, as it allows the learners to reflect upon their individual experiences. Audio recording tools are also helpful in facilitating reflection, as audio reflections tend to be richer and more extensive in content than written reflections. In this phase of the SOURCES framework, the instructor may provide a prompt related to a primary source or historical event, reflective questions to consider, or other parameters that guide the overall reflective process and can be responded to via a text or audio reflection. This reflection may be kept private, or it can be shared with others for discussion purposes. Teachers may also prompt students to reflect on various interactions they had with primary and secondary sources, as well as with other learners, and how these might have impacted their final narratives.

Many of the tools we have discussed can be used to facilitate reflection, but in this chapter we are going to provide a couple of final tools with extensive functionality and potential uses in all phases of the SOURCES framework. We will highlight applications that support reflection, but also the diverse functionality of tools to support varied pedagogical approaches. In examining pedagogical strategies for this final stage, we will explore how we can combine a variety of tools addressed throughout the SOURCES framework to facilitate summarizing final thoughts. Specifically, we will explore media development tools, such as H5P web authoring tools, to support collecting and housing reflections via electronic portfolios or other structures, and conclude this chapter with a discussion of Bulb, a digital portfolio application that supports learners in showcasing their work. We will also examine how the reflection process can be used to illustrate growth in student knowledge and understanding in the historical inquiry process.

H5P. The open-source framework H5P (h5p.org; Figures 12.1–12.2) allows for the development, publication, and sharing of diverse HTML5-based interactive content for inclusion in a number of web-based platforms including learning management systems such as Moodle, Canvas, and Blackboard, and content management systems such as WordPress and Drupal. Users can create multimedia-based elements, including interactive videos, presentations, audio recordings, interactive sequences of images, collages, hot-spot–infused images, timelines, virtual tours, and more. Users can generate question-based content including forms, drag-and-drop tasks/images, image pairs, questionnaires, image questions and answers, and more. Although many of these tools support other parts of the SOURCES framework as well, they can be used either alone or in conjunction with other tools to facilitate rich learner reflection.

Figure 12.1. H5P Tool Collection, Part 1

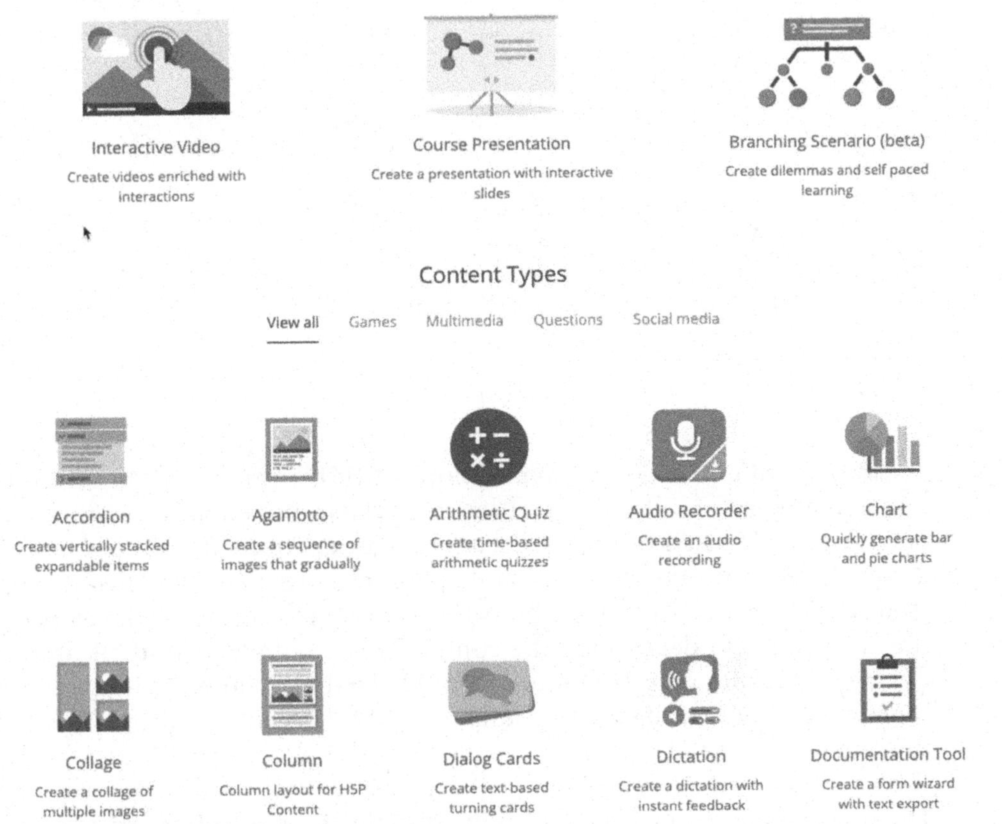

Figure 12.2. H5P Tool Collection, Part 2

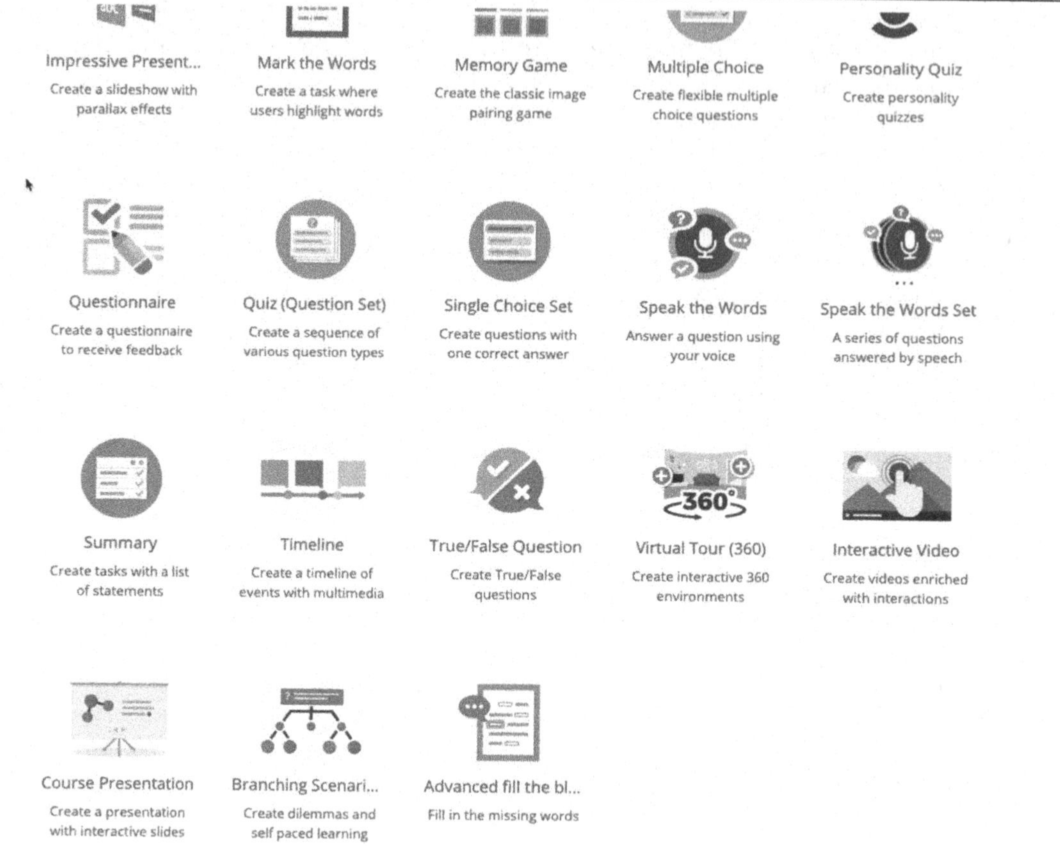

In exploring pedagogical applications of H5P, instructors can create content and integrate it into their web-enabled classroom environments or develop reflection-focused prompts that allow learners to make content and then embed it into a number of web-based platforms. Two key benefits of H5P include the extensive variety in the types of content that can be developed and the ease of use in developing the content. For example, a student prompted to create an audio reflection journal could use the audio recorder tool in H5P (Figure 12.3), which includes a simple "Audio Recorder" button. Then, after the audio is recorded, it can be downloaded and integrated with a web editor such as Weebly, a cloud storage site such as Dropbox, or another application. Thus, over time, extensive collections of reflections or other artifacts can be created, collected, and organized in a manner that supports deep reflection on a lengthy and comprehensive learning plan, allowing students to visualize growth over a period of time.

Figure 12.3. H5P Audio Recorder Interface

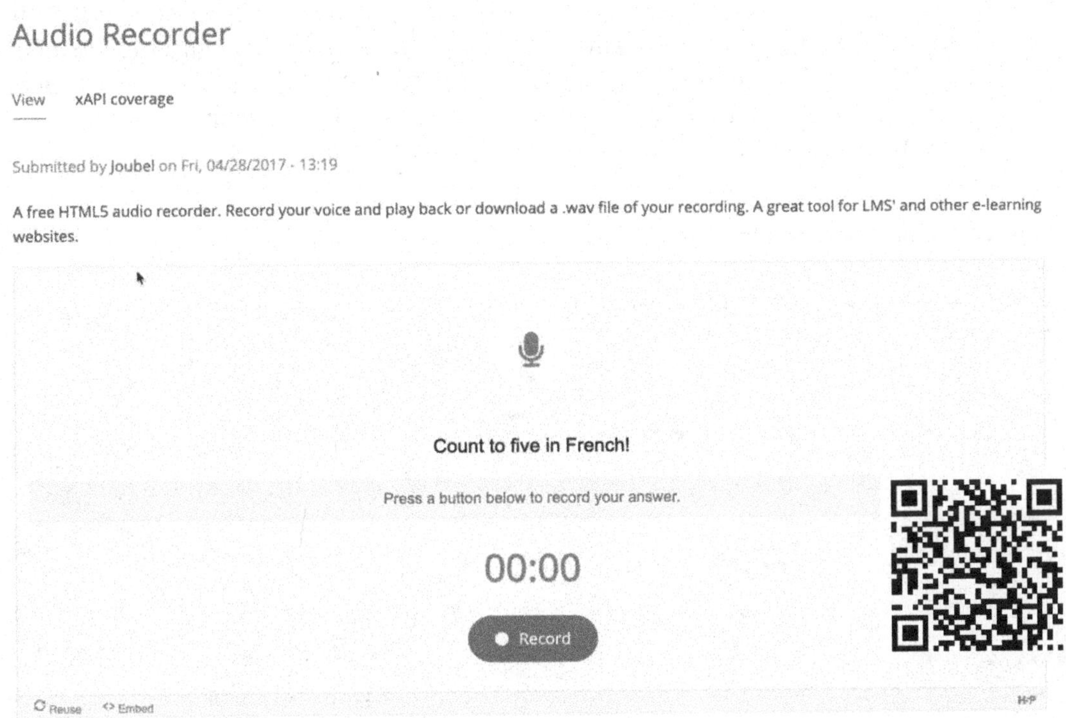

See *H5P* in action using the QR code shown.

Bulb. A browser- and mobile application-based tool, Bulb (www.bulbapp.com; Figures 12.4–12.5) supports the development and sharing of student digital portfolios. Digital portfolios are excellent instructional tools, as they allow learners to explore processes, see growth, and publish their work. Bulb is easy to use and has a minimally distracting environment. It gives teachers a platform for organizing and sharing lessons, exemplars, and other resources, while providing a venue for learners to design, develop, and reflect on a given topic or event. Additional functionality includes (a) the ability to create collaborative groups; (b) an easy-to-use library of personal content; (c) integration with Google Drive and most school-based file formats; and (d) mobile application editing.

As Bulb serves as a digital repository and portfolio, maintaining collections of a variety of sources, the development of artifact-driven pedagogical approaches that support reflection is enabled. For example, learners can be prompted to rank artifacts by order of importance to a particular stance, to highlight work that illustrates greatest "aha" moments in a particular unit or term, or simply to reflect on the selection process of particular resources in corroborating or refuting a particular perspective and how that informed the resulting narrative. Simple text-based reflections on the learning process, points of pride, process struggles, and more are also easily supported. Bulb allows for blogging or journaling, two very powerful pedagogical approaches that can facilitate learner reflection. Lastly, Bulb can be used for peer-to-peer interactions, so peer feedback can be utilized to facilitate deep and rich reflections to support the final phase of the SOURCES framework.

Figure 12.4. Bulb Collection Interface

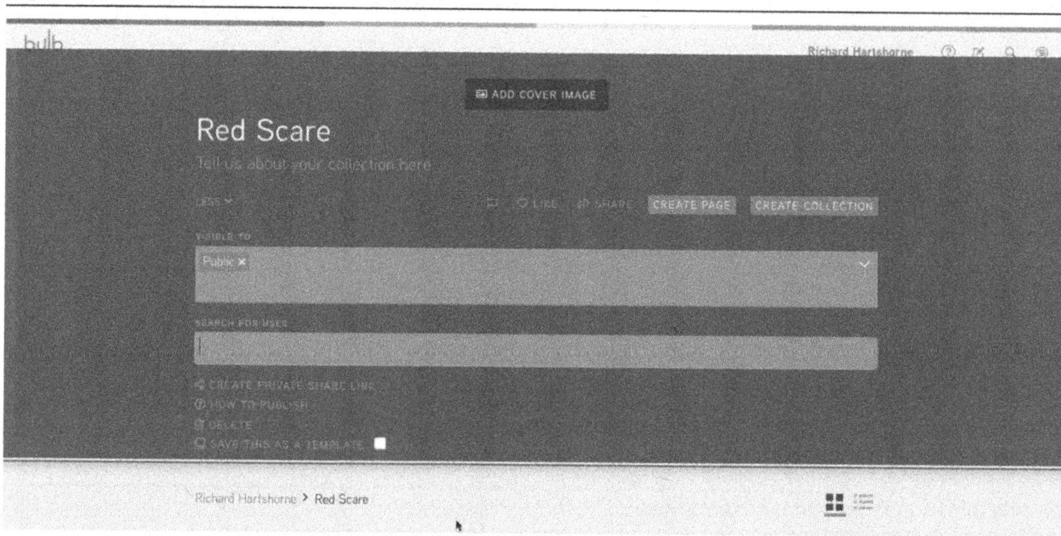

Figure 12.5. Bulb Page Interface

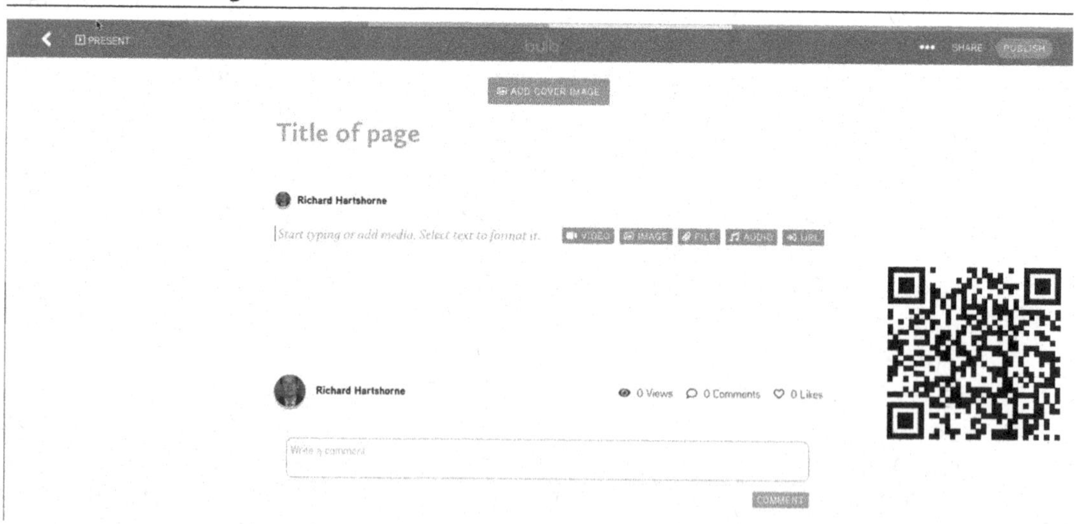

See *Bulb* in action using the QR code shown.

CONCLUSION

In this chapter, we presented student-centered pedagogical strategies and emerging technologies that support the seventh, and final, phase of the SOURCES framework, *Summarizing Final Thoughts*. We provided a series of emerging technological applications (multimedia development, student publication, interactive multimedia production tools) that enable and extend the instructional approaches that facilitate the production of both simple text-based products as well as media-rich products that allow students to provide comprehensive summaries of their understanding of concepts, events, and other content. We introduced the importance of giving learners opportunities to both individually and collaboratively summarize their views and supplement what they know and what they have learned throughout the historical inquiry process. The tools described offer comprehensive features and functionality, and support both simple and interactive media, allowing for a wide array of venues for summarizing final thoughts, as well as pedagogical strategies that can take advantage of such a broad swath of reflective illustrations. In the next chapter, we will provide an Appendix, highlighting additional resources and issues to consider (e.g., analysis sheets, copyright) and primary source repositories and resources (e.g., Library of Congress, university repositories), and we will situate these resources, issues, and repositories within the SOURCES Framework for Teaching with Primary and Secondary Sources.

Pro Tip 6: Bookmark These Websites

Now that you have almost finished this book, let us keep the momentum going. Technological tools, and even pedagogical strategies, are constantly evolving. Although we previously mentioned joining a professional organization, attending a conference, or joining a SIG or other community as a tool to keep up with the constant technological and pedagogical evolution, there are other ways to do this from the comfort of your computer. There are a variety of experts and organizations that host blogs, podcasts, and other resource sites targeted at improving the integration of technology into the educational landscape. Five of our favorites are listed below, but you may want to do some exploration on your own and develop your list of favorites, perhaps using the list below as a starting point. As you begin to curate your collection of resources, we would suggest creating a bookmarked folder, perhaps using one of the tools mentioned in this book (e.g., Tizmos, Zotero, Diigo). It might also be useful to join groups aligned with specific tools that you might opt to use, such as Google for Education (edu.google.com), as these settings are useful for finding training and support resources, specific instructional resources, product information, and news and notes about upcoming changes or resources on the platform.

Cool Cat Teacher (by Vicki Davis) — **coolcatteacher.com**

Provides a collection of tools, newsletters, podcasts, and other continually updated resources for integrating technology into the classroom.

The Ed Tech Round Up — **edtechroundup.org**

Blog format that provides a collection of lesson plans and other resources for integrating technology into the classroom, as well as a regularly updated platform addressing educational technology tools and news.

Free Technology for Teachers (by Richard Byrne) — **freetech4teachers.com**

Started by a former high school social studies teacher, this site provides free technological tools and support resources for teachers, aimed at helping them effectively integrate technology into their classroom.

Shake Up Learning Blog and Podcast (by Kasey Bell) — **shakeuplearning.com/blog**

shakeuplearning.com/shake-up-learning-show-podcast-with-kasey-bell/

Provides a collection and discussion of technology issues, tutorials, resources, and tips for using different types of educational technology in K–12 settings.

TeacherCast (by Jeff Bradbury) — **teachercast.net**

Offers a collection of blog posts and podcasts related to improving the integration of technology into the classroom, for all levels of experience.

APPENDIX

Additional Resources and Considerations

In this final chapter, we offer additional resources such as analysis sheets and online primary source repositories, consider important factors like image quality and copyright issues, and review the SOURCES Framework for Teaching with Primary and Secondary Sources. The framework, the sources, and the resources provided throughout this book allow educators to consider the potential and possibilities of teaching with primary and secondary sources and emerging technologies, and to more energetically and optimistically approach this teaching. Our hope is that all who read this book can make the most of the inquiry process with their own students.

IMPLEMENTING THE SOURCES FRAMEWORK: ADDITIONAL RESOURCES

Analysis Sheets

As students begin an investigation using the SOURCES framework or analyzing primary and secondary sources in isolation, they have several resources on the Internet that will assist them. Primary-source analysis sheets are vital to the process, especially for novice-level thinkers, and there are online PDF versions available for download:

- www.archives.gov/education/lessons/worksheets
- www.loc.gov/teachers/usingprimarysources/guides.html
- www.mdhs.org/education/teachers/primary-source-worksheets
- www.calisphere.universityofcalifornia.edu/themed_collections/pdf/6cs_primary_source.pdf

There are also web-based forms on which students can enter their observations, thoughts, and questions and download and save their responses as a PDF, print out their work, and/or send it as an email. One such site is the one provided by the Library of Congress for the Observe, Reflect, and Question Primary Source Analysis Tool (www.loc.gov/teachers/primary-source-analysis-tool).

Image Quality and Digital Benefits

To assist students in the process of scrutinizing a primary source in detail, it is vital to provide them with the highest-quality images and media possible, and luckily many of the primary-source repositories are providing high-quality files on their websites. For example, if you were teaching students about late-19th-century America, or how Washington, DC, has evolved through time, or looking at different ways to map or depict geographic locations, you might use the image entitled View of Washington City (Figure A.1), found on the Library of Congress website. Analyzing the view can be done with a print version of this image; however, when viewing the image directly on the website (www.loc.gov/resource/g3851a.pm001066), students can zoom in and analyze it in great detail (Figure A.2). Many of the minute details are missed when analyzing the print version.

Figure A.1. View of Washington City

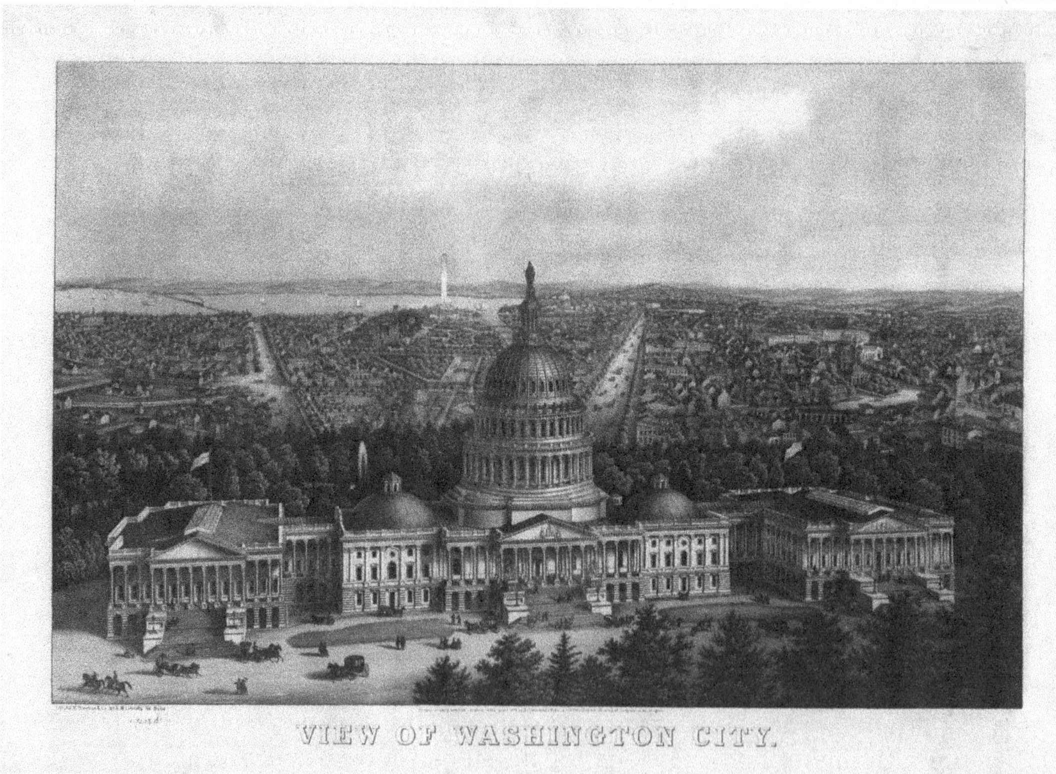

Figure A.2. Zoomed Section of View of Washington City

PRIMARY SOURCES AND COPYRIGHT

Although it typically is not of the utmost concern, it is important to remember that when students are using primary sources in the construction of assessments and projects they should be mindful not to break copyright law. To better inform students about copyright, one can begin by viewing a short video (Teacher Resource: Copyright Quick Check) found on the Library of Congress's website (www.loc.gov/item/webcast-6804). Other resources are the Cornell Law School website (www.law.cornell.edu/uscode/text/17/110) and the U.S. Copyright Office website (www.copyright.gov/help/faq/faq-fairuse.html); these help educators and students better understand Section 110 of the copyright statute, which addresses copyright exemptions and rights that apply to display of materials in nonprofit and educational settings, both physical and digital. Further, as stated by the experts at the Library of Congress, the user should consider three questions prior to the distribution or use of a source, as a single "yes" to any of these questions means that you probably will not need to conduct a fair-use evaluation:

1. Will I just link to this primary source, instead of reproducing it?
2. Was this primary source published before 1924?
3. Was this primary source created by U.S. federal employees as part of their job?

Although you may determine that the answer to a question is yes, you should still always check the rights and reproduction statements associated with any sources that are to be reproduced or disseminated, as one may learn that there are restrictions on use of the item that are not immediately clear.

If the answer is no, then the individual wishing to use the source must conduct her own assessment of its "fair use." Although the language defining fair use may not be clear to everyone, the determining factors are listed in Section 107 of the statute, here italicized and followed by further information from the U.S. Copyright Office:

- *Purpose and character of the use, including whether the use is of a commercial nature or is for nonprofit educational purposes*: Courts look at how the party claiming fair use is using the copyrighted work, and are more likely to find that nonprofit educational and noncommercial uses are fair. This does not mean, however, that all nonprofit education and noncommercial uses are fair and all commercial uses are not fair; instead, courts will balance the purpose and character of the use against the other factors below. Additionally, "transformative" uses are more likely to be considered fair. Transformative uses are those that add something new, with a further purpose or different character, and do not substitute for the original use of the work.
- *Nature of the copyrighted work*: This factor analyzes the degree to which the work that was used relates to copyright's purpose of encouraging creative expression. Thus, using a more creative or imaginative work (such as a novel, movie, or song) is less likely to support a claim of a fair use than using a factual work (such as a technical article or news item). In addition, use of an unpublished work is less likely to be considered fair.
- *Amount and substantiality of the portion used in relation to the copyrighted work as a whole*: Under this factor, courts look at both the quantity and quality of the copyrighted material that was used. If the use includes a large portion of the copyrighted work, fair use is less likely to be found; if the use employs only a small amount of copyrighted material, fair use is more likely. That said, some courts have found use of an entire work to be fair under certain circumstances. And in other contexts, using even a small amount of a copyrighted work was determined not to be fair because the selection was an important part—or the "heart"—of the work.
- *Effect of the use upon the potential market for or value of the copyrighted work*: Here, courts review whether, and to what extent, the unlicensed use harms the existing or future market for the copyright owner's original work. In assessing this factor, courts consider whether the use is hurting the current market for the original work (for example, by

Primary Sources and Copyright Resources

Teacher Resource: Copyright Quick Check	www.loc.gov/item/webcast-6804/
Cornell Law School website	www.law.cornell.edu/uscode/text/17/110
U.S. Copyright Office: FAQ	www.copyright.gov/help/faq/
University of Minnesota's site for "Thinking Through Fair Use"	www.lib.umn.edu/copyright/fairthoughts
U.S. Copyright Office: Fair Use Index	www.copyright.gov/fair-use/
U.S. Copyright Office: What Does Copyright Protect?	www.copyright.gov/help/faq/faq-general.html#protect

> displacing sales of the original) and/or whether the use could cause substantial harm if it were to become widespread. (United States Copyright Office, 2019, para. 2)

You can learn more about copyright basics from the U.S. Copyright Office or through their site outlining "What does copyright protect?" (United States Copyright Office, n.d.). The University of Minnesota's site for "Thinking Through Fair Use" (www.lib.umn.edu/copyright/fairthoughts) can be quite helpful for educators determining fair use in their classroom.

PRIMARY SOURCE REPOSITORIES AND RESOURCES

There are numerous locations for finding primary and secondary sources for use in the classroom, as well as sites that provide resources for teachers and students. Here are a few we have found particularly useful.

Library of Congress

The Library of Congress (www.loc.gov) is the largest library in the world. Luckily, efforts have been made to digitize many sources found in its collections, so one can find millions of books, recordings, photographs, newspapers, maps, manuscripts, and other sources on the library's website. The Library of Congress is the main research arm of the U.S. Congress and the home of the U.S. Copyright Office. Although there are many sections of the website that would be of interest to many educators, one of the most valuable is the one dedicated to education. In the Teachers section of the website, the user can find information on classroom materials, professional development, using primary sources, and other topics. We would suggest taking a look at the Classroom Materials section, as there are premade primary sources sets, lesson plans, presentations, and classroom-based activities provided there. The primary sources sets can easily be modified for use with the SOURCES Framework for Teaching with Primary and Secondary Sources. Although these resources are extremely helpful, keep in mind that there are millions of other sources available through general searches or browsing the collections.

Educational Projects Supported by the Library of Congress

The following are projects that have been funded through the Library of Congress's initiative Teaching with Primary Sources. They are terrific resources for extending the learning and inquiry process and for finding additional primary sources.

DBQuest (www.icivics.org/products/dbquest) is a site that introduces students to major questions in civics and history through the use of primary sources and necessitates the use of evidence in the process of answering "Big Questions." A Big Question acts as a guiding light for deep examination of three selected primary resources. Each document challenges students to dig into the text itself and find the relevant information through document-based supporting questions and helps to get students writing strong arguments based on evidence.

Case Maker (mycasemaker.org) is a customizable system for inquiry-based learning for Grade 6–8 students using primary sources from the Library of Congress. Modeled after the "observe, reflect, question" framework developed under the Teaching with Primary Sources program, Case Maker guides students to review a challenge question, collect evidence, and make a case.

Eagle Eye Citizen (www.eagleeyecitizen.org) engages middle and high school students in solving and creating interactive challenges on American history, civics, and government with Library of Congress primary sources in order to develop students' civic understanding and critical-thinking skills.

Engaging Congress (engagingcongress.org) is a series of game-based learning activities that explores the basic tenets of representative government and the challenges that it faces in contemporary society. Primary-source documents are used to examine the history and evolution of issues that confront Congress today.

KidCitizen (www.kidcitizen.net) introduces a new way for young students (K–5) to engage with history through primary sources. In KidCitizen's nine interactive episodes, children explore civics and government concepts by investigating primary-source photographs from the Library of Congress. They also connect what they find with their daily lives. KidCitizen includes cloud software tools that let educators create their own episodes and share them with students.

National Archives and Records Administration

The National Archives and Records Administration (NARA; www.archives.gov) was established in 1934 by President Franklin Roosevelt and is considered the record-keeper of the United States. Its major holdings date from 1775 and include a

> sweep of the past: slave ship manifests and the Emancipation Proclamation; captured German records and the Japanese surrender documents from World War II; journals of polar expeditions and photographs of Dust Bowl farmers; Indian treaties making transitory promises; and a richly bound document bearing the bold signature "Bonaparte"—the Louisiana Purchase Treaty that doubled the territory of the young republic. (National Archives and Records Administration, n.d., para. 5)

Library of Congress–Funded Primary Sources Repositories and Resources	
Library of Congress: American Memory	memory.loc.gov/ammem/index.html
iCivics DB Quest	www.icivics.org/products/dbquest
Case Maker	mycasemaker.org
Eagle Eye Citizen	www.eagleeyecitizen.org
Engaging Congress	engagingcongress.org
KidCitizen	www.kidcitizen.net

The sources that NARA keeps are those considered to have "continuing value." These sources number around 10 billion pages of text, 12 million maps, charts, and drawings, 25 million photographs and graphics, 24 million aerial photographs, 300,000 reels of motion picture film, 400,000 video and sound recordings, and 133 terabytes of electronic data. A wide variety of items can be found on the website (www.archives.gov), so the user should take time to search and browse this amazing resource. However, for teachers, one of the most valuable areas of the NARA website is the Educator Resources section, which includes DocsTeach (www.docsteach.org). DocsTeach was made for classroom use, and has excellent ready-to-use activities, digital versions of important sources, and tools that can assist students in analyzing sources and thinking historically. One of the most valuable educational projects of NARA is the Our Documents initiative (www.ourdocuments.gov). This site examines the top 100 milestone documents of the United States, so teachers can access digital versions of the Lee Resolution (1776) to the Voting Rights Act (1965) when teaching the history of our nation.

Smithsonian Institution

The Smithsonian Institution, founded in 1846 with funds donated by James Smithson (1765–1829), is the world's largest museum, education, and research complex. Its goal is to shape "the future by preserving our heritage, discovering new knowledge, and sharing our resources with the world" (Smithsonian Institution, n.d., para. 1). The Explore & Learn section of the website (www.si.edu) provides a variety of sources, resources, activities, and research tools for teachers and students. In the Smithsonian Learning Lab (learninglab.si.edu), students can find more than one million resources, create personal collections and educational experiences, and share their creations and work.

University Repositories and Projects

Various universities throughout the United States have online repositories of primary and secondary sources, as well as educational and research-based resources for visitors to their sites. We suggest that you search the many university-based repositories and projects focused on teaching and learning with primary sources. For an example of a university repository, the University of North Carolina's Documenting the American South (DocSouth) is a digital publishing initiative (docsouth.unc.edu) that provides access to texts, images, and audio files related to Southern history, literature, and culture. Among the many collections, the First-Person Narratives of the American South (docsouth.unc.edu/fpn) offers many Southerners' perspectives on their lives by presenting letters, memoirs, autobiographies, and other writings by slaves, laborers, women, aristocrats, soldiers, and officers. One university-based site that includes sources as well as instructional approaches and resources is the Stanford History Education Group's (SHEG) website (sheg.stanford.edu). SHEG seeks to improve education by conducting research, working with school districts, and reaching directly into classrooms with free materials for teachers and students. The Reading Like a Historian curriculum (sheg.stanford .edu/history-lessons) has been created to authentically engage students in historical inquiry. Each lesson revolves around a central historical question and features a set of primary documents designed for groups of students with a range of reading skills.

eBay and Other Online Auctions

One type of resource that may not immediately come to mind in a search for unique primary sources is the online auction site, for example, eBay (www.ebay .com). For those not familiar with online auctions, they are somewhat similar to face-to-face auctions for selling items ranging from antiques to sports collectibles to electronics to cars and homes. Educators might not think of online auctions as resources, but many offerings there pertain to the content covered in K–12 classrooms. The items available for sale open opportunities for utilizing primary sources and exposing students to multiple perspectives, as well as allowing them to see cultural artifacts from all over the world that they otherwise might never have the opportunity to see.

Similar to the marketing of a home, sellers create an advertisement of the item for sale, which includes a title, description, picture of the item, location of the seller, starting price, and shipping and handling charges. As with items being auctioned in a traditional format, a beginning bid price is set, as well as a timetable for the duration of the auction. Users are able to submit a single bid, a maximum bid, or may have an opportunity to buy the item at a desired price preset by the seller.

One important thing that users should be aware of prior to purchasing anything through an online auction site is the seller's ratings and shipping and handling charges. Buyers are encouraged to provide details of their buying experience, so as a potential buyer, you should review some of the previous transactions of the seller and look at the seller's rating and number of positive and negative reviews. Many of the sellers are quite knowledgeable about the items that they sell, are antique dealers, and have done some research prior to purchasing the item themselves. As with any purchase, buyers must beware and should carefully read the transaction stipulations, in order to protect themselves and be sure that the item for sale is what is expected. Sellers typically welcome questions from the potential buyer, so you should feel free to contact them to clarify any questions about the item for sale prior to purchase.

School budgets for purchasing instructional materials are often minimal or nonexistent, so educators may want to use online auctions as electronic resources for bolstering their own knowledge about a topic of study or for printing the images of the items for sale there, as they are typically quite clear and of high quality. The descriptions can help create background or supplemental information for teachers and, depending on their age, for students as well. Educators can select the images posted for an item for sale and save them for printing and for use in a variety of ways.

Links to Primary Source Repositories and Resources

National Archives and Records Administration: Archives	**www.archives.gov**
National Archives and Records Administration: DocsTeach	**www.docsteach.org**
National Archives and Records Administration: Our Documents	**www.ourdocuments.gov**
Smithsonian Learning Lab	**learninglab.si.edu**
University of North Carolina's Documenting the American South	**docsouth.unc.edu**

Links to Primary Source Repositories and Resources *(continued)*

Stanford History Education Group	sheg.stanford.edu	
Annenberg Media: Teaching with Primary Sources	www.learner.org/series/social-studies-in-action-a-teaching-practices-library-k-12/using-primary-sources/	
Beyond Google Searching: Ask A Historian	teachinghistory.org/digital-classroom/ask-a-digital-historian/24089	
National Archives: Lessons	www.archives.gov/education/lessons	
PBS Teachers	www.pbslearningmedia.org	
ProTeacher: Using Primary Sources in Social Studies	www.proteacher.com/090093.shtml	

One area on the eBay site that can be quite useful is the Collectibles & Art section. Within the collectibles section, items for sale are categorized within subgroups, such as comics, sci-fi and horror, photographic images, advertising, ethnic and cultural, and historical memorabilia, all ranging from pre-1700 to the present day. One area that has been useful for educators is that related to the home front in the United States during the Second World War. For example, when searching eBay for items related to the American home front during the Second World War, one can start with Collectibles and follow links to arrive eventually at Original WW II US Home Front Collectibles. This section typically has anywhere from 8,000 to 12,000 items for sale at any one time. As this is a continually updated auction, the offerings are different each time a visitor comes to the site. Perusing the American home front catalog, one can find ration stamp books, magazines, letters, diaries, photo albums, advertisements, posters, war bonds booklets, and other ephemera. Once again, one could choose to save or print the images rather than purchasing them, if funds are not available for this purpose.

SOURCES FRAMEWORK FOR TEACHING WITH PRIMARY AND SECONDARY SOURCES

As demonstrated throughout the book, the SOURCES Framework for Teaching with Primary and Secondary Sources was developed to give students a structured way to utilize primary and secondary sources in an authentic historical inquiry-based approach to learning about the past. Through the seven stages of the SOURCES framework, the students' learning process is carefully planned and scaffolded in order to allow each individual opportunities to examine primary and secondary sources, question their understandings about a historical event, develop background knowledge, find supporting and corroborating evidence, construct source-based narratives, and critically analyze the learning process and findings, as well as consider questions that were not answered.

We argue that not only do students need the critical-thinking skills necessary to progress through the seven stages of the SOURCES framework, it is essential that they have opportunities to engage with the past while utilizing the technologies of today and the future. These are all key elements to becoming more engaged and participatory citizens in a democracy. This is why we determined that in this book, we would in Part I demonstrate the power of the SOURCES Framework for Teaching with Primary and Secondary Sources, and in Part II show how teachers can utilize emerging technological applications, alongside the SOURCES framework, to empower students, provide agentic and critical-thinking opportunities, and creatively extend instructional approaches.

The SOURCES Framework for Teaching with Primary and Secondary Sources

1. Scrutinizing the Fundamental Source(s)
2. Organizing Thoughts
3. Understanding the Context
4. Reading Between the Lines
5. Corroborating and Refuting
6. Establishing a Plausible Narrative
7. Summarizing Final Thoughts

THE FUTURE, POSSIBILITIES, POTENTIAL ROADBLOCKS, AND MAKING THE MOST OF THE HISTORICAL INQUIRY PROCESS

Over the past 20 years or so, the availability of and accessibility to a wide variety of primary and secondary sources has greatly increased. Where once a history teacher would have to purchase primary source kits or visit a museum or library to access primary and secondary sources, there are now billions of sources available in a matter of moments. The struggle, for many, has been how to properly integrate these sources, as well as the plethora of emerging technologies, into the history classroom in a seamless, authentic, and engaging manner. Through the pedagogical approaches, the SOURCES framework, and the resources provided in this book, we hope that we have empowered social studies educators, as well as those in other content areas, with the knowledge and desire to authentically challenge and engage the minds of students across America's classrooms. The skills gained in the process of engaging with primary and secondary sources through the use of the SOURCES Framework for Teaching with Primary and Secondary Sources and the use of emerging technologies give students the power to be productive, informed, and engaged citizens in the ever-changing and complex world around them.

References

Ajjan, H., & Hartshorne, R. (2008). Investigating faculty decisions to adopt Web 2.0 technologies: Theory and empirical tests. *The Internet and Higher Education, 11*(2), 71–80.

Alexander, B. (2006). A new way of innovation for teaching and learning. *EDUCAUSE Review, 41*(2), 32–44.

All-American Girls Professional Baseball League. (n.d.). *League history*. Retrieved from www.aagpbl.org/history/league-history

Allen, J. (1994). If this is history, why isn't it boring? In S. Steffy & W. J. Hood (Eds.), *If this is social studies, why isn't it boring?* (pp. 1–12). York, MA: Stenhouse.

Barton, K. C. (2005). Primary sources in history: Breaking through the myths. *Phi Delta Kappan, 86*(10), 745–753.

Barton, K. C., & Levstik, L. S. (2003). Why don't more history teachers engage students in interpretation? *Social Education, 67*(6), 358–361.

Black, M. S., & Blake, M. E. (2001). Knitting local history together: Collaborating to construct curriculum. *Social Studies, 92*, 243–247.

Britt, J., & Howe, M. (2014). Developing a vision for the Common Core classroom: What does elementary social studies look like? *Social Studies, 105*(3), 158–163.

Callison, D. (2013). CCSS: Primary sources for secondary social studies. *School Library Monthly, 30*(2), 18–21.

Cowgill, D., & Waring, S. M. (2015). Using SOURCES to examine the American Constitution and events leading to its construction. *The Councilor: A Journal of the Social Studies, 76*(2), 1–14.

Ellis, J. J. (2004). *His excellency: George Washington*. New York, NY: Alfred A. Knopf.

Ferdig, R. E. (2007). Examining social software in teacher education. *Journal of Technology and Teacher Education, 15*(1), 5–10.

Fischer, D. H. (2004). *Washington's crossing: Pivotal moments in American history*. New York, NY: Oxford University Press.

Franklin, T., & Van Harmelen, M. (2007). *Web 2.0 for content for learning and teaching in higher education*. London, England: Joint Information Systems Committee.

Frassanito, W. (1975). *Gettysburg: A journey in time*. New York, NY: Scribner.

Freeman, A., Adams Becker, S., Cummins, M., Davis. A., & Hall Giesinger, C. (2017). *NMC/CoSN Horizon Report: 2017 Education Edition*. Austin, TX: The New Media Consortium.

Hancock, J. (1777, January 6–7). *To George Washington from John Hancock, 6–7 January 1777*. Retrieved from founders.archives.gov/documents/Washington/03-08-02-0002

Hartshorne, R., & Ajjan, H. (2009). Examining student decisions to adopt Web 2.0 technologies: Theory and empirical tests. *Journal of Computing in Higher Education, 21*(3), 183–198.

Herlihy, C., & Waring, S. M. (2015). Using the SOURCES framework to examine the Little Rock Nine. *Oregon Journal of the Social Studies, 3*(2), 44–51.

Ketchum, R. M. (1973). *The winter soldiers: The battles for Trenton and Princeton*. New York, NY: Henry Holt and Company.

Knox, H. (1777, January 7). *Letter to Lucy Knox*. Retrieved from www.gilderlehrman.org/collection/glc0243700514

Lamb, A. (2014). Primary source digital documents: CCSS & complexity of text. *School Library Monthly, 30*(4), 5–8.

LaVallee, C., Purdin, T., & Waring, S. M. (2019). Civil liberties, the Bill of Rights, and SOURCES: Engaging students in the past in order to prepare citizens of the future. In J. Hubbard (Ed.), *Extending the ground of public confidence: Teaching civil liberties in K–16 social studies education* (pp. 3–32). Charlotte, NC: Information Age Publishing.

LaVallee, C., & Waring, S. M. (2015). Using SOURCES to examine the *Nadir of Race Relations* (1890–1920). *The Clearing House, 88,* 133–139.

Li, L., & Pitts, J. P. (2009). Does it really matter? Using virtual office hours to enhance student-faculty interaction. *Journal of Information Systems Education, 20*(2), 175–186.

Library of Congress. (n.d.). How to get into Princeton [Video file]. Retrieved from www.loc.gov/item/myloc19

Library of Congress. (2019). *Using primary sources*. Retrieved from www.loc.gov/teachers/usingprimarysources

Maloney, E. (2007). What Web 2.0 can teach us about learning. *The Chronicle of Higher Education, 25*(18), B26.

Maloney, W. (2018). Japanese-America's pastime: Baseball. *Library of Congress Blog*. Retrieved from blogs.loc.gov/loc/2018/05/japanese-americas-pastime-baseball

National Archives and Records Administration. (n.d.). *About the National Archives of the United States*. Retrieved from www.archives.gov/publications/general-info-leaflets/1-about-archives.html

National Council for the Social Studies. (1994). *Expectations of excellence: Curriculum standards for social studies*. Retrieved from www.socialstudies.org/standards/stitle.html

National Council for the Social Studies. (2010). *National curriculum standards for social studies: A framework for teaching, learning, and assessment*. Silver Spring, MD: Author.

National Council for the Social Studies. (2013). *The college, career, and civic life (C3) framework for social studies state standards: Guidance for enhancing the rigor of K–12 civics, economics, geography, and history*. Silver Spring, MD: Author.

National Governors Association Center for Best Practices and Council of Chief State School Officers. (2010). *Common core state standards*. Washington, DC: Author.

Sergeant R______. (1896). The Battle of Princeton. *The Pennsylvania Magazine of History and Biography, 20*(4), 515–519.

Smithsonian Institution. (n.d.). *About the Smithsonian*. Retrieved from www.si.edu/about

Stryker, W. S. (1898). *The battles of Trenton and Princeton*. Boston, MA: The Riverside Press.

Sullivan, T. (1908). The Battle of Princeton. *The Pennsylvania Magazine of History and Biography, 32,* 54–57.

Tanner, H. S. (1816). Affair of Princeton. In James Wilkinson (Ed.), *Diagrams and plans illustrative of the principal battles and military affairs treated of in memoirs of my own times*. Philadelphia, PA: Abraham Small.

Terry, K., & Waring, S. M. (2017). Expanding historical narratives: Using SOURCES to assess the successes and failures of Operation Anthropoid. *Social Studies Journal, 37*(2), 59–71.

United States Bureau of the Census. (1975). *Historical statistics of the United States, colonial times to 1970: Part 1*. Retrieved from www.census.gov/history/pdf/histstats-colonial-1970.pdf

United States Copyright Office. (2019). *More information on Fair Use*. Retrieved from www.copyright.gov/fair-use/more-info.html

United States Copyright Office. (n.d.). *What does copyright protect?* Retrieved from www.copyright.gov/help/faq/faq-protect.html

United States Department of Commerce. (1975). *Historical Statistics of the United States, Colonial Times to 1970: Part 1*. Bureau of the Census. Retrieved from books.google.com/books?id=4uP8TZgLplgC&lpg=PA193&dq=retail%20prices%20of%20selected%20foods%20in%20u.s.%20cities&pg=PA213#v=onepage&q&f=false

Waring, S. M. (2017). Engaging history students through the use of the SOURCES Framework. *In Context, 1*(1), 2–4.

Waring, S. M. (2010). Escaping myopia: Teaching students about historical causality. *The History Teacher, 43*(2), 283–288.

Waring, S. M., & Herlihy, C. (2015). Are we alone in the universe? Using primary sources to address a fundamental question. *The Science Teacher, 82*(7), 63–66.

Waring, S. M., LaVallee, C., & Purdin, T. (2018). The power of agentic women and SOURCES. *Social Studies Research and Practice, 13*(2), 270–278.

Waring, S. M., & Scheiner-Fisher, C. (2014). Using SOURCES to allow digital natives to explore the Lewis and Clark expedition. *Middle School Journal, 45*(4), 3–12.

Waring, S. M., & Tapia-Moreno, D. (2015). Examining the conditions of Andersonville Prison through the use of SOURCES. *The Social Studies, 106*(4), 170–177.

Washington, G. (1776, December 20). *George Washington to Continental Congress*. Retrieved from www.loc.gov/resource/mgw3a.002/?sp=117

Washington, G. (1776, December 27). *From George Washington to Robert Morris*. Retrieved from founders.archives.gov/documents/Washington/03-07-02-0357

Washington, G. (1777, January 5). *From George Washington to Major General Israel Putnam, 5 January 1777*. Retrieved from founders.archives.gov/documents/Washington/03-07-02-0416

Wertenbaker, T. J. (1922). The Battle of Princeton. In *The Princeton Battle Monument: The history of the monument, a record of the ceremonies attending its unveiling, and an account of the Battle of Princeton*. Princeton, NJ: Princeton University Press.

White, S. H., O'Brien, J. E., Smith, A., Mortensen, D., & Hileman, K. (2006). A history lab environment in the classroom brings the standards to life. *Middle School Journal, 37*(4), 4–10.

Wineburg, S. (2010). Historical thinking: Memorizing facts and stuff? *Teaching with Primary Sources Quarterly, 3*(1), 2–4.

Woyshner, C. (2010). Inquiry teaching with primary source documents: An iterative approach. *Social Studies Research and Practice, 5*(3), 36–45.

Zhao, Y., & Hoge, J. D. (2005). What elementary students and teachers say about social studies. *The Social Studies, 96*, 216–221.

Index

About the Authors

Scott M. Waring is a professor and the program coordinator for the Social Science Education Program at the University of Central Florida. He earned his BS. and MA in Education from the University of South Florida and his PhD from the University of Virginia in Social Studies Education, with a minor in Instructional Technology. He teaches courses at the undergraduate and graduate level in social science methodology, research, and theory. While at the University of Central Florida, Dr. Waring has won the Award for Excellence in Research, the Excellence in Graduate Teaching Award, the Excellence in Undergraduate Teaching Award, the Excellence in Academic Advising Award, and the Award for Excellence in Undergraduate Academic Advising. He is the current chair for the Teacher Education and Professional Development Committee of the National Council for the Social Studies (NCSS), chair of the Florida College and University Faculty Assembly (FLCUFA—the higher education research affiliate of the Florida Council for the Social Studies), and the program chair for the SOURCES Conference. Dr. Waring serves as the editor for *Social Studies and the Young Learner, Teaching with Primary Sources Journal,* and *Contemporary Issues in Technology and Teacher Education—Social Studies,* and is the interdisciplinary feature editor for *Social Studies Research and Practice.* He has served as a member of the National Council for the Social Studies (NCSS) House of Delegates, on the Executive Board for the College and University Faculty Assembly (CUFA—the higher education research affiliate of NCSS), and as the Chair for the Society for Information Technology & Teacher Education's (SITE) Social Studies Special Interest Group. He has delivered more than 100 conference and workshop presentations and has written or cowritten grants totaling more than $4 million, including a Teaching with Primary Sources grant from the Library of Congress, a Fulbright-Hays grant (Czech Republic), and three United States Department of Education Teaching American History grants. Dr. Waring has published a book (has four more under contract and in progress), multiple journal articles, and book chapters focusing on the teaching and learning of history, teaching with primary sources, and the utilization of technology in teaching.

Richard Hartshorne is a professor of Instructional Design & Technology and chair of the Department of Learning Sciences and Educational Research in the

College of Community Innovation and Education at the University of Central Florida (UCF). He earned his PhD in Curriculum and Instruction with a focus on educational technology production and technology and teacher education from the University of Florida. At the University of Central Florida, his teaching focuses on the integration of technology into the educational landscape, as well as instructional design and development. His research interests involve primarily the production and effective integration of instructional technology into the teaching and learning environment. The major areas of his research interest are rooted in technology and teacher education, the integration of emerging technology into the K–postsecondary curriculum, and online teaching and learning. His articles have appeared in the *Journal of Technology and Teacher Education,* the *International Journal of Gaming and Computer-Mediated Simulations,* the *Journal of Digital Learning in Teacher Education, Internet and Higher Education,* the *Journal of Educational Computing Research,* and others. He has authored numerous book chapters and serves in editorial capacities for a number of journals in the field of educational technology.